Lars Alvincz

Intelligent Speculative Compiler Optimizations

AF092714

Lars Alvincz

Intelligent Speculative Compiler Optimizations

A Conceptual Framework and its Application to the Optimization of Memory Accesses

Südwestdeutscher Verlag für Hochschulschriften

Impressum/Imprint (nur für Deutschland/ only for Germany)
Bibliografische Information der Deutschen Nationalbibliothek: Die Deutsche Nationalbibliothek verzeichnet diese Publikation in der Deutschen Nationalbibliografie; detaillierte bibliografische Daten sind im Internet über http://dnb.d-nb.de abrufbar.
Alle in diesem Buch genannten Marken und Produktnamen unterliegen warenzeichen-, marken- oder patentrechtlichem Schutz bzw. sind Warenzeichen oder eingetragene Warenzeichen der jeweiligen Inhaber. Die Wiedergabe von Marken, Produktnamen, Gebrauchsnamen, Handelsnamen, Warenbezeichnungen u.s.w. in diesem Werk berechtigt auch ohne besondere Kennzeichnung nicht zu der Annahme, dass solche Namen im Sinne der Warenzeichen- und Markenschutzgesetzgebung als frei zu betrachten wären und daher von jedermann benutzt werden dürften.

Verlag: Südwestdeutscher Verlag für Hochschulschriften Aktiengesellschaft & Co. KG
Dudweiler Landstr. 99, 66123 Saarbrücken, Deutschland
Telefon +49 681 37 20 271-1, Telefax +49 681 37 20 271-0
Email: info@svh-verlag.de
Zugl.: Berlin, Technische Universität Berlin, Dissertation, 2009

Herstellung in Deutschland:
Schaltungsdienst Lange o.H.G., Berlin
Books on Demand GmbH, Norderstedt
Reha GmbH, Saarbrücken
Amazon Distribution GmbH, Leipzig
ISBN: 978-3-8381-1315-9

Imprint (only for USA, GB)
Bibliographic information published by the Deutsche Nationalbibliothek: The Deutsche Nationalbibliothek lists this publication in the Deutsche Nationalbibliografie; detailed bibliographic data are available in the Internet at http://dnb.d-nb.de.
Any brand names and product names mentioned in this book are subject to trademark, brand or patent protection and are trademarks or registered trademarks of their respective holders. The use of brand names, product names, common names, trade names, product descriptions etc. even without a particular marking in this works is in no way to be construed to mean that such names may be regarded as unrestricted in respect of trademark and brand protection legislation and could thus be used by anyone.

Publisher: Südwestdeutscher Verlag für Hochschulschriften Aktiengesellschaft & Co. KG
Dudweiler Landstr. 99, 66123 Saarbrücken, Germany
Phone +49 681 37 20 271-1, Fax +49 681 37 20 271-0
Email: info@svh-verlag.de

Printed in the U.S.A.
Printed in the U.K. by (see last page)
ISBN: 978-3-8381-1315-9

Copyright © 2010 by the author and Südwestdeutscher Verlag für Hochschulschriften Aktiengesellschaft & Co. KG and licensors
All rights reserved. Saarbrücken 2010

Zusammenfassung

In dieser Arbeit stellen wir unser konzeptuelles Framework für intelligente spekulative Compileroptimierungen (*FrISCO, Framework for Intelligent Speculative Compiler Optimizations*) vor sowie die Anwendung des Frameworks, um Speicherzugriffe zu optimieren. Das Ziel des Frameworks ist es, Compilern Wissen über das Laufzeitverhalten von Programmen verfügbar zu machen, um die Kluft zwischen statischen Programmanalysen einerseits und dem dynamischen Programmverhalten anderseits zu überbrücken. Dadurch wird das Problem der Überapproximation gelöst, das den statischen Programmanalysen inhärent ist, und das Optimierungspotential vergrößert.

Die grundlegende Idee unseres Frameworks besteht darin, im Compiler unsichere, aber dafür präzisere Programmanalysen zuzulassen und deren Ergebnisse in spekulativen Optimierungen zu verwenden, um ein präzises Kostenmodell zu erstellen. Dabei wird die Programmkorrektheit in allen Fällen gewahrt. Wir verwenden Heuristiken, um das dynamische Programmverhalten vorherzusagen. Wir stellen ein Verfahren vor, um solche Heuristiken automatisch in einer einmaligen Trainingsphase anhand von Profilingdaten mittels Maschinellen Lernens zu erzeugen. Außerdem schlagen wir vor, ähnliche Programme in Klassen zusammenzufassen. Dies kann automatisch durch eine Clusteranalyse erfolgen. Wir trainieren jeweils eine spezialisierte Heuristik pro Programmklasse sowie einen Programmklassenprediktor. Damit läßt sich das Verhalten beliebiger Programme präzise vorhersagen, indem die am besten geeignete Heuristik ausgewählt wird. Die resultierende kombinierte Heuristik ist hochgradig skalierbar und kann automatisch in ausführbaren, hoch skalierbaren Code überführt werden, der dann in den Compiler integriert werden kann. Wir stellen einen allgemeinen Optimierungsalgorithmus vor, auf den die meisten existierenden Optimierungen abgebildet werden können. Der Algorithmus transformiert das Programm schrittweise und verwendet dabei ein Kostenmodell um sicherzustellen, dass in jedem Schritt die beste Transformation ausgewählt wird.

Das konzeptuelle Framework lässt sich auf eine Vielzahl von Programmverhalten und -optimierungen anwenden. Im zweiten Teil dieser Arbeit zeigen wir die Anwendung des Frameworks auf die Optimierung von Speicherzugriffen. Dies ist ein sehr wichtiges Optimierungsproblem aufgrund des *Memory Gaps*. Für das angewandte Framework stellen wir einen neuen Algorithmus zur spekulative Code-Verschiebung vor, der die effektive Latenz von Ladebefehlen reduziert und dabei sämtliche Arten von Abhängigkeiten überwinden kann. Das Kostenmodell basiert auf den Abhängigkeitswahrscheinlichkeiten für Speicherzugriffe sowie den Latenzen der Ladebefehle. Wir haben das angewandte Framework vollständig implementiert. Als Plattform verwenden wir den Intel Itanium2[1]-Prozessor, der spekulative Optimierung hardwareseitig unterstützt. Unsere Experimente zeigen, dass die Heuristiken das Speicherverhalten von Programmen präzise vorhersagen können, insbesondere dank unseres Konzepts der Programmklassifikation. Weiterhin konnten wir zeigen, dass die spekulative Optimierung dank des Kostenmodells signifikante Laufzeitverbesserungen erreichte sowie in keinem Fall zu einer Verschlechterung führte.

---
[1] *Intel* und *Itanium2* sind eingetragene Warenzeichen der *Intel Corporation* oder ihrer Tochterunternehmen in den USA und anderen Ländern.

Abstract

In this thesis, we present a conceptual *Framework for Intelligent Speculative Compiler Optimizations (FrISCO)* and its application to the optimization of memory accesses. The framework aims at providing compilers with knowledge about the run-time behavior of programs to bridge the gap between static program analyses on the one hand and dynamic program behavior on the other. This solves the problem of over-approximation, which is inherent to static program analyses, and increases the optimization potential. We use machine learning to make the knowledge available to the compiler.

The principal idea of our framework is to admit unsafe, yet more precise program analyses within the compiler and to use their results in speculative optimizations, which use the information to derive precise cost models and which guarantee program correctness in case of misspeculation. In our approach, we use heuristics to predict the dynamic program behavior. We present a method to generate such heuristics automatically in a one-off training phase from profiling data using machine learning. Additionally, we propose to perform program classification to group programs with similar behavior together, which can be done automatically via cluster analysis. Based on the clustering, we train one specialized heuristics for each class as well as a program class predictor. With that, we can precisely predict the behavior of arbitrary programs by selecting the most appropriate heuristics. The obtained overall heuristics is highly scalable and can be automatically translated to executable code to be integrated within the compiler. We present a general optimization algorithm, onto which most existing optimizations can be mapped. The algorithm iteratively transforms the program. To ensure that the best transformation is found in each step, it uses a cost model that is evaluated with the help of the heuristics.

The conceptual framework is applicable to a wide range of program behavior and program optimizations. In the second part of this thesis, we show the application of the framework to the optimization of memory accesses, which is a highly important optimization problem due to the *memory gap*. For the applied framework, we present a novel optimization algorithm that performs speculative code motion to reduce the effective latency of load instructions. During code motion, the algorithm overcomes memory dependencies, register dependencies, and control dependencies, and it maintains a precise cost model which captures the effect of each transformation on the latency of the optimized load. The cost model relies on information about the memory behavior of a program, namely the probability of memory dependencies and load latencies. We present how to build heuristics for that via machine learning. We fully implemented the instantiated framework targeting the Intel Itanium2[2] processor, a modern VLIW processor with hardware support for speculation. In our experiments, we could first show that the heuristics predict the memory behavior precisely, especially due to our concept of program classification. Second, our run-time experiments demonstrate that our speculative optimization, with the help of the heuristics, significantly improves program performance and avoids performance degradation due to the cost model.

---

[2] *Intel* and *Itanium2* are registered tradenarks of *Intel Corporation* or its subsidiaries in the United States and other countries.

Danksagung

Die vorliegende Arbeit entstand während meiner Tätigkeit im DFG Aktionsplan Informatik „Verifikation und Optimierung bei der Übersetzung höherer Programmiersprachen", geleitet von Prof. Dr. Sabine Glesner. An dieser Stelle möchte ich mich bei allen bedanken, die zum Gelingen dieser Arbeit beigetragen haben.

Zuallererst möchte ich meiner Betreuerin Prof. Dr. Sabine Glesner herzlich danken, die maßgeblich zum vorliegenden Ergebnis beitrug. Sie begleitete diese Arbeit über den gesamten Entstehungsprozess und war bei Fragen und Problemen immer ansprechbar, woraus zahlreiche ergiebige Diskussionen entstanden. Gleichzeitig ließ sie mir Freiräume, meine eigenen Schwerpunkte zu setzen, und half mir, dabei den richtigen Weg zu finden. Meinem zweiten Gutachter, Prof. Dr. Jens Knoop, bin ich ebenfalls sehr dankbar verbunden für seine freundliche Unterstützung und seine inhaltlichen Anregungen.

Auch die Arbeitsatmosphäre, in der diese Arbeit entstand, war äußerst produktiv. Meinen Kollegen danke ich für viele Diskussionen, die das Entstehen der Arbeit vorangetrieben haben, sowie für die nötige Ablenkung, sei es am Kaffeetisch, im Kickerraum oder in der Kletterhalle. Insbesondere ein großes Dankeschön an Paula für das Gegenlesen der Arbeit und für ihr äußerst hilfreiches Feedback. Vielen Dank auch meinen Diplomanden, die ebenfalls zu dieser Arbeit beigetragen haben. Vor allem das Engagement von Dirk und Stefan war enorm.

Zu guter Letzt danke ich meiner Familie, die mich stets unterstützt hat, und meinen Freunden für die Auszeiten zwischendurch. Mein ganz besonderer Dank gebührt Dir, Andrea, für Deine Liebe und Unterstützung, und unserem Jonathan, der mit einem kleinen Lächeln unbeschreibliches Glück entstehen lässt.

Contents

1 Introduction   **11**
    1.1   Problem 11
    1.2   Objectives 13
    1.3   Proposed Solution 14
    1.4   Motivation 17
    1.5   Research Area 20
    1.6   Main Contributions 20
    1.7   Outline 22

2 Background   **23**
    2.1   Compilers 23
        2.1.1   Front End 24
        2.1.2   Intermediate Representation 25
        2.1.3   Program Analyses 31
        2.1.4   Optimizations 34
        2.1.5   Code Generation 37
    2.2   The Role of Memory in Compilers 38
    2.3   Analysis of Memory Accesses 40
        2.3.1   Dependence Analyses 41
        2.3.2   Alias Analyses 42
    2.4   Speculative Optimization 45
        2.4.1   Data Speculation 45
        2.4.2   Control Speculation 46
        2.4.3   Recovery Code 48
        2.4.4   Required Hardware Support 49
        2.4.5   Hardware Support in Modern Processor Architectures . . 51

2.5 Machine Learning 52
       2.5.1 Classification Learning 53
       2.5.2 Cluster Analysis 60
       2.5.3 Predictor Precision 60
  2.6 Summary 63

3 Related Work   65
  3.1 Machine Learning in Compilers 65
       3.1.1 Program Behavior 66
       3.1.2 Optimization Sequences 66
       3.1.3 Optimization Parameters 68
       3.1.4 Discussion 68
  3.2 Memory Dependencies 69
       3.2.1 Collection of Memory Dependencies via Profiling . . . 69
       3.2.2 Alias Analysis 70
       3.2.3 Discussion 72
  3.3 Optimization of Memory Accesses 73
       3.3.1 Conservative Optimizations 74
       3.3.2 Speculative Optimizations 75
       3.3.3 Discussion 77

4 A General Framework for Intelligent Speculative Optimizations   79
  4.1 Overview 80
  4.2 Analysis 82
       4.2.1 Program Analysis 83
       4.2.2 Profiling 84
  4.3 Machine Learning 84
       4.3.1 Behavior Predictor 85
       4.3.2 Identification of Program Classes 87
       4.3.3 Program Class Predictor 88
       4.3.4 Repository of Behavior Predictors 89
       4.3.5 Combination with Conservative Analyses 89
  4.4 Speculative Optimizations 90
       4.4.1 Search Space Exploration 91
       4.4.2 Increased Optimization Potential 92
       4.4.3 Cost Model 93
  4.5 Instantiation of the General Framework 95
  4.6 Summary 96

5 Intelligent Speculative Optimization of Memory Accesses — 99

- 5.1 Speculative Optimization of Memory Accesses 100
  - 5.1.1 Optimization Problem 100
  - 5.1.2 Abstraction Level 102
  - 5.1.3 Optimization Algorithm 103
- 5.2 Cost Model 108
  - 5.2.1 Conservative Code Motion 109
  - 5.2.2 Data Speculation 110
  - 5.2.3 Control Speculation 113
  - 5.2.4 Load Address Computation Chains 117
  - 5.2.5 Crossing Check Instructions 119
- 5.3 Learning the Memory Behavior of Programs 121
  - 5.3.1 Collection of Training Data 121
  - 5.3.2 Identification of Program Classes 126
  - 5.3.3 Repository of Predictors 130
  - 5.3.4 Combination with Alias Analyses 130
- 5.4 Summary 131

6 Implementation — 133

- 6.1 Overview 133
- 6.2 Analysis Phase 137
  - 6.2.1 Suite of Representative Programs 137
  - 6.2.2 Static Program Features 137
  - 6.2.3 Static Code Features 138
  - 6.2.4 Profiling Load Latencies 140
  - 6.2.5 Profiling Memory Dependence Degrees 140
  - 6.2.6 Combination of Code Features and Profiling Data . . . 143
- 6.3 Machine Learning 144
  - 6.3.1 Data Preparation 145
  - 6.3.2 Predictor Construction 145
  - 6.3.3 Program Classification 146
  - 6.3.4 Construction of the Behavior Predictor Repository . . . 148
  - 6.3.5 Generation of Executable Code from the Predictors . . . 149
- 6.4 Speculative Optimization 150
  - 6.4.1 Itanium Backend 150
  - 6.4.2 Static Branch Predictor 151
  - 6.4.3 Alias Analysis 152
  - 6.4.4 Speculative Upwards Code Motion 152
- 6.5 Summary 155

7 Experimental Results — 157
- 7.1 Evaluation of the Predictors 157
  - 7.1.1 Validation Methods 158
  - 7.1.2 Program Suite 158
  - 7.1.3 General Applicability of Machine Learning 161
  - 7.1.4 Program Classification 165
  - 7.1.5 Predictor Precision for the Validation Set 173
- 7.2 Optimization 177
  - 7.2.1 Experimental Setup 177
  - 7.2.2 Results 178
- 7.3 Summary 183

8 Conclusion — 185
- 8.1 Results 185
- 8.2 Discussion 187
- 8.3 Outlook 188

List of Figures — 193

List of Tables — 197

Bibliography — 199

1 Introduction

In software engineering, compilers play a major role in creating executable applications from programs in high-level programming languages. While well-researched, the steadily increasing expectations on computer performance as well as the continuous evolution of new computer architectures raise an urgent need for novel compiler techniques. A major challenge lies in the fact that compilers are typically static and have to face the problem of obtaining information about the dynamic run-time behavior to achieve correct, yet efficient programs.

1.1 Problem

Modern compilers try to optimize programs with respect to a given objective function (for example, program performance or memory consumption). To achieve high optimization gains, the optimizations rely on program analyses which investigate properties of the considered program. This includes information which is only available at program run-time and, thus, has to be approximated. When transforming the program, optimizations must maintain program correctness under all circumstances. To that end, special program analyses as, *e.g.*, dependence analyses are used. Optimizations are only allowed to perform transformations that are deemed as admissible by the results of such analyses. The demand for correctness forces the program analyses to err on the safe side, *i.e.*, to over-approximate the behavior whenever no exact solution can be found. This may have severe consequences for the optimization: First, advantageous program transformations may not be chosen due to the over-approximation. Second, and even more importantly, a significant fraction of program transformations may appear inapplicable due to the static analyses being overly conservative. This problem is intrinsic to the scenario of a static compiler: The run-time behavior of a program cannot be predicted in general at compile-time because even the much simpler *Halting Problem* is undecidable. Hence, we have a gap between the static program analyses in the compiler on the one hand and the dynamic behavior of the program under compilation on the other. As a consequence, the run-time performance of the generated programs is severely limited.

One way to overcome this problem lies in bridging that gap by making more precise information about the dynamic run-time behavior available to the compiler optimization. The significant imprecision of static analyses is caused by their over-approximation, which is in turn required for the analyses to be *safe*. Hence, a way to significantly increase precision is to admit *unsafe* analyses. With that, the analyses can focus on the relevant program behavior instead of considering all eventualities. As a consequence, the optimizations that make use of the analyses become *speculative*. Whenever an optimization uses unsafe information about the program behavior, it has to ensure that the program correctness is maintained in all cases by adding so-called *recovery code*. In case the information on the program behavior turns out to be correct, the optimization has exploited more optimization potential than a classic optimization that relies on conservative analyses. Otherwise, the recovery code reconstructs the correct system state. This may entail an additional overhead on program performance, which makes a precise cost estimation vital. Hence, to overcome the problem of the gap between static compilers and dynamic run-time behavior, we need unsafe, but more precise analyses to predict the program behavior together with speculative optimizations that make use of this information to exploit the full optimization potential. This problem concerns different kinds of program behavior and of optimizations. Thus, to obtain a general solution to overcome the gap, we need a conceptual framework for speculative optimizations that provides a mean for obtaining such precise analyses and for describing the speculative optimization. At the same time, it is also important to evaluate the practical applicability of the conceptual framework by applying it to a certain optimization problem.

An example for that the over-approximation of static analyses has severe consequences is the optimization of memory accesses. Because memory accesses have become increasingly expensive over the past years due to the *memory gap*, program performance is often dominated by the memory system. However, because the dependencies amongst memory accesses are hard to predict statically, state-of-the-art alias analyses are highly imprecise. As a consequence, conservative optimizations are severely limited in their optimization potential and can hardly mitigate the implications of the memory gap. Hence, to evaluate the practical applicability of the conceptual framework, we consider its application to the optimization of memory accesses. In the following, we develop objectives to decide whether or not a given framework meets our demands, for the conceptual framework as well as for its application.

1.2 Objectives

As general objectives, we require a conceptual framework for speculative optimizations to provide efficient methods for program analysis and program optimization, to be modular, and to be generally applicable to different kinds of program behavior and different program optimizations. To assess the quality of a framework, we use the following criteria:

- **Generality of the Optimization** The conceptual framework should be general enough to be applicable to a wide range of compiler optimizations.

- **Generality of the Regarded Behavior** The framework should be general enough to be used for a wide range of kinds of dynamic behavior, no matter at which abstraction level it is observed (*e.g.*, on instruction level or on basic block level).

- **Generality of the Analyses** The framework should make it possible that a comprehensive range of programs with differing dynamic behavior can be optimized. This requires the analyses to be generally applicable instead of being specialized to programs with a certain kind of dynamic behavior.

- **Modularity** The framework should be modular, such that analyses can be combined arbitrarily with optimizations.

- **Scalability of the Analyses** While an initial preparation phase is allowed to be time-consuming, the resulting analyses have to be highly scalable to be of practical use.

- **Precision Measure** Because the results of the analyses are used to determine the cost of transformations, it is important that the analyses yield precise results. Hence, the framework has to provide a mean to assess the precision of the obtained analyses.

- **Cost Model** While speculative optimizations allow for more optimization potential, in case of misspeculation, the recovery code poses an additional overhead to the execution time. Hence, it is important that the optimizations use the information from the analyses to rate the expected gain of a given transformation precisely.

To assess the quality of a given application of the general framework to a certain optimization, we additionally propose the following criteria:

- **Precision of the Analyses** For a precise cost estimation, it is important that the regarded dynamic behavior is precisely estimated by the analyses. Due to the *generality of the analyses* that we demanded from the conceptual framework, this has especially to hold for a wide variety of programs with different characteristics.

- **Program Correctness** Because the optimization transforms the program speculatively, it is important that misspeculation is taken care of. The program correctness must be guaranteed in all cases.

- **Optimization Gain** The cost model has to be used to guide the optimization. By that, the optimization can perform the best available transformation w.r.t. the cost model. At the same time, the cost model ensures that performance degradation is avoided.

1.3 Proposed Solution

In this thesis, we present a general *Framework for Intelligent Speculative Compiler Optimizations*, which aims at bridging the gap between static compilers and dynamic program behavior by providing the compiler with knowledge, or intelligence, about dynamic program behavior. This aim is pursued by three central ideas:

1. We propose to admit potentially unsafe **heuristics** to analyze the dynamic program behavior. With that, we can overcome the problem of over-approximation and increase the optimization potential.

2. We propose to automatically generate those heuristics using **machine learning techniques**. By that, we obtain precise and highly scalable heuristics, which only require static information to predict the dynamic behavior of programs and, thus, can be used in a static compiler.

1.3 Proposed Solution

3. We propose to use **speculative optimizations**, which use the results from the heuristics to derive a precise **cost model** to achieve high optimization gains and, at the same time, ensure program correctness under all circumstances.

In the following, we explain those ideas in more detail.

The first idea is to allow possibly *unsafe*, but *more precise* information as a result of program analyses. The optimizations based on that information become then *speculative* and have to cope with the case of wrong analysis results. As a consequence of admitting unsafe analyses, heuristics can be used to implement program analyses. Heuristics can be more precise because they need only cope with the most common (instead of all possible) cases. Hence, the severe problem of over-approximation, inherent to static analyses, is overcome. At the same time, machine learned heuristics are typically less computationally complex than the corresponding program analyses. Thus, they scale significantly better with respect to program size.

The second idea is to use machine learning techniques to automatically generate the heuristics. In general, the information about the dynamic behavior of programs can be collected by profiling. However, this has the following disadvantages: First, it induces a significant overhead on compilation[1]. Second, it requires an input set to execute the program under compilation. Third, the information is highly specialized to the encountered input set but may not be correct at all for another input set. We propose to use profiling in an initial preparation phase to collect the regarded dynamic behavior, and to use machine learning to abstract from that concrete information and to automatically generate general models. In the preparation phase, we perform profiling for a representative set of programs on typical sets of input. Then, we use classification learning to learn the relationship between static code features, which are collected in the compiler, and the regarded dynamic program behavior. This allows for the creation of heuristics, which predict the dynamic behavior solely based on static code features. To face the fact that there is a wide variety of programs with differing characteristics, we additionally propose to perform *program classification*. Using cluster analysis, we automatically group similar programs together and construct one heuristics for each program class. This allows the compiler to rely on a heuristics tailored to the program class of the program currently under compilation. By that, the precision of the heuristics

---

[1] It is not uncommon that profiling increases the compilation time by a factor of 40, as it is the case for the approach presented by Chen et al. [CLD+04], which collects dependencies amongst memory instructions.

should increase significantly. In [Ges08], we already sketched the idea of using machine learning to obtain scalable program analyses. In [AG09], we showed how we obtained precise heuristics for predicting memory dependencies, especially due to our concept of program classification.

The third idea proposes to use *speculative optimizations*. The additional precision of the heuristics significantly increases the optimization potential. Because the analyses are unsafe, the optimizations that use their results become speculative. When speaking of speculation, it is clear that program correctness must never be touched. Hence, the optimizations have to cope with the case that the information is incorrect. To that end, special recovery code is added, which is executed in case of misspeculation. This also shows that deriving a precise *cost model* during the optimization is important: The expected performance gain in case of successful speculation has to be weighed off against the possible additional overhead of executing the recovery code. This allows for identifying the applicable transformation that yields the highest optimization gain at each optimization step. In [GG08], we already could show the benefits of a cost model for speculative optimizations. In that work, we presented an algorithm for speculative register promotion for global variables, which performs a cost estimation to decide which globals to optimize. Due to the cost model, we could optimize many programs of the SPEC CPU2006 benchmark suite while avoiding a performance degradation in all cases.

Our general framework for intelligent speculative compiler optimizations is applicable to a wide diversity of optimizations. To show its practical applicability and to obtain a solution for an important optimization problem, we apply the conceptual framework to the optimization of memory accesses. To that end, we first develop a speculative optimization which performs speculative code motion of load instructions. The optimization can overcome all kinds of dependency by speculation, namely memory dependencies, control dependencies, and register dependencies. Next, we present a cost model, which is vital to decide whether or not a given transformation can be expected to pay off. It captures all different kinds of speculation and thereby models the estimated optimization gain precisely. Additionally, the cost model is parametrized by hardware-dependent information and thus can be tailored to different target architectures. To estimate the performance gain, the cost model requires information about the dynamic behavior of the considered program, namely the expected latency of load instructions as well as the expected probability that two memory accesses refer to the same data. To that end, we show how machine learning techniques can be used to automatically generate precise heuristics, which predict the required information.

1.4 Motivation

Compilers give the programmer the freedom to develop software in abstract programming languages, which allows him to focus on the idea instead of dealing with tedious details of the hardware of the considered target machine. It is the task of the compiler to translate the programmer's idea correctly to an executable binary. At the same time, compilers typically optimize the program with respect to a given objective function. Common examples are to improve run-time performance, memory consumption, or code size. The process of compilation poses several subtasks, ranging from reading in the source program, analyzing and optimizing it, and generating code for the target machine. For some of those subtasks, the underlying problems are so complex that they still are not solved completely by today, leaving much room for improvement. This is especially the case for the optimization problem. Additionally, optimizations have to estimate the dynamic run-time behavior to find advantageous program transformations as well as to ensure that program correctness is maintained. To that end, they typically consult static program analyses, which over-approximate the run-time behavior. This over-approximation may be enormous, which severely reduces the optimization potential of the optimizations and thereby leads to a limited program performance. One example for that the over-approximation of the analyses has severe consequences on the program performance is the optimization of memory accesses. This is caused by a phenomenon termed as *Memory Gap*.

The *Memory Gap*, also known as *Memory Wall*, describes the fact that, while both CPU and memory speed have been growing exponentially over the past decades, the speed of memory did not manage to keep pace with that of CPUs. Figure 1.1 illustrates the evolution (note the logarithmic y-axis). We see how the clock rate of CPUs (solid line) grows exponentially since 1980[2]. The speed of memory (shown by the dotted line) is also steadily increasing, but at a lower rate[3]. We see that for modern systems, CPU speed and memory speed differ by two orders of magnitude. In other words, memory

---

[2]The numbers show the clock rates of Intel processors.
[3]For the various kinds of memory technologies, we collected the average time for a random memory access. From that, we obtained the average access frequency by taking the reciprocal. For example, an average access time of 50ns becomes a frequency of 20 MHz.

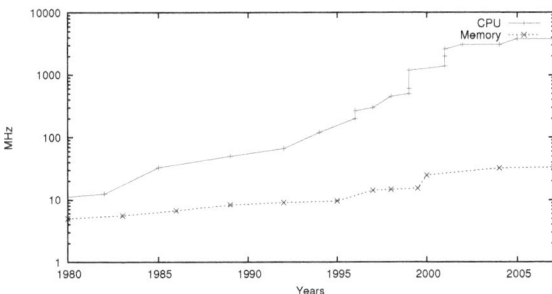

Figure 1.1: The Memory Gap

became slower (in terms of CPU speed), which means that the CPU may have to wait several cycles until a requested value is ready. This has dramatic consequences on the run-time performance: Whereas in the beginning of the computer era, performance was mainly limited by the operation speed of the CPU (*i.e.*, *computing* actually meant *computing*), it is now also limited by the availability of data, which has to be fetched from memory. In the extreme case, this can even mean that run-time performance is dominated by memory speed. While this has been known for a long time (*e.g.*, see Wulf et al. [WM95]), current compilers still perform poorly on optimizing memory performance. This is due to the inherent difficulty of the static analysis of memory behavior of programs, which is dynamic. Empirical studies have shown that only a small fraction of the statically predicted dependencies actually occur at run-time. Mock et al. [MDCE01] measured the average number of targets a pointer may point to, once via a static analysis at compile-time, once via profiling at run-time for a given program input. The considered programs originate mostly from the SPEC CPU2000 benchmark suite. While the alias analysis reported an average number of 25.56 targets per pointer, at run-time, on average only 1.08 targets were accessed by a pointer. In other words, at run-time, most pointers only pointed to one target. This supports the intuitive assumption that programmers use pointers for a certain aim, even if that is not obvious to program analyses at first glance. As a consequence of this significant over-approximation, the optimization potential is drastically limited. The effect is especially bad for *Very Long Instruction Word (VLIW)* processors, which are not capable of dynamic code optimizations at run-time. If a memory stall is encountered, the processor has to wait until the value is available. As a consequence, novel optimization techniques are heavily required, which reduce the impact of the memory gap.

1.4 Motivation

To face the memory gap, speculative optimizations of memory accesses have been proposed. The idea to optimize speculatively and to ensure correctness by special run-time checks was initially proposed by Nicolau [Nic89]. Since then, various approaches have been proposed to optimize load instructions speculatively (e.g., Mahlke et al. [MCH+92], Lin et al. [LCH+04], Rabbah et al. [RSEW04], Dai et al. [DZHY05]). However, all approaches rely solely on implicit cost models (if at all). Furthermore, the information about memory dependencies used in these optimizations is highly imprecise and distinguishes at most between three classes of dependency: no dependency, unlikely dependency, potential dependency. This limits the optimization potential of the optimizations and prevents a precise cost estimation. Another problem on a different level is that all approaches present a solution for the specific problem of optimizing memory accesses. They fail to develop a general framework, which can model a broader range of speculative optimizations.

For machine learning, there are several examples that it can be used to make compilers smarter (e.g., Wu et al. [WL94], Almagor et al. [ACG+04], Panait et al. [PSW04], Cavazos et al. [CFA+07]). However, as for the proposed optimizations, those approaches focus to use machine learning for a specific application scenario, instead of painting the picture how machine learning techniques can be used to improve the compiler in general. The prediction of dependence probabilities has never been investigated before. For load latencies, there is one related work by Panait et al. [PSW04], but their approach is very coarse because it only considers two classes of loads (cache-hit vs. cache miss) instead of predicting the actual latency.

Different from previous work, in this thesis, we develop a general framework how to achieve and exploit a higher optimization potential by using machine learning techniques together with speculative optimizations. With our precise and parametrized cost model and with our concept of program classification to increase the predictor precision, we present further novel ideas not investigated in related approaches. The chosen application scenario, namely, the optimization of memory accesses, is highly relevant due to the memory gap. We use machine learning to precisely predict the memory behavior of programs (load latencies and probabilities of memory dependencies), and use the results in a general speculative optimization, which can overcome all kinds of dependencies.

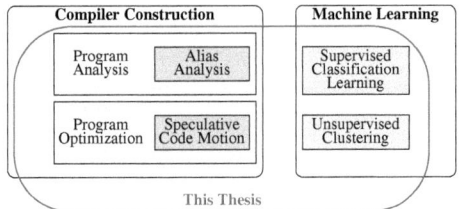

Figure 1.2: Covered Fields of Research

1.5 Research Area

Figure 1.2 shows the fields of research covered by this thesis. Because we apply machine learning techniques in compiler construction, the two broader areas of research this thesis is embedded in are given by those fields. Compiler construction, which is a subfield of software engineering, investigates methods to generate executable code from high-level programming languages. Central questions are how to optimize the program w.r.t. a given objective function and how to map the abstract program to the target machine. Machine learning, a subfield of artificial intelligence, uses statistical methods to automatically create models from training data, which explain some aspect of that data. The knowledge represented in these models can be used to make predictions for previously unseen data. Having a closer look at our approach, for the compiler area, the heuristics we generate are used as program analyses in program optimizations. To generate the heuristics, we use classification learning. The precision is increased by program classification, which is done by cluster analysis. In the application of our conceptual framework, we generate heuristics which predict the latency of a load and the probability of a memory dependency between two memory accesses. The latter can be seen as a probabilistic alias analysis. The optimization using those heuristics performs speculative code motion to reduce the effective latency of load instructions.

1.6 Main Contributions

This thesis makes the following main contributions:

1.6 Main Contributions

General Framework for the Use of Machine Learning in Compilers While it has been previously proposed to use machine learning techniques in compiler construction, previous work has only focused on concrete applications instead of developing a general framework. We propose a general framework to automatically generate heuristics from profiling data and to use them in speculative optimizations.

Program Classification and a Repository of Heuristics To face the fact that the run-time behavior of applications may differ broadly, we automatically perform program classification to group similar programs together. Then, we automatically generate one specialized heuristics for each program class. This yields a two-stage heuristics: To predict the behavior of a program, we first determine its program class and, second, select the appropriate specialized heuristics.

Generic Optimization Algorithm For optimization, we use a generic algorithm that transforms the program iteratively. In each step, all applicable transformations are determined, and the cost model together with the heuristics is used to rated the candidates w.r.t. their expected optimization gain. This allows for selecting the best transformation in each step. Most existing optimizations can be mapped to that algorithm.

Heuristics for Probabilities of Memory Dependencies As one result of the application of our general framework to the optimization of memory accesses, we obtain a precise heuristics that predicts the probabilities of memory dependencies, solely based on static code features. To the best of our knowledge, such a heuristics has never previously been proposed.

Intelligent Optimization of Memory Accesses We present a novel optimization, which performs speculative code motion to reduce the effective latencies of load instructions. The optimization can overcome all kinds of dependencies by speculation.

Precise Cost Model We precisely model the expected performance gain of different speculative transformations in a cost model. This has not been done for speculative optimizations by any other previous work. The cost model can be tailored to different target architectures by hardware-dependent parameters. It allows our optimization to select the transformations with the highest gain.

Practical Evaluation We performed a detailed evaluation of the application of our framework. We completely implemented our framework for the optimization of memory accesses within our compiler framework. We target the

Intel Itanium processor, for which we have established a complete compiler platform within our framework. In our experiments, we first investigated the precision of the predictors. Second, we performed run-time experiments and discuss the results. With our results, we could show that we obtained precise heuristics for memory behavior, namely memory dependencies and load latencies. With the help of these heuristics, our speculative optimization achieved a significant performance improvement for most programs of the SPEC CPU2006 benchmark suite, while avoiding a performance degradation in all cases.

1.7 Outline

This thesis is structured as follows. Chapter 2 describes the necessary background for both compiler construction and machine learning. Especially, we describe the role memory plays in compilation and proposed techniques to optimize speculatively. For machine learning, we introduce the concepts of classification learning and cluster analysis, which are central for our approach. In Chapter 3, we compare our approach with related work, distinguished by the different fields of research our approach covers. Chapter 4 presents our general framework. We give an overview of the framework and describe the phases it comprises in detail. We also give examples how the framework can be applied in practice. At the end of the chapter, we revisit our criteria for the general framework and discuss whether or not they are met by our approach. Chapter 5 presents the application of our general framework to the optimization of memory accesses. We first describe the speculative optimization we have developed to mitigate the impact of the memory gap. Based on that, we derive a cost model which is necessary to estimate the performance gain of different transformations. Finally, we describe the initial training phase, in which heuristics for predicting the memory behavior of programs are automatically generated. At the end of this chapter, we use the criteria that we have defined to evaluate applications of our general framework to assess our approach. Chapter 6 gives details on the implementation of the applied framework. In Chapter 7, we present the results of the empirical evaluation of the applied framework that we performed. We first describe the setup for the machine learning part and assess the precision of the automatically generated predictors. Then, we present and discuss results of run-time experiments we performed to determine the performance gain our optimization achieves. Chapter 8 summarizes the results of this thesis and gives an overview of future work.

2 Background

In this thesis, we present a framework for intelligent speculative compiler optimization as well as its application to the optimization of memory accesses. Thus, compilers and memory accesses in programs are central background topics. To make the framework intelligent, we consider using machine learning, which constitutes the third relevant background topic. We start with describing the structure of a compiler and its central parts, namely its intermediate representation, program analyses, and program optimizations. For the application of our framework, the role memory plays in the compiler and during program execution is important. We describe the implications the usage of memory has for the compiler, depending on the considered target architecture, as well as techniques to analyze the memory dependencies of a program. After that, we present optimization techniques that have been proposed to mitigate the impact of the memory gap by speculating on dependencies. Finally, we describe machine learning techniques, especially classification learning and cluster analysis, which we use in our approach to make the compiler intelligent.

2.1 Compilers

Compilers are programs that take source code in a given language and translate it to a given target language. We consider especially compilers that translate from a programming language (*e.g.*, C) to executable machine code for a given target machine. The advantage of compilers is that they allow the programmer to develop software in higher-level programming languages, which abstract from the details of the machine. By that, the development process is alleviated. One major challenge for compilers is to generate efficient programs that exploit the capabilities offered by the targeted hardware architecture. To that end,

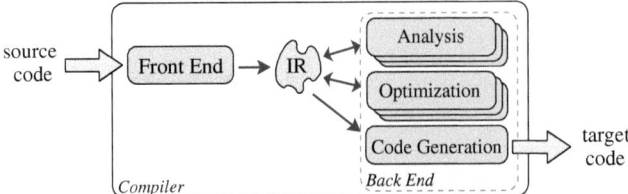

Figure 2.1: Architecture of a Compiler

the compiler tries to optimize the program with respect to a given objective function[1]. Common examples for that are to minimize the execution time of the generated program, its memory consumption, its energy consumption, or its code size. Most of those optimization goals contradict each other.

The architecture of a typical compiler is shown in Figure 2.1. The *front end* translates the source into an abstract *Intermediate Representation (IR)*. Various analyses and optimizations are performed upon the IR, and in the end code generation yields the target program. This part of the compiler is termed as *Back End*. Code generation can be seen as a special optimization, since the translation of the abstract IR to the concrete target level offers many choices and constitutes a vital step in the program optimization. In the following, we consider the central concepts of a compiler in turn, starting from left to right, or, from front end to back end.

2.1.1 Front End

The front end analyses the source code and transforms it into the IR. It starts with a *lexical analysis* of the code, which groups the stream of characters of the source file into meaningful *tokens* (*e.g.*, keywords and identifiers). Then, the *parser* performs a *syntactical analysis* and checks whether the program conforms to the (context-free) grammar of the considered programming language. On success, the result is the *Abstract Syntax Tree (AST)*. Additionally, the *symbol table* is constructed, which contains the defined variables. After that, the *Semantic Analysis* extracts context-sensitive information, *e.g.*, *scopes* of variable definitions are identified and type checks are performed. The AST as well as the symbol table are annotated with semantic information. The

---

[1] Strictly speaking, the term *optimize* is misleading, since most compilers merely *improve* (or try to) the program w.r.t. the objective function, but do not guarantee that the optimum is actually found.

IR is built from the AST by making the control structure (loops, if-then-else) explicit.

2.1.2 Intermediate Representation

The IR represents the program which is considered for compilation. During the translation in the compiler, it passes through various levels, starting from the (high) source level and ending at the (low) target level of the considered machine. The work of a compiler can be correspondingly decomposed into a sequence of steps, which subsequently process the IR. Each step performs one of the following actions:

Analysis The IR is analyzed w.r.t. certain properties and the result is annotated again in the IR. This information can then be used by subsequent optimizations.

Optimization Optimizations transform the representation with the aim of improving it w.r.t. an objective function, under consideration of the IR together with its annotations.

Lowering The IR is transformed to a lower level. Typically, this means that it is enriched with information about the target level (*e.g.*, size of data types) or that constructs like loops are broken down into simpler code (`if` and `goto` statements). *Lowering* is a special case of an optimization.

Figure 2.2 sketches the translation process for a typical compiler, together with the corresponding IR level. The front end translates the source code via a syntax tree into *High-Level IR (HIR)*. In the following, a mixture of the three kinds of steps presented above is performed. First, machine-independent optimizations (*e.g.*, algebraic transformations or constant propagation) can be performed. Then, more specific optimizations will be performed, and the IR is gradually lowered. In the *Medium-Level IR (MIR)*, some notion of the target platform is introduced. At the end, code generation yields the *Low-Level IR (LIR)*, which is very close to the final assembler code. After final optimizations, the assembler code is emitted.[2]

---

[2]In the compiler community, the notion of HIR and LIR is common practice, whereas MIR is often subsumed under HIR.

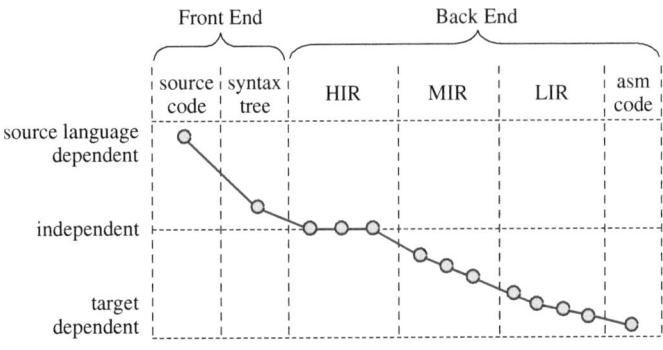

Figure 2.2: Compiler IR

The IR typically represents each function of the program as a *Control Flow Graph (CFG)*, which is generated from the *Abstract Syntax Tree (AST)* of the source file. One important task in CFG creation is to identify the control flow in the program as induced by loops and other control structures. As a result, statements that are always executed together (*i.e.*, which have no intervening branches) are grouped to *Basic Blocks*, which constitute the nodes of the CFG. The edges connecting them represent the control flow. Each CFG has exactly one entry block (the first block of the function) and one exit block (the block with the `return` statement). If a function has multiple `return` statements, the last property can always be achieved by adding a special exit block and making it the successor of all blocks with `return` statement. Analyses will add further information to the CFG or add special edges, *e.g.*, to indicate data dependencies among the statements. Besides the CFG, the IR also contains the data types and variables defined in the program. As data dependencies are important to most program optimizations, it is common practice to annotate this information in the CFG. The resulting graph is called *control data flow graph (CDFG)*.

Figure 2.3 gives a short example for CFG construction. On the left, we see a small function which calculates the greatest common divisor of two numbers. The resulting CFG is shown on the right. It consists of three basic blocks, labeled 1 to 3, and has several control flow edges which connect the blocks. Note the conditional edges from block 1 to blocks 2 and 3, respectively. The loop of the C program is expressed by the loop in the CFG between blocks 1 and 2.

2.1 Compilers

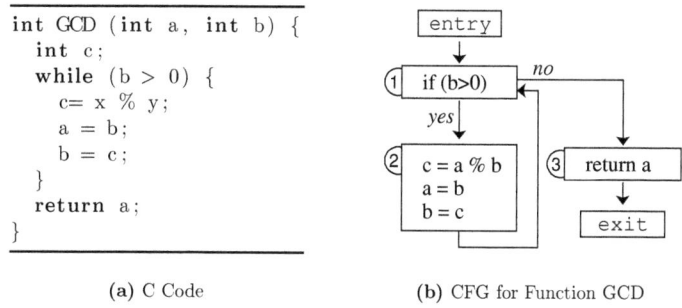

(a) C Code   (b) CFG for Function GCD

Figure 2.3: C code and resulting CFG

As the order of instructions has an impact on correctness as well as on run-time performance, the concept of *dependencies* amongst the statements of the CFG is vital for compiler analyses and optimizations. There exist two types of dependencies: data dependencies and control dependencies. Data dependencies refer to the data flow in the program and cover the intended use (a written value is used) as well as re-use of variables (a variable is re-defined/overwritten). Control dependencies are created by branches, which stem from control constructs (like if-then-else or loops). Within a basic block, we have only data dependencies because all instructions of a basic block are always executed together. Control dependencies occur between merely between basic blocks. In the following, we consider data flow and control flow in turn.

Data Flow

Most optimizations require information about data dependencies, since they perform code motion, which is only allowed if all data dependencies are considered. An example is *Loop Invariant Code Motion*, where expensive code fragments are pre-executed before a loop instead of being re-executed with every loop iteration. This is of course only admissible if the code fraction does not interfere with the remaining loop body. Another example is code scheduling. The dependence information is represented by the *Data Dependence Graph (DDG)*, which contains all statements of the program. Its edges connect statements (or the contained variables) that refer to the same data (*e.g.*, registers or memory locations). Evidently, the DDG is acyclic and transitive. Since each statement may read or write given data, there are four kinds of dependencies:

RAR *(read after read)* Two instructions read the same data.

RAW *(read after write, true dependency)* One instruction reads data that was written by a previous one.

WAR *(write after read, anti dependency)* One instruction writes data that was previously read by another one.

WAW *(write after write, output dependency)* One instruction writes data that was previously written by another one.

Of those, RAW dependencies are those which one has naturally in mind: Data is calculated by one instruction and then used by another one. RAR dependencies indicate shared usage and can be safely ignored. The remaining dependencies, WAR and WAW, are dependencies which are introduced by limited resources and redefinition of variables. For example, they are caused by variable definitions in a loop or by register allocation, where only a limited number of registers are available and thus have to be re-used. To ensure correctness, all but RAR dependencies must not be violated. The DDG is generated by *Dependence Analyses*, which will be described in Section 2.3.1.

When lowering the IR to LIR during code generation, different kinds of data dependencies can be distinguished. During the lowering, the compiler decides which variables will be held in memory and which in registers (see Section 2.2). This requires additional memory instructions (loads and stores) to bring data from the memory in registers for performing calculations on them. Thus, we now have data dependencies amongst registers and those amongst memory locations. Dependencies amongst registers can be exactly determined at compile-time. Memory dependencies, on the other hand, can only be approximated, since in general, the address an instruction references is not known before run-time. The problem of identifying memory dependencies is described in Section 2.3.

As an example for dependencies amongst registers, consider Figure 2.4, which shows a short fragment of assembler code together with the induced dependencies for register r1. Obviously, the RAW dependency between *a)* and *b)* represents a true dependency in the sense of intended information flow. This also holds for the dependency between *a)* and *c)*. Between *b)* and *c)*, a RAR dependency exists (shown by the dotted arrow), which can be safely ignored.

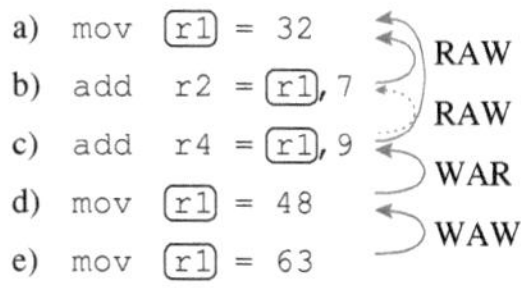

2.1 Compilers

```
a)  mov   [r1] = 32
b)  add   r2 = [r1], 7
c)  add   r4 = [r1], 9
d)  mov   [r1] = 48
e)  mov   [r1] = 63
```
RAW
RAW
WAR
WAW

Figure 2.4: Data Dependencies for Registers

The other dependencies shown are simply due to the re-use of resources (in this case, registers). WAW dependencies among registers will not be found in final machine code, since the first instruction (here: *d)*) can be safely removed. However, for dependencies among memory accesses, it cannot always be determined whether or not a dependency is WAW (this requires evidence that both instructions will always write to the same memory address).

Control Flow

Many optimizations move code from its original basic block to other basic blocks. In doing so, the control dependencies of the CFG must be regarded. It has to be guaranteed that when reaching the original block, the moved code was executed before. Since there are typically various different paths to reach a block, this may entail code duplication. We first focus on *paths* in the CFG. Then, we introduce the *dominance relation*, which helps to decide to which blocks the code has to be moved while limiting the impact on code growth.

The CFG is a graph of basic blocks, connected by directed control flow edges. The entry and the exit block of a CFG are unique and are denoted as **entry** and **exit**, respectively. A *Path* is a sequence of basic blocks such that there is a control flow edge between each pair of succeeding nodes. We treat a path as an ordered set of basic blocks. For a CFG with loops, there may be an infinite number of paths (in case of infinite loop bounds). Hence, to keep the number of paths finite, we consider only acyclic paths. For two blocks blk_1 and blk_2, $PathsBetweenBlocks(blk_1, blk_2)$ yields all possible paths from blk_1 to blk_2. With that, we can define the *dominance relation*.

Dominance Relation   *A block dom is said to* dominate *another block blk if on all paths from the CFG's entry block to blk, dom is executed before blk:*

$$\forall path \in PathsBetweenBlocks(\textbf{entry}, blk) : dom \in path.$$

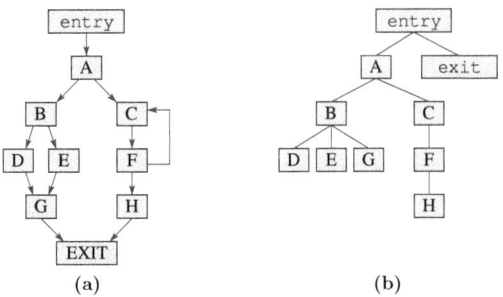

Figure 2.5: (a) Control Flow Graph (b) Dominator Tree

The dominance relation is reflexive, transitive, and anti-symmetric. Each block has at least one dominator, and each block is dominated by the entry block. Figure 2.5 shows a CFG together with the resulting *dominator tree*. It contains all basic blocks of the CFG, and each node immediately dominates its children. The dominator tree can be constructed in linear time (see Harel [Har85]).

When moving code upwards, it has to be ensured that the code has been executed when reaching the original block. To that end, one solution is to move the code into one of the dominator blocks. However, depending on the structure of the CFG, the number of blocks between the dominator and the original block may be enormous. This increases the likeliness of dependencies between the moved code and the intermediate blocks and therefore can make code motion inadmissible. For that case, the concept of the *dominance front* is better suited.

Dominance Front *A set of blocks DomF is the* dominance front *of a block blk if on all paths from the CFG's entry block to blk, exactly one $d \in DomF$ is executed before blk:*

$$\forall path \in PathsBetweenBlocks(\mathtt{entry}, blk) : \exists! d \in DomF : d \in path$$

This is equivalent to say a set of blocks $DomF$ is the *dominance front* of a block *blk* if for the graph obtained by merging all blocks $DomF$ to a single block *dom*, *dom* dominates *blk*. As a special case, if $DomF$ contains only one block, the dominance front is at the same time the dominator of *blk*. An example is given in Figure 2.6. On the left, we see a dominance front for the exit block. On the right, we see the subgraph induced by merging the dominance front

2.1 Compilers

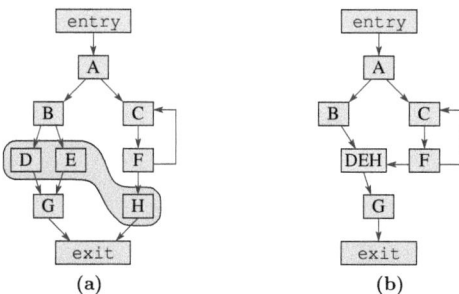

Figure 2.6: (a) CFG with a Dominance Front for the Exit Block (b) Induced Subgraph after Merging Blocks

into one block. This shows that D, E, and H are actually a dominance front, since the obtained merge block DEH dominates the exit block.

2.1.3 Program Analyses

For the decision where and to which extent to optimize, optimizations need various information about the properties of the considered program. Examples are data dependencies among the instructions (see Section 2.1.2), liveness of variables and the redundancy of expressions. This information is collected by *Program Analyses*. They can be categorized along the following dimensions:

Safe/Unsafe In some cases, optimizations require *safe* information. This is the case for data-dependence information, where wrong results may lead to wrong code. Some information, on the other hand, only affects the optimality of the transformation and hence may be *unsafe*. An example is branch prediction, which can be used by many optimizations.

Static/Dynamic *Static* analyses are invoked at compile-time and can only analyze the considered program code. *Dynamic* analyses (or profiling) examine the run-time behavior of the program for a given input. This information can then be used in a subsequent (static) compiler run for optimization. Static analyses can consider all possible cases and are thus necessary to achieve safe results. Dynamic analyses, on the other

	Static	Dynamic
Safe	Conservative Program Analyses	–
Unsafe	Heuristics	Profiling

Table 2.1: Categorization of Program Analyses

hand, consider only a subset of all possible program behavior and are hence inherently unsafe.

Table 2.1 shows the resulting analysis classes. They are discussed in more detail in the following.

Conservative Program Analyses A program analysis observes the CFG and infers the expected dynamic behavior from that (for example, detect redundant computations, determine dependencies amongst variables). The analysis will iterate over the CFG and eventually annotates the resulting information at each statement. If there are different possibilities at a given program point (for example, when control-flow merges after an `if-then-else`), over-approximation takes place, in order to make the analysis safe.

For example, the *Reaching Definitions* analysis annotates at each program point the currently valid definition sites for every variable (a *site* refers to a location in the source code). Hereby, a program point represents the moment just before or after the execution of a statement. Hence, for every statement s, we want to determine the set of valid definition sites before and after s, denoted by $def_{in}(s)$ and $def_{out}(s)$, respectively. Initially, def_{in} is set to the empty set for all statements, and def_{out} is set to (s, x) if s defines x and to the empty set, otherwise. Then this information is propagated along the CFG. The def_{in} information merges the information of its potential predecessors, *i.e.*, the predecessors in the CFG for the first statement of a basic block or the immediate predecessor within a basic block otherwise. The def_{out} information is updated appropriately. A statement keeps all definitions of the def_{in} set except for those that are overwritten by the statement itself. This iteration is repeated until the fixed-point is reached. The existence of the fixed-point can be proved by modeling the information as a lattice. Finiteness of the lattice (every program has only a finite number of statements and variables) and monotonicity of the update function directly show the existence. The result can be used to construct *use-definition* chains, which connect every use of a

2.1 Compilers

variable with the corresponding potential definition sites, as well as to build *definition-use* chains, which represent the dual case where every definition of a variable is linked with its potential uses. Both kinds are important for most optimizations.

The presented example belongs to a class of data-flow analyses that is based on monotone frameworks. An analysis is characterized by the underlying lattice, the direction of the analysis (forward, as in our example, or backwards), a function to combine the information from the predecessors of a node (in our example, a set union), and the update function (*i.e.*, how the information is affected by a statement). These analyses can be implemented efficiently and are linear in the number of program points. For details see *e.g.* Nielson et al. [NNH99]. Other examples are *available expressions analysis* (was *expr* already computed before?) and *live variables analysis* (is x still alive, *i.e.*, will its value be used again?).

The advantage of program analyses is that the information is safe, *i.e.*, optimizations can rely on them, which is important to maintain program correctness. The analysis results are valid for all possible program runs, even corner cases are covered. The disadvantage lies in the over-approximation, which may lead to suboptimal results.

Profiling For profiling, the program is executed on certain input data and the regarded information about the dynamic behavior is collected. Then, this information is used to optimize the program accordingly. The advantage is that the information is very precise and will lead to a strong improvement for the considered input set. However, at the same time, this is the disadvantage of profiling. It is not guaranteed that the program will behave similarly for other inputs, and thus we have very precise information for similar program runs and unprecise or possibly wrong information in all other cases. Besides, profiling requires that input data is available and can significantly increase the overall compile-time. The efficiency of profiling depends on the data to be collected. For counting the frequencies of CFG edges and of CFG paths, efficient algorithms with a run-time overhead of 16% and 31%, respectively, have been proposed (see Ball et al. [BL94], Ball et al. [BL96]). However, in general, the costs of profiling can be expected to be higher by several orders of magnitude. For example, Chen et al. [CLD+04] present an approach to profile data dependencies. While their approach is tuned for efficiency, the required run-time is about 40 times higher than without profiling.

Heuristics Like conservative program analyses, heuristics observe the CFG to predict the dynamic behavior. However, heuristics may yield incorrect results. Thus it is important that their results are not used in a way that correctness could be affected. The heuristics may either be specified by the programmer (rules of thumb) or may be automatically extracted from previous observations of the program behavior. This entails a previous dynamic profiling phase, which executes programs on typical input sets, collects the regarded information and derives from that the heuristics, which can be later on invoked statically. Heuristics may either predict functional or non-functional program behavior. In the first case, heuristics can augment or replace conservative program analyses. Since heuristics are unsafe, the optimization must ensure program correctness in case of wrong predictions. In the second case, wrong predictions merely may lead to less performance gain and, hence, maintaining program correctness is not an issue. Heuristics combine the ideas of profiling and program analyses: They can be more precise than program analyses, since they need not to be correct in all cases, and they avoid the overfitting as inherent to profiling, since they are not tailored to a special program run.

In this section, we discussed how information about the program can be collected by program analyses. In the next sections, we see how this can be used by optimizations.

2.1.4 Optimizations

As described above, there are many different kinds of optimization. One criterion to classify optimizations is the IR level they work on. This ranges from high-level optimizations to low-level optimizations. Another criterion, which is orthogonal to the IR level, is the functionality of the optimization. The following shows a functional classification, which covers most optimizations (based on Cooper et al. [CT04, p.495])

- **Dead Code Elimination:** Remove unrequired code. Reasons may be that its result is not used or that it cannot be reached at run-time.

- **Specialize** Consider the code context to find a specialized and more efficient version (*e.g.*, *Constant Propagation*, *Strength Reduction*).

- **Inlining/Unrolling:** Reduce the overhead of function calls/loops. Additionally, this allows for further optimizations, *e.g.*, loop unrolling can allow for more parallelism in the code.

2.1 Compilers

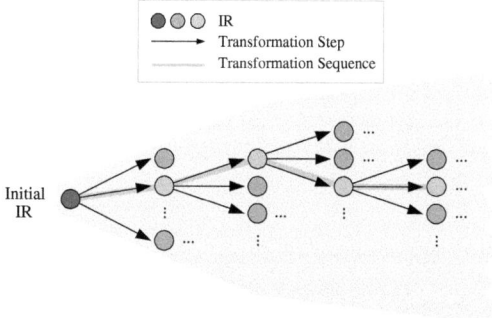

Figure 2.7: Tree of Possible Transformation Sequences

- **Code Motion:** For example, move code from blocks to less frequently executed predecessors if admissible (*Loop Invariant Code Motion*)
- **Redundancy Elimination:** Re-use already computed values. This can be implemented using code motion.

Some of these optimizations can be applied on different abstraction levels. For example, dead code elimination can be applied first on the high-level IR and then again on the low-level IR, since during the course of optimizations, parts of the code may have become dead code.

Orthogonal to these classifications, optimizations can be either categorized as *optimal* or as *heuristic*. A given optimization has several opportunities in deciding in which way the code should be transformed. Typically, the resulting overall transformation can be decomposed into a sequence of simpler transformation steps, which are similar to each other. For example, for Code Motion, a transformation step would mean to move a piece of code to another place. During the optimization, it has to be decided *which* code should be moved *where*. As a consequence, for each optimization, the applicable transformation steps span a search tree that contains all possible versions of the program the optimization can yield (see Figure 2.7). Starting with the initial program version as root node, the successors of a node are obtained by applying each of all possible transformation steps. Each path that starts at the root represents a certain transformation sequence (see the highlighted path in the figure). If we assume that each program version can be labeled by its cost (*e.g.*, estimated execution time or estimated power consumption), the goal is to find the version with the minimal cost. If the optimization explores the search space *exhaustively*, it can find a program version that is guaranteed to be optimal (w.r.t. the capabilities of the currently regarded optimization), and hence the optimization is termed *optimal*. However, for most optimizations, the search space grows rapidly due to combinatorial explosion, and exhaustive exploration is very expensive or even unfeasible. This problem is met by *heuristic* optimizations, which only explore the search space *partially*. For example, a greedy optimization could construct the transformation sequence iteratively by always selecting the best applicable transformation step and disregarding all other options. While the result is not guaranteed to be optimal, it is mostly considered sufficiently good. Besides, it can be obtained in reasonable time, which is necessary for compilers used in practice. It depends on the application as well as on the optimization, whether optimality is required or whether a solution yielded by a heuristic approach is sufficient.

In case of *optimal optimizations*, all relevant aspects of the program are formalized in a model, which captures the optimization problem. Based on that, an *objective function* is specified, which expresses the aim of the regarded optimization. This is used to find a solution to the problem, which is guaranteed to be the best one w.r.t. the objective function. One popular technique that is generally applicable to solve such optimization problems is *Integer Linear Programming (ILP)* (Nemhauser et al. [NW88]). The advantage lies in the guaranteed optimality. However, the more complex the optimization problem gets, the less feasible it is to find the solution. Winkel [Win07] presents an approach to use ILP for scheduling. The required time to find the solution grows rapidly with the considered code size. For up to 100 lines of code, a solution is found within seconds. For up to 200 lines, it is found in 20 minutes on average. Beyond that, no numbers are given, but high computation times can be expected. Hence, optimal optimizations via ILP can be applied to hotspot optimization, which only target selected pieces of the code (*e.g.*, loops) that have a major impact on program performance. In some cases, instead of the general ILP, a specialized formalization can be derived, and more scalable techniques can be used to find a solution. Scholz et al. [SHK04] present an approach for speculative partial redundancy elimination, which models the problem as a network flow problem, for which efficient solution techniques are available. To sum up, optimal approaches exist and are used where resources are extremely limited. For a certain optimization, they consider the complete optimization space and select the solution guaranteed to be best. However, the challenge lies in deriving a compact formalization of the underlying optimization problem and in choosing an appropriate algorithm to find the solution, which is important to avoid or at least limit combinatorial explosion. Besides,

2.1 Compilers

optimality is only guaranteed w.r.t. the specified objective function. Hence, if the model of the optimization problem contains approximated parameters, the optimality of the solution is put into perspective.

Heuristic optimizations, on the other hand, trade off guaranteed optimality of the solution for scalability. Opposed to the optimal approach, only a small part of the search space spanned by all possible optimizing transformations is explored. While it is not guaranteed that the resulting optimization is optimal, mostly, it can be obtained efficiently, which is in many cases indispensable. Besides, heuristic approaches are more suitable for approximated information.

2.1.5 Code Generation

Code generation is a special case of a low-level optimization. This transformation is a vital transformation step in the compiler. It maps the abstract IR onto the concrete target machine. This mapping is ambiguous, and the choice made here influences heavily the performance of the generated program. It includes the three phases *instruction selection*, *instruction scheduling*, and *register allocation*. Those phases are highly interdependent and each phase alone constitutes an NP-hard optimization problem. Typical compilers solve this problem by implementing these phases separately and calling them in a fixed order, which sacrifices optimal results, but makes the problem manageable. The typical sequence is: 1. instruction selection, 2. pre-scheduling, 3. register allocation, 4. post-scheduling/packing. The *pre-scheduling* aims at reordering the instructions to minimize register pressure (*i.e.*, to cut down the number of required registers), the *post-scheduling* tries to minimize the execution time.

Instruction Selection For instruction selection, one common technique is tree pattern matching with a bottom-up rewrite system. A set of rules specify how the IR should be mapped to assembler code. Each rule states how a certain tree pattern, which will be matched against the IR, can be reduced to a so-called *non-terminal* symbol, and which assembler code should be emitted. The *non-terminals* can occur in the tree pattern of the rules, which allows for chaining different rules together. Instruction selection typically considers one statement at a time and tries to find a rewrite sequence that transforms the statement to a single node. Usually, the rules are associated with costs, and a cost-optimal rewrite sequence is searched for. This technique allows for retargetable compilers: The instruction selection mechanism is generic. When retargeting to a new platform, only the corresponding rewrite rules have to be implemented.

Register Allocation Before register allocation, the compiler uses an arbitrary number of virtual registers for intermediate results. Register allocation maps this set to the real set of available registers. This includes the insertion of spill and fill code, which swaps registers in and out of memory if the number of registers is exhausted, and code for saving and restoring register values at the begin and the end of a function, respectively.

(Post-)Scheduling The scheduler rearranges the instructions to minimize execution time, which can be achieved by executing expensive instructions (*i.e.*, those which take a long time) first, so that the waiting time is hidden by other instructions. This especially applies to memory accesses, which may experience latencies of 100 cycles or even more. However, during the re-ordering of code, the compiler must not violate any dependency, since then, the correctness of the program is not guaranteed. Thus, the opportunities for optimizations of the scheduler highly depend on the precision of the information about data dependencies.

2.2 The Role of Memory in Compilers

During compilation, the compiler also decides about the data layout of the program (*i.e.*, global data and stack frames), and it decides whether or not variables have to reside in memory. Primitive data types typically fit in registers and thus do not have to be put in memory generally[3]. Complex structures, like lists or trees, require a special treatment. If they are defined through a declaration, the compiler will allocate enough space in the corresponding stack frame or in the global data section (depending on whether the declaration has local or global scope). If they are allocated dynamically (*i.e.*, by calls to special functions like `malloc` in C), the memory allocation happens at run-time. In the first case, the compiler knows the exact addresses. In the latter case, it cannot determine them at compile-time. As a further complication, the same allocation site can lead to multiple allocations at run-time if it lies within a loop or within a function which is called multiple times.

---

[3]An exception has to be made if, somewhere in the program, the address of the variable is taken. Then, the variable must be in memory, since it may be referred to by its address.

2.2 The Role of Memory in Compilers

This complicates the dependence analysis considerably, and to ensure program correctness, a dependency between two memory accesses has to be assumed unless proved to be absent.

The implications of the memory gap, the discrepancy between the speeds of CPU and main memory, lead to a potentially drastic impact on program performance. The compiler plays a major role in mitigating this impact. It can reorder instructions, so that the long latencies of load instructions are hidden. The impact of the memory gap depends on the selected architecture.

Systems with Limited Resources

For these systems, which are frequently used in embedded systems, in many cases, dynamic memory allocation is not admitted. This simplifies the dependence analyses significantly, since now mainly scalars and arrays have to be analyzed, for which efficient analyses are available. Another consequence is that the memory traffic is more predictable, since all data is either on the stack or in the (typically continuous) global data area. This allows for a better exploitation of the caches. Both factors limit the impact of the memory gap. Additionally, these systems often have a comparatively low CPU frequency, which reduces the memory gap in the first place.

Sequential Systems

For these systems, the compiler has to cope with imprecise information on data dependencies due to dynamic memory allocation and pointer arithmetic. However, the absence of parallelism helps the compiler slightly: To reduce the impact of the memory gap, other instructions are scheduled between a long-latency load and the corresponding use. Since all those instructions are executed sequentially, the reduction of the effective latency is higher than it would be on a parallel machine. Still, for memory-intensive programs and high load latencies, this will not be sufficient to hide the memory gap completely.

Super-scalar Processors

These processors can execute multiple instructions in parallel. The parallelism is decided dynamically at run-time. The processor receives the code sequence and creates a schedule. This requires complex hardware, since the processor must be able to perform a dependence analysis at run-time. Again, the compiler can assist the processor by previously reordering the instructions to hide the latencies. However, since the processor is parallel, the required number of instructions to hide a given load latency increases with the parallelism offered by the processor. This makes it harder to hide the latencies. However, for super-scalar processors, the processor can ignore false dependencies that could not be proved absent by the static compiler. In case of a memory stall, it can look for other instructions which are ready to execute.

VLIW Processors

Very Long Instruction Word (VLIW) processors also allow for parallelism, which makes it harder for the compiler to hide the latencies. As opposed to super-scalar processors, however, the processor is rather simple and requires the compiler to derive a schedule of the code. That means that it lies in the responsibility of the compiler to arrange the code and to decide which instructions can be executed together. The advantage is that the compiler has a global view of the whole program and that it can take its time. On the down side, the compiler has only static information, which is less precise than the information that would be available in a super-scalar processor at run-time. If the processor stalls, nothing can be done but to wait for the memory command to finish. This puts the compiler into a strong responsibility, since it is solely liable for the schedule and therefore for the program performance.

For the considered system classes, the compiler has an increasingly important influence on mitigating the memory gap. Hence, for VLIW processors, it is most important to focus on optimizing memory accesses, since otherwise, the run-time performance of programs may be dominated by stalls caused by the memory system. For that reason, we target VLIW processors in the application of our proposed framework.

2.3 Analysis of Memory Accesses

As we have seen previously, the compiler needs to regard the data dependencies of the program to keep the program correctness. In the following, we sketch how the dependence information can be determined in general. Then, we describe alias analyses, which determine the memory dependencies of a program.

2.3 Analysis of Memory Accesses

2.3.1 Dependence Analyses

Dependence analyses are vital to construct the DDG for a program, which is used by nearly all optimizations to decide about the correctness of a given transformation. The analyses can be categorized into one of the following three types according to the class of data types they focus on:

Scalars For scalar variables, the *def-use* analysis can be used to yield the dependencies. If the IR obeys the *SSA (Static Single Assignment)* form (into which it can be transformed easily, see Cytron et al. [CFR+91]), the dependencies among scalars are directly visible because for every redefinition of a variable, a new version of that variable is introduced. Classic SSA form assumes un-aliased variables. However, extensions to cope with aliases have been proposed, *e.g.*, by Chow et al. [CCL+96].

Arrays For arrays, the situation is more difficult, since the expression to calculate the index can be complex. However, if only linear expressions are allowed, *Diophantine Equations* can be used to efficiently decide about dependency (Kennedy et al. [KA02, pp. 94-96]).

Any In the generic case, however, when also arbitrary variables and pointer expressions are considered, dependency is undecidable (Landi [Lan92]). *Alias analyses* approximate the information which variables may be aliases of each other. This has to be regarded during the construction of the DDG.

All possible dependencies have to be reported to ensure correctness. Here again the problem of over-approximation takes effect: Most dependencies depend on input data, which is not known at compile-time. Hence the analyses have to act conservatively. This leads to more edges in the DDG, which hampers code optimizations.

In the presence of pointers and structures on the heap, alias analyses are vital to cut down the number of edges in the DDG. In the next section, we briefly present the problem of aliases in more detail.

```
int a,b, *p,*q;
p=&a;
if (cond) q = &a;
else q = &b;
...
*q = 20;
a = 2*a;
```

	Points-To Targets	
	maybe	*must*
p		a
q	a,b	

(a)   (b)

Figure 2.8: (a) Sample Code with Aliasing (b) Resulting Points-To Table

2.3.2 Alias Analyses

A variable is an *alias* of another variable if it can be used to refer to and modify the latter one. This can already occur at function calls with call-by-reference arguments and is especially relevant for languages with pointer-arithmetic as *e.g.* C. Alias analyses typically collect *points-to* sets that contain for every pointer the set of targets it may point to. Figure 2.8 gives a short example for aliasing. We have integer variables a and b and integer pointers p and q. p is set to the address of a, *i.e.*, it is now an alias of a. The value of q depends on a condition *cond*. If *cond* is true, q is set to the address of a, otherwise to that of b. In Figure 2.8b, the result of an alias analysis is shown: For every variable, we see a list of targets. As shown here, it may be distinguished whether a variable points *definitely* or only *potentially* to a target. The second to last line of the code in Figure 2.8a shows the importance of the aliasing relation. A value is written to the address contained in q. This means that either a or b are changed. Hence, there is a potential dependency between the last two lines, since the last line reads and writes a. As we see here, alias analysis gets complicated in the presence of branches. This is even more the case if we take aliasing across functions into account.

Alias analyses iterate over the program code and collect possible targets of pointers. Table 2.2 lists the classes of statements which are relevant for the analysis (following Steensgaard [Ste96b]). The type of the statement determines in which way the points-to information is affected by it. Depending on the type of the alias analysis, not all listed statements may be relevant. For example, the easiest analysis *Address-Taken* assumes that all variables, which have their address taken, are aliased by any pointer. This analysis would only have to consider *Address Assign* statements and collect the variables on the

2.3 Analysis of Memory Accesses

$x = y$	Simple Assign	$x = alloc(..)$	Allocation
$x = \&y$	Address Assign	$*x = y$	Assign to Pointer
$x = *y$	Pointer Assign	$fun(x_1,..,x_n) \to y$	Function decl
$x = op(y_1,..,y_n)$	Operator Assign	$x = f(y_1,..,y_n)$	Function call

Table 2.2: Types of Statements

right hand side. Then, the points-to sets for all pointers would consist of this collected list.

There are various dimensions to distinguish different analyses (for a more detailed discussion, see, *e.g.*, Hind et al. [HP00]):

data-flow   *sensitive* vs. *insensitive:* Is the data flow considered, which is induced by the instructions? While this is the case for most analyses, it is not for the *Address-Taken Analysis*, which simply looks at the right hand side of certain assignments.

control-flow   *sensitive* vs. *insensitive:* Is the control flow considered? If so, the analysis has to merge the information whenever control merges, *e.g.*, after an *if-then-else*. This also means that different possible points-to sets have to be maintained at the same time. In the extreme case, one points-to set for every path.

context   *sensitive* vs. *insensitive:* Is the calling context at function calls considered? Otherwise, the analysis assumes values could flow from a call through the function and return to another caller.

scope   *inter-procedural* vs. *intra-procedural:* Is only one procedure considered at a time, or is the whole program considered? For C programs, which may consist of several separate files, there is *inter-procedural (intra-file)* as an intermediate level.

heap   *aware* vs. *unaware:* Are the various dynamically allocated memory areas distinguished from each other? If not, the heap would appear as one object, and all dynamically allocated variables would be assumed to be aliased.

structure *aware* vs. *unaware:* What is the granularity of the analysis? Are different fields of a structure or different elements of an array distinguished?

Generally, the analyses have to trade off precision for scalability, and the various criteria have a different impact on that. Data-flow-sensitivity is hardly under discussion, since without it, the results would be extremely imprecise, and the introduced overhead is low. The same holds for whether or not making the analysis inter-procedural, which gives more precision at acceptable overhead. Also heap-awareness is important for meaningful analysis results, since otherwise all heap references would be reported as aliased. Besides, the additional overhead of distinguishing the different allocation sites is limited. Compared to that, structure-awareness leads to only a slight increase in precision, but leads to a higher overhead. The remaining choices have a major impact on the scalability of the overall analysis. Control-flow-sensitivity collects the alias information for each program point, hence it is very memory intensive. Context-sensitivity, on the other hand, needs to collect the alias information for every possible calling context, which also jeopardizes scalability. Typical alias analyses, as found in compilers, are data-flow-sensitive, control-flow-insensitive, inter-procedural, context-sensitive, and heap- and structure-aware. Recently, scalable analyses that are control-flow-sensitive as well as context-sensitive have been proposed (see Section 3.2.2).

However, even the most precise alias analysis can do nothing more than to over-approximate the actual aliases present at run-time significantly. This was shown by an empirical study by Mock et al. [MDCE01], which measured the average points-to size predicted by different alias analyses and compared them with the size of the actual points-to sets experienced at run-time for given input data. While the actual points-to sets had an average size of about one target, the analyses predicted average target sizes per program ranging from 1 to 450, with an overall average ranging from 26 to 80. Moreover, most of the pointers had only one actual target at run-time. This illustrates the imprecision of the analyses, which is caused by their overly conservative over-approximations.

2.4 Speculative Optimization

The problem with alias analyses is that they have to be conservative, since they have to be correct. They have to consider all possible dependencies, whether or not they may actually occur at run-time for realistic input data. To overcome this problem, *speculative optimization techniques* have been proposed. The idea is to speculatively ignore unlikely memory dependencies. Then, the DDG will have fewer edges, and the optimizations have more opportunities at their disposal. Of course, it has to be made sure that the program behavior remains the same if the ignored dependencies actually *do* hold at run-time. This will be dealt with by special checks and recovery code, which is issued when speculation fails.

The use of speculation now admits *unsafe* alias analyses. While conservative analyses have to report a dependency *unless proved to be absent*, speculative analyses have the freedom to do the opposite and report only dependencies *proved to exist*. Of course, precise results are still important, since misspeculation comes at the price of additional overhead. But it enables the alias analyses to become realistic instead of overly pessimistic.

Speculative optimizations can ignore data dependencies. This is termed *data speculation*. However, to allow for optimizations across basic block level, it has to be speculated on control flow, since a load may be newly introduced to a path. This is referred to as *control speculation*. Both techniques are orthogonal to each other, hence a combination is possible. Finally, in case of misspeculation, the correct system state has to be re-established. This is done by recovery code. In the following, we look at data and control speculation as well as recovery code generation in more detail. After that, we discuss to which extent hardware support is required and, also, present in current architectures.

2.4.1 Data Speculation

Data speculation ignores data dependencies and moves loads across possibly dependent stores to issue them earlier and to thereby hide their latency (at least partly). An example is given in Figure 2.9. On the left, we see an excerpt of a basic block, in which we load a value and use it. As it may happen, the loaded value is not cached. Therefore, it has to be fetched from main memory, which will take a long time, in which the processor is deemed to wait (denoted by the cloud). However, nothing can be done, since the load

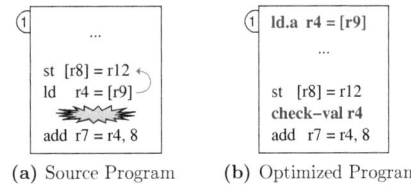

(a) Source Program   (b) Optimized Program

Figure 2.9: Data Speculation

is immediately preceded by a store, for which the alias analysis reported a possibly data dependency. Conservative optimizations would stop here, since no optimization can be statically guaranteed to be correct: The value to be loaded may be changed by the store instruction, hence it cannot be issued before it. However, if we have some evidence that the reported dependency is unlikely, we can optimize speculatively and deal with correctness dynamically at run-time. The result is shown on the right: We move the load to the top of the block. The load is now marked as an *advanced load* (*ld.a*) to indicate that it is speculative. To ensure correctness, after the possibly conflicting store, we have to check whether the value is still valid. This is done by a special *check* (*check-val*). If we detect that everything went well, we can proceed and use the value. If not, we have to reload the value from memory. This is dealt with by *recovery code*, which is discussed in more detail in Section 2.4.3. In this example, the load was moved only across one store. In general, data speculation can move the load over an arbitrary number of stores.

For speculation, loads have to be issued non-blocking, which means that the stall does not occur on the load instruction itself, but only when the value is actually used by another instruction. Despite that, further hardware support is not required, but advantageous, as we will see later.

2.4.2 Control Speculation

While data speculation ignores data dependencies, control speculation ignores control dependencies to increase the optimization potential. Since basic blocks are only of limited size, the presented data speculation may not suffice to hide a significant amount of the latency. Instead, speculative optimization across block boundaries offers more potential to reduce the latency. This requires limited hardware support. If a load is moved speculatively into another block, it may happen that it is newly introduced to a path through the program,

2.4 Speculative Optimization

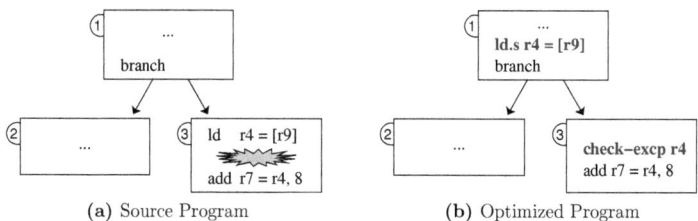

(a) Source Program (b) Optimized Program

Figure 2.10: Control Speculation

on which it was not present before. This is acceptable for loads with valid addresses. But if, for example, the address is invalid, an exception[4] would be introduced on a path where it would not have occurred before. Hence, in this case, the load has to suppress potential exceptions, and they have to be deferred to the original block.

An example is given in Figure 2.10. On the right, we see the original code. In block 3, a value is loaded and used. Again we assume that the load leads to a long stall. With data speculation, we cannot optimize, since the load cannot be safely moved to block 1. There exists a path $1 \rightarrow 2$, onto which the load would be newly introduced. If the load did raise an exception, the program behavior would be changed. But with control speculation, we can move the load in block 1 and mark it as *speculative* (*ld.s*). This means that exceptions which may potentially be raised are deferred. Hence, the behavior of the path $1 \rightarrow 2$ remains unchanged. Before the use, a special check is added (*check-excp*). In case of a deferred exception, it will be reported now. Note that control speculation *per se* does not entail data speculation, especially, misspeculation is not an issue[5]. The value loaded is known to be unchanged, the only issue is the deferral of exceptions to be able to optimize across block boundaries. Since both techniques are orthogonal to each other, they could and should be combined. Control speculation can be seen as a mean to apply data speculation at a broader context.

---

[4]For example, a page fault or a segmentation fault.
[5] Of course, when a load is introduced on a new path, it has to be ensured that the target register of the load does not overwrite a register used on that path. This can be achieved by register renaming.

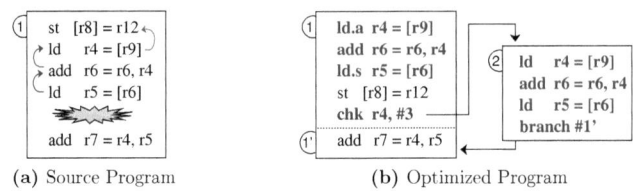

Figure 2.11: Speculation with Recovery Code

2.4.3 Recovery Code

In case of misspeculation, the correct system state has to be recovered. This can be done by branching to a newly added basic block, which contains the recovery code and jumps back right to the use of the value. So far, we speculated only on single load instructions. In this case, the recovery code only consists of the original load instruction. In the general case, the speculatively loaded value can be used by further instructions. If a load together with its dependent instructions is optimized speculatively, in case of misspeculation, the load together with its dependants has to be re-executed by the recovery code. Figure 2.11 gives an example. On the left, we have a chain of instructions that loads an address, adds a value to that, and loads from the resulting address. The second load leads to a stall. However, since a potential dependency is reported between the first load and the preceding store (*i.e.*, the addresses in $r8$ and $r9$ may overlap), no optimization can be done. Speculation allows us to ignore this dependency if it is deemed unlikely. The result is shown on the right: All three instructions are moved across the store. Before the use of the finally loaded value, it has to be checked whether the first load is still valid. This is done by the check instruction. Other than before, in case of misspeculation, a chain of recovery code has to be executed. In that case, the check instruction jumps to block 2, which contains the recovery code and jumps finally back right to the use. Clearly, in that case, we have a higher gain, but also a higher overhead. Note that this does not require additional hardware support. For data speculation without hardware support, an extra block for recovery code has to be added even for the simple case of optimizing only one single load.

2.4 Speculative Optimization

2.4.4 Required Hardware Support

As mentioned previously, speculation benefits from hardware support, but does not depend on it. The only requirements to hardware is the availability of non-blocking loads and, in case of control speculation, the possibility to defer exceptions (like page faults). However, hardware support can help to improve the efficiency of speculation, namely for the validity check and for the execution of recovery code.

In case of data speculation, the validity of the speculatively loaded value has to be checked before using it. In other words, it has to be ensured that no intervening store has changed the loaded value, which means that for each store, the target address must not overlap with the address of the loaded value. This check can be performed with and without hardware support, making it more or less efficient, respectively. In case of hardware support, the check can be made efficient by adding a small table to keep track of the speculatively loaded values. Whenever an advanced load is issued, its address is added to the table, and every store that is executed checks whether an overlapping address is in this table. If so, it is removed. Then, the check can be performed by a table lookup: If the corresponding address is in the table, the value is still valid. Otherwise, the corresponding recovery code has to be executed. Without hardware support, data speculation causes more overhead. For every intervening store, instructions have to be inserted to explicitly compare the target address with that of the considered load. If store and load are equally aligned and if both have the same size, one check for equality of the corresponding addresses is sufficient. In the general case, two checks are necessary to prove that the load and the store do not conflict. For example, consider a 4-byte store to an address $addr_1$ and an 8-byte load from address $addr_2$. To determine whether both instructions are independent, we need to check if either $addr_1 + 4 <= addr_2$ or $addr_2 + 8 <= addr_1$. If one of these checks fails, recovery code has to be issued. Clearly, without hardware support, speculation leads to more overhead, which increases with every intervening store (remember that with hardware support, misspeculation cost does not depend on the number of stores). However, for load instructions with a very high latency, this can still pay off in the end. The gain of speculation amounts to the number of cycles saved by issuing the load earlier (*i.e.*, the number of cycles the intervening instructions consume) minus the overhead for the validity check in the positive case, and to the overhead for the check plus the time needed for the reload in

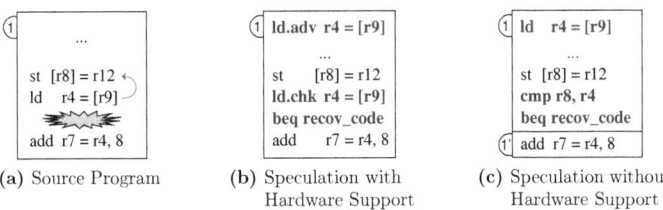

Figure 2.12: Speculation with and without Hardware Support

the negative case. Hence, even if not the entire latency of the load is hidden, at least it is reduced.

Hardware support can also reduce the overhead of recovery code execution, which is relevant for both data and control speculation. In general, before the use, a special check has to ensure the validity of the value, which jumps to the recovery code if necessary. For speculation of single loads, in which case the recovery code would only consist of the load instruction, hardware can offer a special instruction, which performs check and reload (if necessary) at once. This saves the overhead of two branches and makes speculation especially efficient.

In Figure 2.12, we see another example which contrasts speculation with and without hardware support. On the left (Figure 2.12a), we see a sequence of assembler code. A value is loaded into register $r4$ and then used. If the value does not happen to be in the cache, this will lead to a long stall. Moving up the load is not safe in general, since $r8$ and $r9$ may refer to the same address. However, if our speculative alias analysis tells us that the addresses are probably different, we can optimize speculatively. First, we consider speculation with hardware support (see Figure 2.12b). We move the load across the store and make it an *advanced* load, which is comparative to a binding prefetch. Then, after the store, we check whether the loaded value is still valid. If so, we avoided a long stall. Otherwise, we simply reload again, and the program run-time is similar to the left program. It is important to note that speculation does not sacrifice correctness. If we misspeculate, we only get additional overhead but the results stay correct. Without further hardware support for speculation, additional instructions must be inserted to check whether the addresses overlap and to execute recovery code to reload the value if necessary (see Figure 2.12c).

2.4.5 Hardware Support in Modern Processor Architectures

Because the concepts of speculation have been proposed over twenty years ago and because the memory gap has grown and leads to significant, if not drastic performance limitations, it can be expected that speculation will be increasingly used in new processor architectures. One architecture that already offers hardware support for speculation is the Intel Itanium processor. We use this processor as platform in our case study. The Intel Itanium, and especially its capabilities concerning speculation, will be presented in the following.

The Intel Itanium processor has an *EPIC (Explicitly Parallel Instruction Computing)* architecture, which is an extension of the VLIW architecture. It has an issue width of 6 instructions per cycle. However, the instruction format is more general: The instructions are packed into bundles of 3 instructions each. Instructions that should be issued at the same cycle, form *instruction groups*. Those groups can span several cycles, and the processor can choose how many instructions to execute at once. With that, the same instruction format can be used for different issue widths. The Itanium supports *predication* to increase basic block size. Basically, predication enables the conversion of control flow into data flow. For example, an *If-Then-Else* region can be merged into one *hyperblock*. The comparing instruction of the *if* sets two boolean predicates (contained in special registers on the Itanium), with the first containing the result of the comparison and the other containing the negative value. The *then*- and the *else*-branch are each marked with the corresponding predicate. Instructions that have a false predicate have no effect at run-time. Thus, both branches can be executed, and the predicates take care that only the correct one has an effect. This helps to increase block size, which leads to less branches and therefore decreases branch misprediction stalls. Additionally, an increased block size means also more potential exploit the parallelism of the processor because it offers the scheduler more instructions to choose from.

Data and control speculation are supported by special hardware. For data speculation, the *Advanced Load Address Table (ALAT)* contains all values that were loaded in advance (indicated by *ld.a*). For every store instruction, the ALAT is considered, and conflicting entries that are invalidated by the store are removed. The check instruction consults the ALAT table. If its address is within the table, the loaded value is still valid. Otherwise, it has to be reloaded again. If only one single load has been optimized, the *ld.c* instruction can perform both check and reload (if necessary) at once. Otherwise, a check instruction detects misspeculation and branches to recovery code. Control

Cache Level	Size (bytes)	Latency (cycles)
L1	16k D + 16k I	1
L2	256k	min 5 (FP: 6)
L3	1.5M	min 12
Main Memory	1G	min 180-225

Table 2.3: Configuration of the Intel Itanium2 McKinley 900MHz Processor

speculation can be indicated by a special flag on the load ($ld.s$). In that case, every exception is deferred and not reported until the corresponding $ld.c$ is encountered. All registers have an additional *Not a Thing (NaT)*-bit, which is set if the value is invalid due to an exception. Data and control speculation can be combined ($ld.sa$).

The cache architecture and the corresponding latencies are shown in Table 2.3 (taken from [Int04, pp. 33, 34, 48]). The actual latencies can be higher than the shown values. There are two L1 caches for data and instructions, respectively. The other caches are unified (*i.e.*, contain both). For the L2 cache, the minimum latency depends on whether the data is integer or floating-point (FP). For speculation, the following latencies have to be considered. On success, the check load has a one cycle latency. Misspeculation leads to an additional overhead of 8 or 18 cycles, depending on whether or not the value is in the cache, plus the cycles required to load the value from memory if necessary. If recovery code has to be executed (via the *chk* instruction), the overhead further increases due to branching. Speculation should be applied carefully. On the one hand, the overhead of misspeculation has to be regarded. On the other hand, the ALAT table is of limited size (32 entries in case of the Itanium). Hence, too aggressive speculation could cause the eviction of entries from the ALAT table, which can lead to spurious misspeculation (*i.e.*, actually successful speculation is interpreted as misspeculation, since the corresponding entry remains no longer in the ALAT).

2.5 Machine Learning

Machine Learning (ML) techniques can be used to automatically infer information from a series of observations. Machine learning can either be *unsupervised* or *supervised*. In the first case, we know what to learn. For example, in case

2.5 Machine Learning

of classification learning, each observation is annotated with a class label (that is, it belongs to one of a fixed number of categories). The aim of learning is to identify the relationship between an observation and its corresponding class. This allows us to classify new, previously unseen data. In the second case, for unsupervised learning, the observations have no annotations. For example, in case of cluster analysis, the goal is to group the observations together. This can be seen as first defining a set of classes and second defining the class of each observation. Opposed to supervised learning, we have no means of knowing whether or not the annotated classes are correct. In this thesis, we use both techniques. We use classification learning to learn the relationship between code properties and run-time behavior. From that, we can generate heuristics. We use cluster analysis to perform program classification, such that similar programs are put together in one class. This allows for having a set of specialized heuristics, which we expect to increase the precision of the predictions. In the following, we consider classification learning and cluster analysis in turn. After that, we discuss how the precision of a predictor obtained by classification learning can be assessed.

2.5.1 Classification Learning

For classification learning, we have a set of observations annotated with their classes. From that, a model is built (or trained) to explain the relationship between observations and their classes as precise as possible. This is illustrated in Figure 2.13a. We have six observations, each described by a feature vector and by its class, and build a model from that. This model can then be used as a predictor to classify new, previously unseen observations based on their feature vectors (Figure 2.13b). To validate the precision of the predictor, it can be applied to the training data, and the predictions can then be compared with the known correct classes. This yields a measure for the precision of the model w.r.t. the training data. However, typically, the learned model is used to classify new, unseen data. Thus, a more realistic estimate of the precision of the model is given by applying the model to a new set of data, for which the correct classes are known as well, and by comparing the predictions with the actual classes (Figure 2.13c). One pitfall in learning is *overfitting*. This occurs if the model explains the training data precisely, but performs worse on new data. In other words, the model failed to generalize and instead focused on the peculiarities of the training data. The risk of overfitting can be reduced

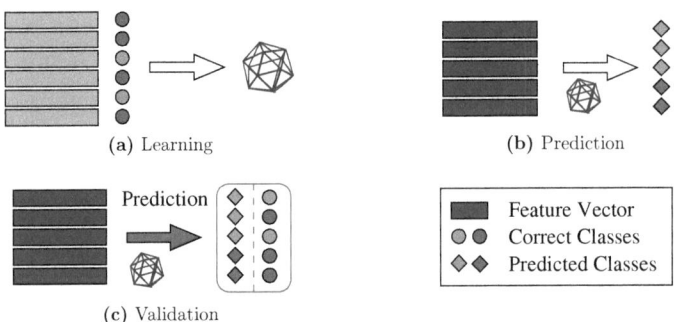

Figure 2.13: Machine Learning

by data preprocessing and by selecting sensible parameters for the considered learning algorithm.

More formally, the problem solved by classification learning is the following: We have a set of m observations, $O = (o_i)$. Each observation o is described by an n-element feature vector $Feat(o) \in \mathcal{F}$, which collects its properties. Additionally, we have a set of k classes, $\mathcal{C} = (\mathbf{c}_j)$, and for each o we know the corresponding class c. The aim is to model the relationship between features and classes. This yields a predictor function $p : \mathcal{F} \to \mathcal{C}$, which can be also applied to new observations. The features can be thought of as a $m \times n$ matrix $F = (f_{i,j})$, where $f_{i,j}$ denotes the j-th feature for the i-th observation. Besides, we have an m-element vector $C = (c_i)$, which contains the corresponding (correct) classes. The predictor function p can be used to yield an m-element vector $\widehat{C} = (\widehat{c}_i)$, which contains the predicted classes. The columns of F (the features) are also called input (or explanatory, dependent) variables, and C is called response or dependent variable. For the training data, we have the feature matrix F_{train} together with the vector of the corresponding classes, C_{train}. Similarly, we have F_{test} and C_{test} as test data. Training yields the model M_{train}. This model can be applied to the corresponding data sets to yield the predicted classes $\widehat{C}_{train}$ and $\widehat{C}_{test}$, respectively.

The whole process consists of the following phases:

- **Data Preprocessing** The features may have to be preprocessed, depending on the selected learning algorithm.

2.5 Machine Learning

- **Learning Phase** The model is trained with the training data using a certain learning algorithm. The resulting model can then be used to predict the classes for new, unseen data sets.

- **Application** The model can finally be used as a predictor or oracle in the corresponding application area.

In the following, we regard each phase in turn.

Data Preprocessing

The different columns of the feature matrix F, *i.e.*, the properties, can be of different type, also termed as *levels of measurement*. The following types of data are distinguished:

- **Nominal Data** Discrete data that has no order. Each value is unique and incomparable with others. Also termed as *Categorical Data*. Examples: {*red, green, blue*}, {*north, east, south, west*}.

- **Ordinal Data** Discrete data that is ordered. On ordinal data, no distances can be calculated. Hence, instead of a mean value, only the median can be determined. Examples: {*low, medium, high*}, {*no,maybe,yes*}.

- **Quantitative Data** Data that can be freely used for calculations. Especially, this means that the distance between two values can be determined, and that interpolation makes sense. Examples: $\mathbb{R}, \mathbb{N}$.

For classification, the response variable (c_j) is discrete and may be nominal, ordinal, or quantitative. If the classes are ordered, the response variable is ordinal. If furthermore a distance can be determined upon the classes (for example, if the classes represent a degree), the response variable is quantitative. Otherwise, if different classes are incomparable, the response is nominal. The features play a crucial role for the precision of the predictor. A relationship between features and class can only be learned if it is actually extractable from the features. Hence, it is important to find a good set of features as well as to normalize their values.

Feature Selection One approach is to start with as many features as possible. While this is a good starting point, this may slow down the learning phase. Besides, it may also lead to models which consider unimportant features more relevant than necessary (overfitting). This makes feature selection important.

Various techniques for feature selection can be used. As with learning, this can happen either *unsupervised* or *supervised*. In the first case, only the features alone are considered to determine the most important ones, in the last case, also the corresponding classes are regarded. Typically, most techniques are parametrized by the number k of desired remaining features. Unsupervised selection could consider those features with the highest variance. Another way is to use *Principal Components Analysis*, where the features are transformed to a new space, in which the new features are sorted decreasingly by their importance (w.r.t. variance). Supervised selection can *e.g.* select only those features with the highest correlation with the given class vector. Another way is to iteratively select different sets of features, train the predictor, determine the prediction error and finally take those features that performed best.

Normalization If the data contains undefined values, it may be necessary to either replace them or to omit the corresponding entry completely from the data set. However, some learning algorithms can cope with undefined values, in this case, no special treatment is necessary. Ordinal and nominal data can be transferred to numeric data if required by the learning algorithm. In the first case, this can be easily done by mapping the ordered k values to the interval $[0, k]$. In the latter case, this can be done by replacing the nominal feature with $k - 1$ new features, where k is the number of nominal values, as follows: For the first value, all new features are 0. For the i-th value ($i > 1$), the $(i-1)$-th value is set to 1, the others to 0. Quantitative data as well should be normalized. For example, if the values have a huge data range, taking their logarithmic values can be beneficial. For some learning algorithm (*e.g.*, Neural Networks), it is necessary to finally transform the data, such that all features are centered around 0 and have a unit variance. This can be simply done by calculating $(x - \mu)/\sigma$ for every feature, where x denotes the regarded feature values, and μ and σ refer as usual to the mean value and the variance.

It is important that the resulting transformation (feature selection plus normalization) is also used to prepare new data when making predictions. That is, after the training phase is finished, all data that is fed into the predictor has to be transformed appropriately.

Learning Phase

Various learning algorithms have been proposed. Most algorithms use statistics to build a model that explains the training data with minimal error. The

2.5 Machine Learning

choice of the algorithm is determined by characteristics of the data set and by the intended use of the model. The algorithms can be divided into two classes, depending on how the model is represented. In case of an *explicit/intelligible representation*, the representation is directly readable and understandable. The advantages are a compact representation, identification of overfitting, and possibly an insight into the structure of the considered data. The other class of algorithms has merely an *implicit representation*. A model is constructed and can be used for predictions, but it acts as a black-box. In the following, we give popular examples for both classes.

Explicit/Intelligible Representation

Naive Bayes This algorithm does not consider the features at all. The probability distribution of the classes of the training data is estimated and used to predict new values. This distribution constitutes the model.

Decision Trees The data is partitioned recursively into smaller subsets until all objects in a partition have the same class. This yields a decision tree, which has a conditions at each inner node and a class label at each leaf node. On construction, a feature together with a cut-point is chosen that partitions the regarded subspace best with regard to error minimization. This can be thought of as dividing the n-dimensional feature space into boxes, such that for each box, all contained objects have the same class. In other words, the feature space is partitioned into hyper-boxes (*i.e.*, hyper-rectangular regions, bounded by hyper-planes orthogonal to the axes). This feature selection and partitioning is repeated iteratively until a certain precision or a given node depth is achieved. The model is represented as the decision tree with conditions on the inner nodes and the predicted classes at the leaves. This can be interpreted as a set of rules, one for each leaf. Figure 2.14 illustrates how a decision tree is trained. On the left hand side, we see the hyper-boxes (for 2 features, we have simply rectangles) which partition the space. On the right, we see the resulting tree, which can be used to classify new examples based on their attributes.

Random Forests For random forests (Breiman [Bre01]), a collection of decision trees is trained (a typical number is 500). Each tree is trained with a different, randomly selected subset of the training data, and also the selection of the features to partition the space is influenced by random. For prediction, each of the trees is consulted, and majority vote is used to determine the class

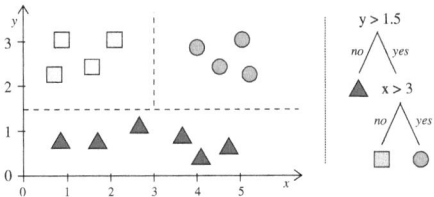

Figure 2.14: Decision Trees

to predict. Random forests are more stable than decision trees and yield often more precise predictors.

Linear Discriminant Analysis While for decision trees, the hyper-planes have to be orthogonal, in linear discriminant analysis, arbitrary hyper-planes are allowed to separate the data. Nesting of planes is not allowed. Hence, the model is a set of hyper-planes, together with the predicted class for the induced subspaces. A variant is *Quadratic Discriminant Analysis*, which allows for parabolic hyper-planes. Figure 2.15 gives an intuition. On the left, we see how the space is separated by hyper-planes (or in 2D, by lines) using linear discriminant analysis. Newly encountered examples will be classified depending on the area they reside in. On the right, we see the same for quadratic discriminant analysis.

Implicit Representation

Nearest Neighbors The training data is fully stored. A prediction for a new object is made by finding the nearest neighbor among the training data in the feature space, and using its class as prediction. An extension is *k-nearest neighbors*, where the k nearest neighbors are determined together with their classes, and majority vote is used to make the prediction. The model is given

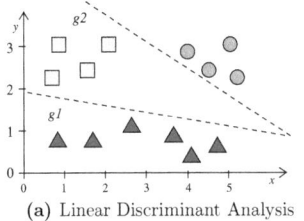
(a) Linear Discriminant Analysis

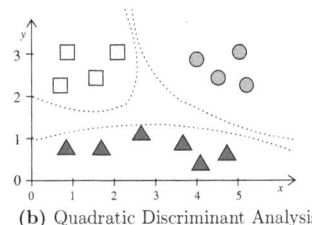
(b) Quadratic Discriminant Analysis

Figure 2.15: Discriminant Analysis

2.5 Machine Learning

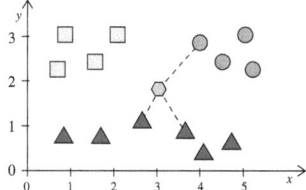

Figure 2.16: k-nearest Neighbors ($k = 3$)

by the whole training data. Figure 2.16 gives an example. We see how a new example (the gray hexagon) is classified by determining its three nearest neighbors. In this case, the majority vote would be *triangle*.

Neural Networks A network with as many input nodes as features, as many output nodes as classes, and arbitrarily many intermediate layers is constructed. Connections are only allowed between two adjacent layers and are annotated with a weight. For prediction, the values of the features are propagated through the net, and the class with the highest weight is predicted. In learning, the weights of the network are adjusted corresponding to the features and the class of each training example. Different learning rules are possible. The model is given by the topology of the network and the weights.

The advantages of an explicit representation of the learned model are that the model is concise as well as understandable. The conciseness allows for efficiently making predictions, which is required to obtain highly scalable heuristics. The understandability of the model allows us to identify which features contribute most to the model, which enables the construction of a simplified model. Hence, we consider learning algorithms with an explicit representation.

Application

To use the predictor in practice, the model as well as the corresponding algorithm has to be implemented. For algorithms with a concise representation of the model, which is the case for algorithms with explicit representation as well as for, *e.g.*, neural networks, this can easily be done. For example, the implementation of a decision tree is straight-forward. A decision tree has a condition $feat <= value$ at each inner node, which determines whether to branch left or right. The leaves of the tree contain the predicted class. Hence, a decision tree can be implemented by nested `if`-constructs. Random forests are constituted by a set of decision trees. Thus, for implementation, all trees have to be consulted, and the most frequently predicted class is returned as overall prediction. In case of nearest neighbors, on the other hand, the whole training data has to be stored. For each prediction, the considered feature vector has to be compared to every feature vector of the training data to determine the nearest neighbors. For a given learning algorithm, the implementation can be automatically generated from the learned model. Hence, it is important to consider learning algorithms with a concise representation of the trained model. This allows for the automatic generation of efficient and highly scalable heuristics.

2.5.2 Cluster Analysis

With cluster analysis, a set of objects $\mathcal{O} = \{o_1, o_2, \ldots, o_n\}$ is automatically grouped together to build a set of clusters, such that similar objects are put together and that dissimilar objects reside in different clusters. The resulting clusters $cl_1, \ldots, cl_m$ build a partition of $\mathcal{O}$, that is: $\mathcal{O} = \cup_{i=1}^{m} cl_i$ and $cl_i \cap cl_j = \emptyset$ for $i \neq j$. To decide about similarity, the cluster analysis requires a distance measure amongst the objects. For n objects, the distance measure can be represented as an $n \times n$ matrix. One popular class of clustering algorithms is *hierarchical clustering*. In that case, the resulting clustering is iteratively built. For *agglomerative hierarchical clustering*, we start with each object being in a cluster of its own and successively merge clusters together. For *divisive hierarchical clustering*, initially, all objects reside in one cluster, and we successively split one cluster at each step. In both cases, the distance measure is used to decide which clusters to join and split, respectively, Hierarchical clustering yields a hierarchy of clusters, which contains for each $i \in \{1..n\}$ a clustering with k classes (c_i). To obtain the resulting clustering, we can either specify a k and select the corresponding clustering, or we can define a quality measure upon the clusterings and select the best one. For more details on cluster analysis, see, *e.g.*, Kaufman et al. [KR90]. The result of a cluster analysis can also be seen as a new classification of the objects, which assigns a class $c_k, k \in \{1, \cdots, m\}$ to each object o. Once the classification has been obtained by clustering, classification learning can be used to identify the relationship between the features of the objects and their corresponding classes.

2.5.3 Predictor Precision

To validate the precision of a predictor, it is applied to a data set for which the correct classes are known. Then, the predictions are compared with the

2.5 Machine Learning

correct classes. To obtain realistic results, the data to which the predictor is applied should be different from the data it was trained with. There are many ways to define precision, and it depends on the intended application which is the right choice. Some error measures are only applicable for quantitative classes. In the following, let m be the number of classes, n the number of observations, $C = (c_i)$ the vector of the actual classes, and $\widehat{C} = (\widehat{c}_i)$ the vector of the predicted classes. $||.||$ denotes the cardinality of sets.

Error Rate/Accuracy One straight-forward way to assess a predictor is to determine its error rate, i.e, the rate of wrong predictions.

$$ER = \frac{||\{i \mid c_i \neq \widehat{c}_i\}||}{n}$$

Conversely, the accuracy is given by the rate of correct predictions and amounts to $1 - ER$. The error rate gives a good first impression of the performance of a predictor. However, due to its all-or-nothing behavior, also *almost correct* predictions, which may occur for quantitative data, are regarded as incorrect.

Mean Absolute Error For quantitative classes, the mean absolute error is a more accurate measure. It is given by the mean value of the difference between correct and predicted classes.

$$MAE = \frac{\sum_i |\widehat{c}_i - c_i|}{n}$$

The standard deviation σ_{MAE} can be calculated to measure the dispersion.

Δk-Accuracy The mean absolute error gives an idea of the precision, but because it returns only one value, it has limited expressiveness. As example, it is not possible to distinguish whether we have 10 times an error of 1 or once an error of 10. It depends on the application area, whether this distinction is important or not. The Δk-accuracy is a generalization of the accuracy and yields a more precise measure.

$$\Delta k\text{-}Acc = \frac{||\{i \mid |\widehat{c}_i - c_i| \leq k\}||}{n} \quad , \quad k \in \{0, \cdots, m-1\}$$

Δk-Acc is the fraction of predictions with a maximum error of k classes. Clearly, $\Delta 0$-Acc reports the amount of correct predictions and equals to the accuracy as defined above. If we have m classes, $\Delta(m\text{-}1)$-Acc is 1. Like the mean absolute error, the Δk-accuracy requires quantitative classes.

Correlation If the classes are quantitative, the correlation of predicted classes $\widehat{C}$ and actual classes C can be calculated by

$$Cor = \frac{Cov(\widehat{C}, C)}{\sigma_{\widehat{C}} \sigma_C} = \frac{\frac{1}{n} \sum (\widehat{c}_i - \mu_{\widehat{c}})(c_i - \mu_c)}{\sqrt{\frac{1}{n} \sum (\widehat{c}_i - \mu_{\widehat{c}})^2} \sqrt{\frac{1}{n} \sum (c_i - \mu_c)^2}}$$

The result is a degree of the linear relationship between predicted values and correct classes. Degrees close to 1 or -1 indicate a strong linear relationship, degrees close to 0, however, do not mean the absence of any relationship. They merely can be interpreted as the absence of a *linear* relationship.

Discussion The prediction error yields the amount of incorrect predictions. However, all mispredictions are treated equally. This is inadequate for quantitative data because an error of one class is treated like an error of ten classes. The mean absolute error is better suited to assess the precision of a predictor in case of quantitative data. However, in some cases, if the class distribution is extremely skewed, a constant predictor could achieve a low error rate without actually predicting anything meaningful. In this case, the correlation can be consulted for clarification. The correlation is undefined if one of its arguments is constant, and is very low if its arguments are mostly constant. Hence, a non-zero correlation together with a low mean absolute error indicates a good prediction. To get an even more precise picture of the precision of a predictor, the Δk-accuracy can be inspected.

Example To get an intuition of the presented error measures, we consider a small example. Let us assume we have three classes ($m = 3$) and ten training examples ($n = 10$) with corresponding classes $C = (1, 2, 3, 1, 2, 3, 1, 2, 3, 1)$. The predicted classes are $\widehat{C} = (1, 1, 2, 2, 3, 3, 2, 2, 1, 1)$. Then we have:

- error rate: 0.6
- mean absolute error (stddev): 0.7 (0.67)
- Δk-accuracy: $\Delta 0$-$accuracy = 0.4$, $\Delta 1$-$accuracy = 0.9$, $\Delta 2$-$accuracy = 1$
- correlation: 0.29

2.6 Summary

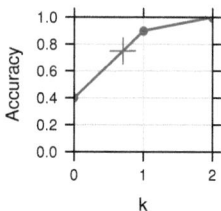

Figure 2.17: Δk-Accuracy

The Δk-accuracy can also be shown graphically, as can be seen in Figure 2.17. The x axis indicates the values of k, and the y axis shows the corresponding accuracies. Because $k \in \{0, \cdots, m-1\}$, the graph is only defined for integer values (indicated in the plot by the dots). The mean error is indicated in the figure by the abscissa of the plus sign. Since we have three classes, the maximum absolute error is 2. For the maximum error, the class deviation rate is always 1, as can be seen in the graph.

2.6 Summary

In this chapter, we presented the structure of a compiler and its essential components. One central challenge during compilation is to optimize the program with respect to its memory behavior. We have reviewed the state of the art techniques to meet this challenge, namely alias analyses that investigate memory dependencies on the one hand and speculative optimizations that allow for more aggressive optimization on the other, and we have seen their limitations: Alias analyses are performed statically and thus estimate the memory dependencies conservative. As a consequence, they tend to drastically overestimate the dependencies, which limits the optimization potential. Speculative optimizations offer a solution to this problem by ignoring unlikely dependencies while maintaining program correctness. This allows for more aggressive optimizations. As speculation introduces a run-time overhead, it is vital to perform a precise cost estimation to achieve a maximal performance gain and to avoid performance degradation (in case of misspeculation). However, to identify unlikely dependencies that could be ignored, the cost estimation requires information about the probability of memory dependencies. We propose to use machine learning to get these probabilities. In the second part of this chapter, we reviewed corresponding techniques from machine learning. We propose to use classification learning to automatically generate heuristics from observations, and to use cluster analysis to automatically derive a program classification to make the heuristics more precise. To assess the resulting predictor, we have presented different means to estimate predictor precision.

3 Related Work

The framework presented in this thesis proposes to use machine learning techniques to automatically generate heuristics that can be used in a compiler. Thus, clearly, work that makes use of machine learning in compilers is related. We apply our general framework to the optimization of memory accesses, which means work on the analysis of memory dependencies in programs as well as work on the optimization of memory accesses (classic as well as speculative) are also related. For each area in turn, we present and discuss related work and compare our approach to that.

3.1 Machine Learning in Compilers

One central idea of using machine learning in compilers is to provide the static compiler with knowledge about the dynamic program behavior at run-time, for example, by automatically deriving heuristics from the observed dynamic program behavior in a one-off training phase. This can entail substantial overhead in the training phase, but the resulting predictors, which can then be used in the compiler, are typically highly scalable and can be implemented efficiently. This approach can be used to enrich or replace all analyses that allow for unsafe information. Another application is to determine in which order optimizations should be applied during compilation. It is obvious that fixed optimization sequences, as used in common compilers, cannot get the best out of every program. However, due to the combinatorial explosion, the search space of all possible optimization sequences cannot be completely explored. Machine learning can be used to learn which sequences are promising candidates, depending on characteristics of the considered program. Thereby, it guides the search space exploration. As a special case, this can also be used to predict parameters for certain optimizations, *e.g.*, the unroll factor for loop unrolling. In the following, we present approaches which use machine learning to respectively obtain predictors for program behavior, good optimization sequences, and good optimization parameters. At the end of this section, we compare our approach with the presented ones.

3.1.1 Program Behavior

One popular example used in many compilers is static branch prediction as proposed by Wu et al. [WL94]. The aim is to statically predict the target of a branch to reduce stalls due to branch misprediction. The authors collected profile data together with program information about the regarded programs. The relationship between various static program properties and the branch direction (*taken/not-taken*) was learned and yielded a couple of predictors. For example, one heuristics predicts a *branch-if-zero* to be *not-taken*. Another one predicts that the branch to a return statement in a function is taken. For branch prediction, the result of all predictions is weighted and then combined to yield the final result. For the considered programs, a perfect predictor would have a miss rate of 10%[1]. The proposed predictor reaches a miss rate of 20%, which is far better than the 50% of a random predictor.

Another approach, which is more related to ours, was proposed by Panait et al. [PSW04]. The authors aimed to find a predictor that identifies *delinquent* loads, *i.e.*, loads that lead to long cache stalls. They extracted static code features out of assembler code and performed program runs to collect loads that missed the cache. With that information, predictors were trained. The resulting heuristics is intuitive, *e.g.*, the more multiplications were used to calculate an address, the likelier is a cache miss. The predictor was able to identify a subset of 11% of the loads that accounted for 96% of all cache misses.

3.1.2 Optimization Sequences

While in a typical compiler, a couple of predefined optimization sequences are available (`-O1`, `-O2`, etc.), it is obvious that there is not one single sequence that is best for all programs. Instead, sequences were chosen that perform well in the general case. On the other hand, it is not feasible to find for each program

---
[1]The underlying assumption is that a predictor makes always the same prediction for a certain branch instruction. Hence, in the presence of conditional jumps, even the perfect predictor is not always correct.

3.1 Machine Learning in Compilers

the best optimization sequence[2]. For example, if we want to choose 10 out of 20 optimizations, we have already $\frac{n!}{(n-k)!} = \frac{20!}{10!} \approx 6.7 \cdot 10^{11}$ different sequences, without considering shorter sequences or sequences in which an optimization is applied multiple times. If we optimistically assume that one sequence can be evaluated per second, this will take over 20.000 years. Typical compilers have about 50 optimizations, and the optimization sequence is of about the same length. Hence, this suggests to use machine learning to learn which sequences may be advantageous for which kinds of programs. This information can then be used to cut down this huge search space by only exploring parts of it.

The process of finding optimal sequences tailored to the considered program is also called *iterative compilation*. Typically, in a first learning phase, a substantial part of the search space is explored exhaustively to train the predictors. Then, the predicted information is used to measure the result for a few interesting sequences. After that, several iterations may follow, which use the run-time results to further explore other sequences. Almagor et al. [ACG+04] investigate the structure of the search space and finds out that many local minima are close to a global minimum. As a consequence, the authors propose to use hill-climbing with different random starts to find good sequences. Their approach is an extension of the work by Cooper et al. [CSS99]. Agakov et al. [ABC+06] first consider only a moderate number of optimizations and collect exhaustive data for this reduced search space (5 out of 14 available optimizations). The authors analyze the structure of the search space and find out that optimal sequences are scattered among the space. To avoid exhaustive search to find any of them, they use *genetic algorithms* together with *Markov models* to guide the search for sequences. As training data, they use the exhaustive information about the small search space (containing 88.000 sequences, and for each sequence code features of the resulting program and its speedup over the unoptimized version). The trained predictor allows for finding good sequences with limited effort. They evaluate their approach by applying the predictor to a more realistic space (20 out of 82 optimizations, leading to over 10^{38} sequences). As a result, the predictor finds good sequences with only a few iterations. This approach is extended by Dubach et al. [DCF+07]. There, the authors aim at actually predicting the performance impact of a given optimization sequence. *Artificial neural networks* are used to build the models. Unlike before, the model is trained only with a small portion of the small search space (512 instead of 88.000 samples). Still, the model can predict

---

[2] And even theoretically it is not possible, since the optimality of a sequence might depend on the encountered program input.

the performance gain precisely, even for the huge search space (in this case, up to 20 out of 54 optimizations or 10^{34} sequences). Cavazos et al. [CFA+07] consider a fixed optimization sequence and aims at determining which optimizations to apply. This leads to a smaller search space of 2^k for a sequence length of k. As features, they use performance counters, which collect many low-level properties of the program (e.g., cache misses or number of branches) and are offered by most modern processors. The model is trained using logistic regression. The resulting performance is on average 17% better than with a commercially available compiler for the considered platform.

3.1.3 Optimization Parameters

As with optimization sequences, a good choice of optimization parameters depends on the considered program. Moss et al. [MUC+98] use classification learning to predict the parameters of a scheduler to find the optimal order of instructions. The result is a *preference* relation, which is used by the scheduler. Similarly, in the work of Stephenson et al. [SAMO03], the priority function of the scheduler is learned automatically via genetic programming. The results are sometimes even better than for manually written priority functions. Cavazos et al. [CM04] present an approach to train a heuristics that decides whether or not to schedule. If compilation time is expensive, it might be advisable to skip scheduling if the improvement is limited. The heuristics could reduce the time spent in the scheduler to 25%, while keeping the same program performance. Cavazos et al. [CO05] show how to learn whether or not a given function should be inlined in Java, based on parameters like *maximum callee size, number of calls in the callee, size of the caller*. For the machine learned heuristics, a significant performance improvement could be achieved compared to other heuristics. Stephenson et al. [SA05] propose to use classification learning to predict loop unroll factors, based on static loop features. The training data is given by a set of loops, each described by its features and the best loop unroll factor (determined empirically). Based on that, the best unroll factor for new loops could be predicted in 65% of the time, which leads to a performance improvement of 5% for the SPEC CPU2000 benchmarks.

3.1.4 Discussion

The previous sections gave an overview of the problems in compiler construction machine learning was used for, to demonstrate how fruitful the combination of both areas can be. The strength of machine learning is that concise models can be automatically constructed from comprehensive training data. These models condense the complex information and yield statically applicable predictors. This can be either used to make huge search spaces manageable or to provide the static compiler with knowledge about the dynamic run-time behavior. The presented approaches are dedicated to a certain problem, for which they use machine learning techniques. In contrast to that, we propose a conceptual framework that can be applied to all kinds of program behavior. Our novel concept of program classification can be used to improve the presented approaches. In the application of our general framework, we focus on learning memory behavior, namely, memory dependencies and load latencies. Learning memory dependencies has never been considered before to the best of the author's knowledge. Hence, we see our approach not as a competitor with the presented ones, but as an extension. For learning load latencies, Panait et al. [PSW04] have proposed a related approach. However, this approach distinguishes only two classes for a load, namely *cache hit* and *cache miss*. In our approach, we use a finer classification. We directly predict the latency of a load with an accuracy of 10 cycles (the load latency is discretized to 11 classes). By that, the load latencies can be estimated more precisely.

3.2 Memory Dependencies

To optimize memory accesses, knowledge about memory dependencies is required. This information can either be collected dynamically by profiling or statically by program analyses. In the following, we describe related work which uses profiling. After that, we give an overview of the state-of-the-art of alias analyses and present the strengths and weaknesses of the different approaches, and we discuss whether or not these static techniques are sufficient for our purposes.

3.2.1 Collection of Memory Dependencies via Profiling

Profiling can be used to measure the actual program behavior at run-time. Since the results are unsafe, it is typically used to collect branch and path counts of a program. This can be used to identify hot regions, which can then be optimized with increased effort. Chen et al. [CLD$^+$04] present an approach to use profiling to collect the actual data dependencies of a program

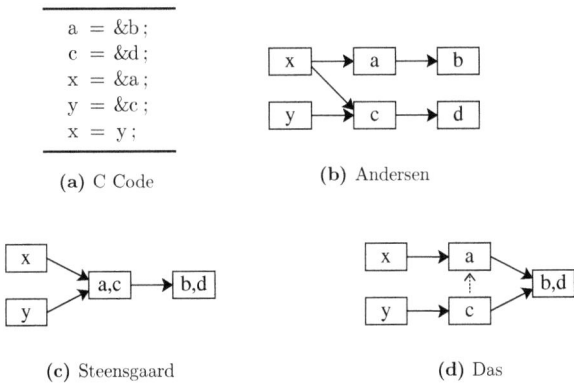

Figure 3.1: C code and Resulting Points-To Graphs

present at run-time for a given input set. To this end, the code is modified such that each memory access is tracked. A virtual representation of the memory (named shadow memory) is built and records for every address the last defining access (*i.e.*, the last store instruction that wrote to that address). This is used to identify actual dependencies between instructions, *e.g.*, which instructions consumed the values written by another one. Since it is not feasible to represent the memory completely, the authors propose to increase scalability by sacrificing precision, and they map the actual address space to the smaller shadow memory by hashing. Even with the thereby limited precision, the run-time for collecting the dependencies is about 40 times higher.

3.2.2 Alias Analysis

For languages with pointer arithmetic like *C*, alias analyses are vital to cut down the number of dependence edges in the DDG. While alias analyses have also been proposed for other languages like Java[3], we focus on alias analyses for *C*.

As we have seen in Section 2.3.2, alias analyses come in different flavors. We briefly present the most popular approaches and compare their results for a running example, shown in Figure 3.1. Since we are interested in scalability, we only consider the class of control-flow-insensitive and context-insensitive

---

[3]Java makes things easier on the one hand, since arbitrary pointer arithmetic is not possible. On the other hand, new issues due to the dynamic type system are introduced, which add other sources of complexity.

3.2 Memory Dependencies

analyses (F^-C^-). Andersen [And94] proposes a *subset-based* algorithm, which is structure-unaware. It is considered to be the most precise approach within the F^-C^- class, since in the constructed points-to graph, the out-degree of a node is arbitrary (see Figure 3.1b). The algorithm is of cubic complexity in the worst case, thus it does not scale too well for huge programs. The major reason for the high complexity is the arbitrary out-degree of the nodes. Consequently, Steensgaard [Ste96b] presents an almost linear alias analysis[4], which enforces an out-degree of one. This algorithm is also structure-unaware, but Steensgaard presents an extension that considers structures [Ste96a]. The analysis is based on type theory and uses equivalence classes, represented by efficient union-find structures. It is also classified as *unification-based*, which means that the direction of a *simple assign* (see Table 2.2) is not considered, which is the case for subset-based algorithms. As a result, the analysis is less precise, compared to Anderson. This is evident in the results for our example shown in Figure 3.1c. The unification-based approach leads to many false dependencies, *e.g.*, the points-to graph reports that y may point to a. Shapiro et al. [SH97] present an algorithm for which the precision can range from Steensgaard to Andersen. They have a parameter k, which denotes the maximum allowed out-degree in the points-to graph. With $k = 1$, we have Steensgaard's algorithm, with $k = \infty$, Andersen's. However, scalability is still bad for higher values of k. Das [Das00] presents another way of combining the benefits of the algorithms of Steensgaard and Andersen. For the first level of indirection, the direction of an assignment is considered, *i.e.*, the algorithm is like Andersen's. This was motivated by the fact that pointers in C are often used to establish call-by-reference for data structures. Hence, for the first level, precise analysis is important. For further indirection, the unification-based approach (like Steensgaard's) should suffice, which keeps scalability of the analysis. The algorithm is of quadratic complexity in the worst case, but scales well. Due to the reported results, the analysis is almost as precise as the (computationally more complex) analysis proposed by Andersen. This can also be observed in Figure 3.1d, which is for the first indirection level equivalent to Figure 3.1b. Note the so-called *flow edge* from the box containing c to that one with a. This edge indicates that the upper box also includes the lower box, and thus establishes a subset-based approach for the first level.

For a broader overview and for a discussion of also control-flow- or context-sensitive algorithms, respectively, there exist comprehensive survey papers, which discuss the relevance of alias analysis, the role of the chosen analysis

---

[4]Its complexity is bounded by α, the inverse of the Ackermann function.

precision and other important aspects like, *e.g.*, choosing the right granularity of the analysis (see Hind et al. [HP00], Hind [Hin01], Ghiya et al. [GLS01], Chen et al. [CLHY02]).

Recently, also alias analyses to yield speculative dependencies have been proposed. Fernández et al. [FE02] consider an alias analysis for assembler code. For the propagation of the alias information along the CFG, the authors use profiling information to only consider frequently executed paths. This makes the result speculative, since not all possible paths are considered. Additionally, also a safe alias analysis is performed. Hence, dependencies that are predicted by the safe but not by the speculative analysis are marked as speculative. Chen et al. [CHJL04] propose a probabilistic alias analysis. However, the probabilities depend on branch probabilities determined by profiling. Besides, their analysis is very expensive and can only deal with code up to 1000 lines of code. Silva et al. [SS06] present a probabilistic alias analysis, which is flow-sensitive. The dependence information is represented by sparse matrices and also relies on branch probabilities. The analysis time can amount to up to 5 hours for real-world programs.

Concerning the complexity classes of the analyses, it has been shown by Landi [Lan92] that for control-flow-sensitive analyses, *may-alias* is not decidable and *must-alias* is not even semi-decidable. Horwitz [Hor97] proves that control-flow-insensitive analyses are NP-hard if arbitrary levels of pointer indirections are admitted.

3.2.3 Discussion

In the previous sections, we presented an approach which collects the actual dependencies for given input data via profiling. Also, the current state-of-the-art of alias analyses was presented, to demonstrate the complexity of the problem on the one hand and the imprecision even of today's analyses on the other. Scalable alias analyses are inadequate for our means, since they are too imprecise in two ways: They report too many false dependencies, which sacrifices optimization potential, and know only (at most) three classes of dependencies, namely *absent, maybe*, and *must*. Two approaches (Fernández et al. [FE02] and Chen et al. [CHJL04]) add a fourth class, *speculative*. While this is a step in the right direction, it is still too imprecise for a precise cost model. However, our approach allows for benefiting from the strength of those approaches. Whenever the alias information reported by the alias analysis is known to be exact (*i.e.*, for the dependence classes *absent* and *must*), we use it. Otherwise, we consult our heuristics. By that, the resulting predicted program behavior can be expected to be much more precise. Alias analyses that do not scale allow for better precision than their scalable counterpart. In case of the approaches of Chen et al. [CHJL04] and Silva et al. [SS06], we even get probabilistic dependence information. The latter approaches could also be combined with our approach. However, until now, they do not scale and cannot be practically used. Besides, it is unclear whether they can be more precise than our approach, hence a comparison would be necessary.

The work by Chen et al. [CLD+04] is the only approach known to the author to consider the actual data dependencies at program run-time. The approach differs from ours in two significant points: First, the authors collect only actual dependencies and not all dependencies. However, this is not sufficient in the presence of code motion, where new dependencies may occur when two instructions refer to the same address. We do not consider dependencies, but accessed addresses, from which we can infer all possible dependencies. This information is stable w.r.t. code transformations. Second, they fail to generalize from the collected data as we do via machine learning. For every program under consideration, the data dependencies have to be collected. This requires representative input data and leads to a significant overhead (the required time for profiling is 40 times the regular execution time). Conversely, in our approach, we only require profiling in the one-off training phase. From the collected information, we generate highly scalable predictors, which can be efficiently implemented in the compiler.

3.3 Optimization of Memory Accesses

Many optimizations have been proposed to reduce latencies induced by loads. Conservative optimizations either perform prefetching to bring the required data into the cache, or they perform code transformations to reduce the number of expensive loads (via partial redundancy elimination) or to reduce the encountered latencies (via code motion). Speculative optimizations also perform the mentioned transformations, but act more optimistically by deliberately ignoring unlikely dependencies. Thus, they can exploit more optimization potential. Prefetching is similar to speculation, since it loads data in advance. The difference is that the prefetched values cannot be used in further computations (*i.e.*, prefetching performs a *non-binding* load), whereas the results of speculative loads can be used (*binding load*)[5]. In the following, we present approaches for conservative as well as speculative optimizations.

3.3.1 Conservative Optimizations

Prefetching

The idea of prefetching is to bring data into the caches before it is actually needed. This can increase cache hit rates and thereby reduce the impact of the slower main memory. Prefetching does not affect functional program correctness, but merely cache behavior and thus program performance. Prefetching requires *non-blocking* load instructions, *i.e.*, loads have to be executed in the background. While its value is fetched, regular execution can continue.

For prefetching, it has to be decided which values to prefetch. This can be done either by software or by hardware. In the latter case, complex logic is required to detect regular patterns and to prefetch automatically. Examples are iterative accesses to arrays within a loop. Software prefetching can be even more complex, since the whole program can be considered. Again, loops are the starting point. Prefetching loads can be used when iterating over arrays or structures. However, prefetching can also impair performance: It leads to an increased memory traffic, increases code size, and may lead to *cache pollution* when applied too aggressively. Cache pollution refers to the eviction of useful entries from the cache to make room for the prefetched values. As consequence, this can lead to additional cache misses which would not have occurred without prefetching.

Vanderwiel et al. [VL00] give a good survey of hardware and software prefetching techniques and also discuss the downside of prefetching. One research topic is to identify the stride value of memory accesses in loops, *i.e.*, for accesses to regular structures, the increment which is added in each iteration. Stoutchinin et al. [SAG+01] present an approach for prefetching, which can also deal with pointer-chasing loops. However, the intrinsic problem is that for structures in the heap, the access sequences are unpredictable, unless the structures were allocated during an initialization phase without any other intervening allocations. Wu [Wu02] determines the stride through profiling.

---
[5]For a *binding load*, the result is stored in a register and thus can be used in the following. This should not be confused with the term *non-blocking load*, which means that the load is executed in the background while following instructions are being executed. Prefetching as well as speculative loads both require loads to be *non-blocking*.

3.3 Optimization of Memory Accesses

Different algorithms are presented and compared. Puzak et al. [PHES05] give a further discussion on the profitability of prefetching.

Code Transformations

Partial redundancy elimination is used in most compilers. It applies to redundancy in general, *i.e.*, to arithmetic expressions as well as memory accesses. However, in the latter case, it is more difficult to determine whether or not a value is still valid, due to the aliases among memory accesses. For code motion, loop invariant code motion is a popular example. The idea is to move expensive instructions out of hot regions, which are executed frequently (*e.g.*, loops). This is only possible if the result is not modified by the other instructions in the region. See, *e.g.*, Muchnik [Muc97] for more details. The mentioned optimizations are important to achieve a good program performance. However, their weakness is that they have to rely on conservative program analyses, since otherwise, program correctness is jeopardized. Especially for programs with many memory accesses, this can mean that much optimization potential is neglected.

3.3.2 Speculative Optimizations

Basically, speculative optimizations allow us to make assumptions, which are not proved to be true. Thus, they allow the compiler to be more optimistic, which is justified, since the over-approximation of static program analyses is often highly imprecise. Speculation can be used to guess about the value of variables, to invoke threads speculatively, and to speculate about memory dependencies. In our approach, we consider the last case. Every classic optimization that regards memory dependencies can be made speculative. This has been done for partial redundancy elimination as well as for scheduling.

Nicolau [Nic89] is one of the first to propose speculation on data dependencies, in this case for array accesses. This enables the compiler to ignore potential dependencies between array accesses, for which the index expressions cannot be proved to be different (*e.g.*, because one of them was non-linear), as long as corresponding check instructions are inserted appropriately. Mahlke et al. [MCH+92] generalize this approach. They propose a framework for speculative scheduling on parallel processors to reduce latencies induced by loads. While they used simulation to evaluate their approach, Rogers et al. [RL92] and

Bringmann et al. [BMH+93] propose hardware extensions to cope with speculation. This idea led to the proposal of the *HP PlayDoh* architecture (mentioned by Abraham et al. [AR94]), which in turn led to the development of the Intel Itanium (see Huck et al. [HMR+00]). Speculation was used in many other generic compiler frameworks, *e.g.*, in the work of Ebcioglu et al. [EGK+94], which proposes speculative code motion, and in the approach of Deitrich et al. [DH96], which considers speculative scheduling. August et al. [ACM+98] present a simulator for the Itanium, for which predication and speculation lead to great performance improvements. From that point on, most approaches for speculation on data dependencies consider the Itanium architecture.

Ju et al. [JNMW00] present a comprehensive framework for speculative optimization during list scheduling, and also considers the optimization of chains of instructions. After scheduling, recovery code is generated where required. Simple heuristics are used to determine whether or not a memory dependency due to aliasing should be marked as speculative (comparison of the corresponding base addresses). Lin et al. [LCH+04] present a compiler framework with a speculative extension of SSA form. Opportunities for speculation are annotated in the IR via the *speculative* flag. As optimization, speculative partial redundancy elimination (SPRE) is presented. This approach is a generalization of the work of Ju et al. [JNMW00]. While the authors propose to annotate whether or not dependencies are speculative, they only use a binary flag, which cannot be used for a precise cost model. Another optimization, speculative register promotion, is presented by Lin et al. [LCHY03]. Scholz et al. [SHK04] propose another solution for SPRE. The authors extend their previous work on classic PRE. Their formalization considers execution time as well as program size and can optimize for a combination of both. Rabbah et al. [RSEW04] consider a more general approach. First, expensive loads are identified (using the results from Panait et al. [PSW04]). Then, the corresponding *load dependence chains (LDCs)*, which are required for, *e.g.*, address calculations, are determined and optimized. The maximum length of an LDC is limited to 7 instructions. The authors report significant performance improvements, however, the results are hard to compare, since only a subset of the SPEC benchmarks is considered. Dai et al. [DZHY05] give a detailed discussion of the different cases in speculative code motion, together with the implications for recovery code generation. Besides, speculative stores are considered, which have to be implemented completely in software, since the Itanium has no hardware support for that. Lin et al. [LHY+06] give further details on the generation of recovery code in the framework proposed by Lin et al. [LCHY03]. In [GG08],

3.3 Optimization of Memory Accesses

we considered the speculative optimization of a certain class of memory accesses, namely those induced by the use of global variables. Those variables have to be reloaded after calls to functions that might change them. However, if the value remains unchanged, the reload is redundant. We performed speculative register promotion for globals to avoid those redundant reloads. The optimization performs a cost estimation to decide which variables to optimize. We could obtain a performance improvement for many of the SPEC CPU2006 benchmarks, while avoiding performance degradation in all cases. Also, finding the optimal solution for speculative scheduling was considered. Winkel [Win04] models the scheduling problem as an *integer linear program*. However, the approach is very expensive, so that only small programs/code regions (hundreds of lines of code) can be considered.

3.3.3 Discussion

In the previous sections, we presented a selection of approaches to optimize memory accesses and to reduce the experienced memory latency. Especially relevant for our approach are existent speculative optimizations. While some approaches propose special speculative optimizations (*e.g.*, speculative register promotion as presented by Ju et al. [JNMW00] and by us in [GG08], SPRE as presented by Lin et al. [LCH+04] and by Scholz et al. [SHK04]), our approach is more general and comparable to the work of Lin et al. [LCH+04] and of Panait et al. [PSW04]. Concerning the code transformation, the latter approaches and ours have similar capabilities. However, in contrast to those approaches, we use a precise cost model to predict the performance gain. This model uses information about expected load latencies, probabilities of memory dependencies, and branch frequencies. Therefore, we argue that costs are much more adequately modeled in our approach, which allows for an increased performance improvement. Additionally, the cost model contains architectural parameters. This makes it possible to transfer our approach to other architectures that do not offer hardware support for speculation.

On top of that, our general framework proposes a unified way of using machine learning for obtaining more precision in the compiler. The framework can be instantiated for various application scenarios. To demonstrate its practical applicability, we applied it to the optimization of memory accesses. To the best of the author's knowledge, a general framework for combining machine learning techniques with speculative compiler optimizations has not been proposed before.

4 A General Framework for Intelligent Speculative Optimizations

Optimizing compilers have to face the challenge to generate programs with an efficient run-time behavior while merely looking at the static program code. The optimizations are guided by program analyses, which estimate the run-time behavior. However, the necessity of correctness forces the analyses to err on the safe side, which may lead to a severe over-approximation. As consequence, the optimizations have overly pessimistic assumptions on the program behavior and cannot exploit the available optimization potential. In this chapter, we present our general *Framework for Intelligent Speculative Compiler Optimizations (FrISCO)*. FrISCO overcomes the problems of conservative analyses by admitting unsafe, but more precise analyses, which are automatically obtained via machine learning, together with speculative optimizations, which ensure the program correctness in all cases.

To automatically construct a model of the dynamic program behavior, we propose to use machine learning techniques. This allows for the automatic construction of heuristics that can be used to predict dynamic behavior solely based on static code features. Training happens in a one-off preparation phase. The resulting predictors are typically based on a simple representation (*e.g.*, decision trees) and are thus highly scalable (*i.e.*, can process many queries in a short time). They can be used in the compiler as oracles, which precisely predict the estimated dynamic program behavior. Hence, instead of considering all cases, including pathological ones, as equally likely, the compiler can focus on the likely behavior.

80 A General Framework for Intelligent Speculative Optimizations

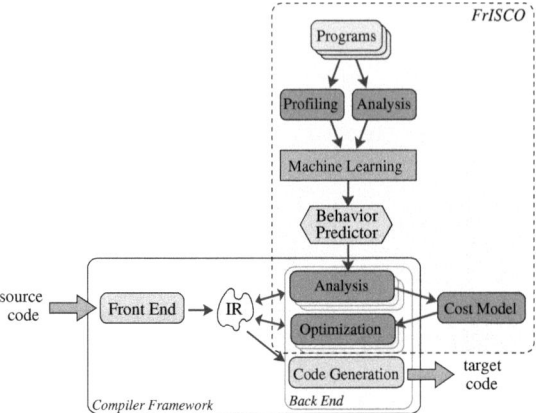

Figure 4.1: Extending Compiler Frameworks with *FrISCO*

4.1 Overview

We propose a conceptual framework that brings intelligence to compiler optimizations by providing them with knowledge about dynamic program behavior. The knowledge is gained automatically by machine learning from profiling data. Our framework can be used to extend existing compiler frameworks, especially their analyses and optimizations. Figure 4.1 illustrates our approach. At the bottom, we see a conventional compiler, which performs several analyses and optimizations. Our framework extends conventional compiler frameworks by intelligent compiler optimizations, together with the corresponding analyses and cost models. The idea of our framework is to first collect static code and program features as well as profiling data for a representative program suite. From that, machine learning automatically generates behavior predictors, which can be used as heuristics to guide the optimization and to estimate the performance gain via the cost model.

Our framework comprises three phases (see Figure 4.2): Analysis, Machine Learning, and Speculative Optimization. As a prerequisite, the framework requires a mean of collecting the desired behavior through profiling as well as a comprehensive and representative suite of programs to obtain the training data. In the first phase (*Analysis*), the compiler translates the program suite to binaries and collects their static code features at the same time. Then, profiling collects information about the dynamic program behavior. This yields

4.1 Overview

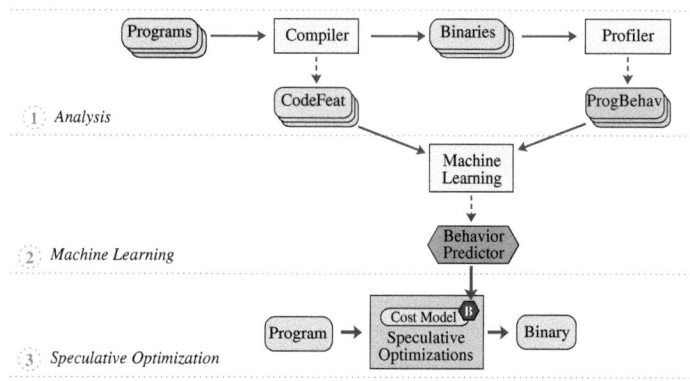

Figure 4.2: Phases in *FrISCO*

the data required by the next phase, namely the code features as well as the corresponding behavior. In the second phase (*Machine Learning*), a model is automatically constructed that explains the relationship between features and behavior. This model yields the *Behavior Predictor*, which can be integrated into the compiler to make predictions for new programs. In the third phase (*Optimization*), the predictor is used by speculative optimizations, which use the predictions for the construction of a cost model, which determines whether or not a given transformation is considered beneficial and should be applied. While especially the first and also the second phase entail a significant overhead, they are only executed initially. The collected data is condensed and abstracted in the generated predictors, which can efficiently be implemented. In the final phase, the compiler consults the predictors. Due to their high scalability, the additional overhead is negligible (and actually lower than those of conservative program analyses).

The framework aims at providing the optimization with heuristics to estimate the dynamic run-time behavior, which are automatically constructed by ML techniques. Since all kinds of programs are considered, the program behavior can differ significantly from program to program. Hence, if only one predictor is trained for all programs, it can be expected that it is either precise for some programs and highly imprecise for the rest or quite imprecise for all programs. As a solution, we introduce *program classes* to group programs with similar behavior together. The idea is that for each program class, one predictor is trained. Since programs in one class behave similarly, the predictor can yield precise results. Instead of having one predictor for all programs, we

82 A General Framework for Intelligent Speculative Optimizations

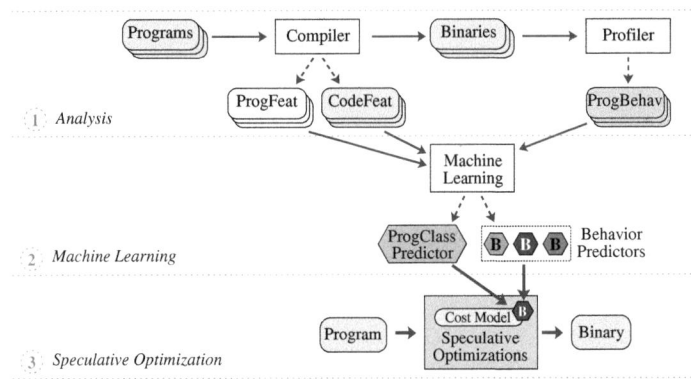

Figure 4.3: *FrISCO*: Extended Framework with Program Classes

now have one predictor per program class. Additionally, we train a *program class predictor*, which determines the program class for a previously unseen program.

The extended framework is shown in Figure 4.3. In the analysis phase, we extend the compiler by also collecting static features of a whole program. This is later required to train the program class predictor. In the learning phase, we automatically group similar programs into program classes. This can be used to train the program class predictor, which learns the relationship between static program features and the corresponding program class. Additionally, we build one behavior predictor for each program class. In the optimization phase, we now have a two-stage process: First, the program class of the considered program is determined. Then, the corresponding behavior predictor is taken, and it is used to derive the cost model and thereby guides the optimization. In the following, we describe each phase of our framework in detail. We start with the one-off training phase, which comprises the analysis phase and the machine learning phase, and show then how the obtained predictors can be used to guide speculative optimizations.

4.2 Analysis

In the analysis phase, we collect the data that is required by the subsequent machine learning phase, namely the code and program features and the program behavior. The investigated program behavior determines the abstraction

4.2 Analysis

level, at which code features as well as the program behavior are analyzed. Examples for the abstraction level are instructions, pairs of instructions, variables, basic blocks, or loops. The abstraction level defines the *entity domain* $\mathcal{E}$, which contains all possible entities (*e.g.*, all possible load instructions) and is infinite. We consider a representative suite of programs $\mathcal{P} = (p_i)$. For each program p_i in turn, the concrete entity domain $\mathcal{E}_i \subseteq \mathcal{E}$ is determined, which contains the entities occurring in the program. These entities constitute the base, upon which the following analyses operate. First, the static features have to be collected for each program in the program suite by a program analysis. This includes the code features, which are collected for the regarded entities of a program, as well as the program features, which represent the characteristics of a whole program. Then, the regarded dynamic behavior for representative input data has to be recorded via profiling. We describe both steps in turn.

4.2.1 Program Analysis

To obtain the static code features for the entities of a program, the compiler has to implement the projection function $\pi_{cfeat} : \mathcal{E} \to \mathcal{F}_{code}$, which maps a given entity to its code feature vector. To that end, the regarded entity together with its context is inspected and properties relevant to the considered program behavior are collected. This yields the feature vector. For example, if $\mathcal{E}$ denotes load instructions, the feature vector could contain information about the data types of the referenced variables, about the complexity of the address calculation, and about the number of memory instructions in the surrounding basic block. Since the collected features are crucial for learning the relationship between feature vector and corresponding class, it is important to collect many features. Later on, *feature selection* can be performed to keep only the most relevant features. By that, the learned model gets simpler and overfitting can be avoided. Based on function π_{cfeat}, we can collect the features for all m entities of a program with the projection $\Pi_{cfeat} : \mathcal{P} \to \mathcal{F}_{code}^m$. For a given program p_i, this yields the code feature matrix $CFeat_i \in \mathcal{F}_{code}^m$.

Additionally, we collect for each program one program feature vector. That vector represents the characteristics of a whole program that are expected to have an influence on the regarded program behavior. For example, the program feature vector could contain the fraction of integer/floating point variables w.r.t. all variables as well as the average basic block size. To obtain the vector, the compiler implements the projection function $\pi_{pfeat} : \mathcal{P} \to \mathcal{F}_{prog}$.

Thereby, we obtain for each representative program p_i the program feature vector $pfeat_i = \pi_{pfeat}(p_i)$. This is later used to train the program class predictor.

4.2.2 Profiling

By profiling, we collect the actual behavior for the entities of p_i, which is used to implement the projection function $\pi_{beh} : \mathcal{E} \to \mathcal{O}_{beh}$. Since at run-time, some parts of a program are executed multiple times, while others are not executed at all, the result of profiling for a program p_i on a given program input is the function $\Pi_{beh} : \mathcal{P} \to \mathcal{P}ot(\mathcal{O}_{beh})$, which maps each entity to a (possibly empty) set of observations. For example, if we consider load instructions as entities and their latencies as behavior, profiling yields for each load instruction of a program a (possibly empty) list of experienced latencies. Since we consider classification learning, we define the classes of behavior $\mathcal{C}_{beh}$ an entity can show, and we specify a function $I_{beh} : \mathcal{P}ot(\mathcal{O}_{beh}) \to \mathcal{C}_{beh}$, which performs the classification for a set of observations. For our example of load latencies, we could take the average of all experienced latencies and discretize this value by defining a finite set of equivalence classes. The observation sets for an entity may be empty, and it depends on the considered behavior, how this should be interpreted. One way is to use a default class for that case. (*e.g.*, for the access frequency of a variable, an intuitive default value would be 0). Another way is to consider only entities for which an observation was made, *i.e.*, for a program p_i, to consider only $\mathcal{E}'_i = \{e \in \mathcal{E}_i \mid \pi_{beh}(e) \neq \varnothing\}$ (*e.g.*, this would be appropriate when predicting the cycle execution time of instructions). As result, profiling yields for each e_j its behavior $beh_j = I(\pi_{beh}(e_j))$, and for the m' entities ($m' \leq m$) of p_i, this constitutes the vector $Beh_i \in \mathcal{C}_{beh}^{m'}$.

Formally, for our program suite $\mathcal{P} = (p_i)$, we now have the program features $PFeat = (pfeat_i)$ and, for each program p_i and for each entity e_j, the static code features $cfeat_j$ and the profiled behavior beh_j, yielding $CFeat_i = (cfeat_j), Beh_i = (beh_j)$ for a program p_i and altogether $(CFeat_i)$ and (Beh_i).

4.3 Machine Learning

In the second phase, we use machine learning techniques to automatically construct models, which explain the relationship between the static code features and the dynamic run-time behavior. To increase precision, similar programs are grouped together into program classes, and a set of specialized predictors

4.3 Machine Learning

is constructed. The phase has three steps: identify the program classes ($\mathcal{C}_{prog}$), train the program class predictor (P_{PC}), and build one specialized behavior predictor for each class (P_{beh}^j), which yields the repository of behavior predictors. In the following, we first regard the overall goal, namely to obtain a behavior predictor. Then, we describe the mentioned three steps to obtain more precise predictions of the run-time behavior via program classification. After that, we discuss how conservative program analyses can be used to further improve the results of the predictions.

4.3.1 Behavior Predictor

From the preceding analysis phase, we have a set of m observations, consisting of static code features together with the corresponding observed dynamic behavior. The domain of one feature vector is denoted as $\mathcal{F}_{code}$. Because we consider classification learning, the regarded dynamic behavior was discretized to a set of classes $\mathcal{C}_{beh}$. Thus, the training data is given by the feature matrix $CFeat \in \mathcal{F}_{code}^m$ and by the class vector $Beh \in \mathcal{C}_{beh}^m$. With that, we can use a machine learning algorithm (*e.g.*, classification trees) to automatically generate a model from the training data. The algorithm aims at finding a model which represents the relationship between features and classes with minimum error. In other words, a model is constructed that explains the relationship best for the considered training data. The model can then be fed with a feature vector and yields as result the predicted class. This can be used to determine the prediction error for the training set. But more interestingly, the model can be used as a predictor and can be applied to new, previously unseen feature vectors. By implementing the underlying algorithm of the considered learning method, an executable heuristics can be automatically generated from the trained model. This heuristics can replace a program analysis in the compiler[1] and provides the optimization as well as the cost model with precise information about the expected run-time behavior.

Because our representative program suite contains multiple programs, we also have multiple sets of training data. This poses the question how to construct *one* predictor from that. To that end, we can choose from two combination techniques: Either, the data sets of the programs are merged and upon this data, one predictor is trained. Or, for each data set, one predictor

---

[1]Note that the considered program behavior may be non-functional (*e.g.*, the execution frequencies of basic blocks) as well as functional (*e.g.*, the values of variables or expressions).

86 A General Framework for Intelligent Speculative Optimizations

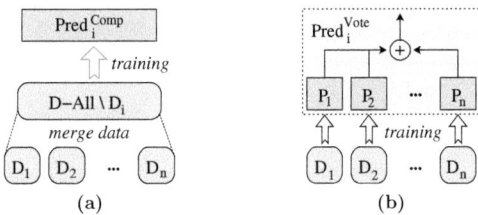

Figure 4.4: (a) Combination of Data *vs.* (b) Combination of Predictors

is trained, and to obtain the resulting predictor, each of these predictors is consulted to derive the final prediction. In the latter case, there are again different possibilities to combine the results, or votes, from the separately trained predictors:

- take the majority vote and break ties by selecting the minimum solution
- take the majority vote and break ties by selecting the maximum solution
- combine all votes and derive an average value if appropriate for the considered behavior (*i.e.*, if the behavior is represented by quantitative classes)

The first case, combination of the training data, is shown in Figure 4.4a. Formally, the new predictor P is constructed as follows (with $CFeat_j$ and Beh_j denoting the training data for each program j):

$P = train(\cup_j CFeat_j, \cup_j Beh_j)$

The second case, combination of the predictors gained for each program, is shown in Figure 4.4b. Formally,

$P = \oplus P_j$, with $P_j = train(CFeat_j, Beh_j)$,

with $\oplus$ either $mode_{min}$, $mode_{max}$, or $average$. The functions $mode_{min}$ and $mode_{max}$ are defined as follows:

$mode_{min}(O) = \{e \in O | \forall e' \in O : ||O||_e > ||O||_{e'} \vee (||O||_e = ||O||_{e'} \wedge e \leq e')\}$

$mode_{max}(O) = \{e \in O | \forall e' \in O : ||O||_e > ||O||_{e'} \vee (||O||_e = ||O||_{e'} \wedge e \geq e')\}$

4.3 Machine Learning

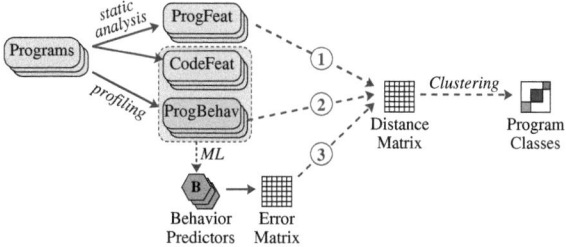

Figure 4.5: Three Ways to Identify Program Classes

4.3.2 Identification of Program Classes

So far, we considered how to construct one universal heuristics for a given behavior, which is expected to predict the behavior of all kinds of programs. Given the great diversity of programs, however, the idea of one universal predictor is not appropriate. Instead, we propose to use program classification to obtain a set of specialized predictors. For a given program which is to be optimized, we can choose the predictor that suits best that program's characteristics to predict its dynamic behavior.

To identify program classes for the programs in the training set, the idea is to group (or cluster) similar programs together. The question is how to define similarity. Based on that definition, a dissimilarity or distance matrix[2] can be constructed, which is then used by clustering algorithms to form the classes. Three different kinds of information can be used to define program similarity (see Figure 4.5):

① **Static Code Features** Define similarity based on the static code features. This puts programs together that have similar code characteristics.

② **Dynamic Behavior** Define similarity based on the dynamic behavior as obtained by profiling. This can be used to group programs with similar dynamic behavior.

③ **Mutual Predictability** Define programs as similar that explain each other with little error. To this end, we train a predictor for each program and use it to predict the behavior for every other program in the training set. If we compare the predictions with the results from profiling, we have

---
[2]While the algorithms for cluster analysis typically use a distance measure, it is obvious that also a similarity measure can be used because the one can easily be transformed into the other.

an error for each pair of programs, which yields an error matrix. This matrix can directly be used as distance matrix for the cluster analysis. As a result, we obtain program classes such that the inner class prediction error is minimized.

Which similarity measure is best depends on the considered behavior as well as the selected programs. In the validation phase, different criteria can be compared by performing the corresponding clustering and measuring the induced error for the behavior predictions. To perform clustering, machine learning offers various unsupervised algorithms, which cluster entities based on a distance measure. Besides, we pose the following constraints to obtain reasonable clustering: To prevent trivial classes, we define a minimal size each class must have ($minClassSize$). Similarly, a minimal number of program classes is defined ($minClassCount$).

At the end of this step, we have identified a set of k program classes $\mathcal{C}_{prog} = \{\mathfrak{c}_1, \mathfrak{c}_2, \cdots, \mathfrak{c}_k\}$. Additionally, each program p_i is assigned to its corresponding class $pc_i \in \mathcal{C}_{prog}$, expressed by the vector $PC = (pc_i) \in \mathcal{C}_{prog}{}^n$.

4.3.3 Program Class Predictor

The idea of the concept of program classes is to obtain more precise predictors for program behavior by grouping programs with similar behavior together and by building a separate behavior predictor for each program class instead of using a general predictor for all programs. This leads to a repository of predictors, which is given by training one behavior predictor per class. Then, for a given program, its program class can be determined to select the appropriate predictor. To this end, the program class predictor is built.

The clustering performed in the previous step yields for the n programs (p_i) the corresponding program classes $PC = (pc_i) \in \mathcal{C}_{prog}{}^n$. In the initial analysis phase, we also collected the static program features of the programs $PFeat = (pfeat_i) \in \mathcal{F}_{prog}{}^n$. From $PFeat$ and PC, we can train a predictor for program classes $P_{PC} : \mathcal{F}_{prog} \to \mathcal{C}_{prog}$, which can be used to predict the program class of a previously unseen program (see Figure 4.6).

This predictor allows the compiler to use a behavior predictor tailored to the considered program. Given that we have one behavior predictor for each program class, the compiler can select the appropriate one. As result, the

4.3 Machine Learning

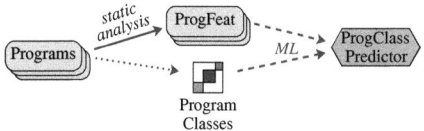

Figure 4.6: Construction of the Program Class Predictor

predictions of the dynamic run-time behavior can be expected to be more precise than if only one general behavior predictor would be used.

4.3.4 Repository of Behavior Predictors

Opposed to Section 4.3.1, where we considered to build only one behavior predictor for all programs of the program suite, we now construct a set of specialized behavior predictors to increase the precision of the predictions. As a result of the identification of program classes, the programs of our representative program suite are grouped into program classes. The idea is now to construct one specialized predictor per program class, which yields the repository of predictors. To obtain the predictor for a given program class, the features and the profiling data sets of the corresponding programs are used as training data $((CFeat_i), (Beh_i))$. As described in Section 4.3.1 the data sets are combined to obtain one predictor. As a result, for each program class j, a behavior predictor P_{beh}^j is constructed. Figure 4.7 shows the overall process.

4.3.5 Combination with Conservative Analyses

While one aim of our approach is to overcome the inherent imprecision of conservative program analyses, our approach also allows for benefiting from them. For example, in many cases, a program analysis can tell whether the reported

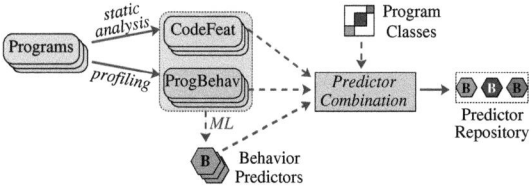

Figure 4.7: Construction of Behavior Predictors

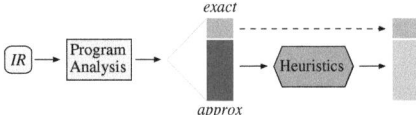

Figure 4.8: Combining Program Analyses and Heuristics

behavior is definitely correct (*i.e.*, exact) or whether it is only approximated due to insufficient information. Then, the result of the program analysis can be used when exact, and otherwise, the heuristics can be consulted. On top of that, the result of the analysis can be even used as input for the heuristics. Figure 4.8 illustrates this idea. As a result, the overall predictions get more precise by combining heuristics with conservative program analyses.

In this section, we have presented how machine learning techniques can be used to automatically construct heuristics from the data collected in the preceding analysis phase, namely static code features together with profiled dynamic behavior. The heuristics predict the dynamic behavior of previously unseen programs, solely based on static features. We also presented how to automatically perform program classification, which leads to a set of specialized predictors. With that, we can select the most appropriate predictor for a given program and thereby obtain more precise predictions. Finally, we have seen how the heuristics can benefit from conservative analyses. With the methods presented in Section 2.5.3, we can assess the precision of a predictor by applying it to new data for which we know the correct classes. We can also compare different parameters of the learning phase against each other and determine which performs best. For example, we can compare the different combination schemes presented in the previous section to find the best one. Or we can perform different program classifications and identify the classification that leads to the highest precision. Especially, this gives us a mean to evaluate the improvement that we obtain by program classification.

4.4 Speculative Optimizations

In the final phase of *FrISCO*, the predictors created via machine learning are used by one or more speculative compiler optimizations. The optimizations use the predictors to estimate the dynamic behavior of the considered program. Using these estimations, a precise cost model is derived, which helps to decide whether or not a given transformation is beneficial. In the following, we first

4.4 Speculative Optimizations

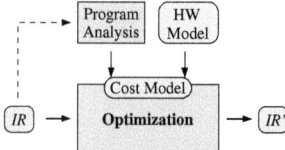

Figure 4.9: Black-box View of Compiler Optimizations

take a closer look at how optimizations explore the search space to find transformation sequences. We focus on *heuristic* optimizations, which only explore the search space partially and which iteratively decide which transformation to apply. We compare speculative optimizations with their conservative counterparts to illustrate how speculation increases the optimization potential. After that, we present how the machine learned predictors are used to build a precise cost model. With that, promising candidates can be selected while at the same time, transformations that would degrade the performance can be avoided.

4.4.1 Search Space Exploration

Compiler optimizations transform the IR of a given program to improve it with respect to the regarded objective function (*e.g.*, efficiency, code size). A black-box view of a compiler optimization is shown in Figure 4.9. The *IR* of the program is transformed to yield the optimized *IR'*. The optimization is performed with respect to a *cost model*, which is used during the optimization. It receives information about the program via program analysis as well as about the considered target architecture via a hardware model[3]. How the actual transformation of the *IR* is performed, varies from optimization to optimization. There is no general approach to model all kinds of optimizations. However, all optimizations can be thought of as a function that transforms the program into another version. The set of all possible program versions an optimization can achieve from the original program constitutes the search space of the optimization. In Section 2.1.4, we have seen that there are *optimal* optimizations, which explore the whole search space and hence yield the best solution (possibly at the price of feasibility), and *heuristic* optimizations, which only explore the search space partially and trade off optimality for efficiency. Optimality, however, is only relative to the considered cost model. If the cost model is based on approximated information, it is questionable whether the

---
[3]In case of machine-independent optimizations, the hardware model is not needed.

92 A General Framework for Intelligent Speculative Optimizations

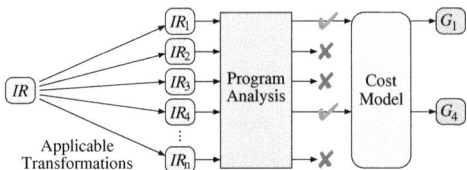

Figure 4.10: Optimization Step for Conservative Optimizations

yielded so-called optimal solution *is* actually optimal. In this situation, heuristic optimizations are preferable. They are naturally suited to approximated information and besides, they perform the transformation efficiently. Hence, we consider the approach of heuristic optimizations, which transform the program iteratively and which explore the search space only partially.

As we have seen in Section 2.1.4, the transformation performed by an optimization can be thought of as a sequence of simpler transformation steps. To construct the sequence, the optimization has to explore the search tree built by all possible transformation sequences. Due to combinatorial explosion, the search tree is huge, and complete exploration is not feasible. Hence, we consider the optimization to be greedy: Instead of actually constructing the complete tree, it is only explored locally. The transformation sequence is built incrementally. At each point, all applicable transformations are determined and rated with their expected gain. Then, the best one is selected and appended to the sequence. This is iteratively repeated until either a given quality of the code is reached, no advantageous transformation steps are left, or a given number of transformation steps was performed. Most proposed compiler optimizations can be mapped to this model. In the following, we take a closer look at the optimization step, which decides which transformation to apply. To illustrate the advantages of speculative optimizations over their conservative counterparts, in the following, we compare both alternatives.

4.4.2 Increased Optimization Potential

The optimization step for conservative optimizations is shown in Figure 4.10. Starting on a given IR, we assume that n transformation steps can be applied, which respectively yield the transformed IR_i. For each IR_i, the estimated dynamic program behavior yielded by program analysis is used to first decide whether the corresponding transformation step is safe, *i.e.*, is guaranteed to maintain the program semantics (shown in the figure by the green check marks

4.4 Speculative Optimizations

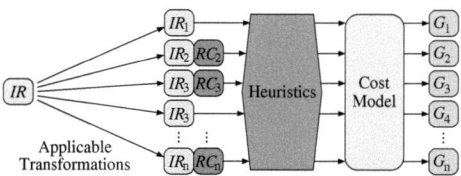

Figure 4.11: Optimization Step for Speculative Optimizations

and by the red crosses, respectively). If so, second, the results from program analysis are fed into the cost model, which yields the corresponding expected performance gain $G_i \in \mathbb{N}$. In case of machine-dependent optimizations, this also takes the hardware model into account. If a transformation step is rendered unsafe, it is not considered for selection. From the safe transformation steps, the best one is selected, and we proceed as before. Since the program analyses are conservative, many if not most of the possible transformation steps will be rendered unsafe. As a consequence, much of the optimization potential is wasted.

Speculative optimizations allow us to overcome the limitations introduced by conservative optimizations and exploit the full optimization potential. The optimization step is slightly changed (see Figure 4.11). As opposed to the conservative case, speculative optimizations consider also *unsafe* transformation steps, which cannot be guaranteed at compile-time to be semantics preserving. In those cases, special recovery code has to be added, which dynamically ensures correctness at run-time (denoted in the figure by RC_i). It checks whether the speculative assumption was true. If that is not the case, *i.e.*, in case of misspeculation, corresponding code is executed which restores the correct system state. The cost model reflects the effects of the transformation step on the *IR* as well as the estimated additional cost for the recovery code in case of misspeculation. For speculative optimization, heuristics instead of program analyses are consulted to estimate the dynamic run-time behavior and to thereby construct the cost model. Since heuristics are allowed to yield unsafe information, they can provide more optimistic and hence more precise information and thus render more transformation steps applicable.

4.4.3 Cost Model

Speculative optimizations allow for performing possibly unsafe transformations, thereby increasing the optimization potential. In doing so, it is im-

94 A General Framework for Intelligent Speculative Optimizations

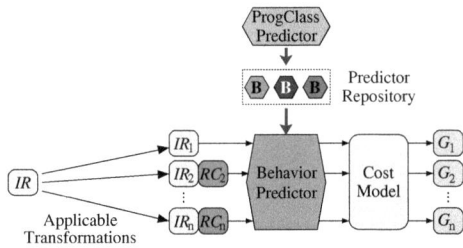

Figure 4.12: Optimization Step in *FrISCO*

portant to perform a precise cost estimation, which rates the optimization candidates, to find good transformation sequences. While speculative optimizations in general allow for using heuristics to rate the candidates, in our proposed *FrISCO* framework, we propose to use machine learning to automatically generate predictors which can be used as heuristics. This allows for the automated construction of precise, highly scalable heuristics. To increase the precision of the predictors, we perform program classification to have one specialized predictor per program class. The corresponding optimization step is shown in Figure 4.12. First, the program class of the considered, previously unseen program is determined by the program class predictor. With that, the appropriate behavior predictor can be selected from the predictor repository. By that approach, the dynamic run-time behavior of a program is precisely predicted by a predictor tailored to its corresponding program class. This in turn leads to a precise cost model, which allows for balancing the expected gain due to speculation against the expected overhead in case of misspeculation. The high scalability of the generated predictors further guarantees only limited compile-time overhead. In fact, since predictors are typically more efficient than program analyses, the overhead can be expected to be less as for program analyses in the case of conservative optimizations.

In this section, we have described a generic algorithm for speculative optimization. The program is iteratively transformed to improve its run-time behavior. At each step, for all applicable transformations, the resulting performance gain is determined with the help of the cost model, and the transformation with the highest gain is selected. Since the optimization is speculative, a transformation may require additional recovery code to guarantee program correctness in all cases. This is considered by the cost model. The cost model relies on the behavior predictor, which was automatically generated via ma-

4.5 Instantiation of the General Framework

Optimize	Predict	Abstraction Level
critical path length	required time (cycles)	instruction
code layout	execution frequency	basic block, trace, function
loop layout	loop iteration count	loops
execution time	recursion depth	function
memory accesses	dependence degree	pair of memory instructions
register promotion	access frequency	variable
memory usage	dynamic size	variable

Table 4.1: Exemplary Instantiations of *FrISCO*

chine learning in the previous phases of the framework, to predict the run-time behavior of the program.

4.5 Instantiation of the General Framework

The presented *FrISCO* framework can be instantiated for different kinds of speculative optimizations[4]. Both the assumptions of the considered dynamic program behavior as well as the model of speculative optimizations are so general that most proposed approaches can be mapped to it. Table 4.1 lists some examples for possible instantiations. The chosen instantiation determines the abstraction level, *i.e.*, at which level the behavior is observed (*i.e.*, it defines $\mathcal{E}$), as well as in which way the behavior is collected (π_{beh}). This also determines which code features are collected ($\mathcal{F}_{code}, \pi_{cfeat}$) and how the behavior is mapped to a class (I). Additionally, we have to determine which program features should be collected for program classification (π_{pfeat}). It is obvious that the analysis part and the optimization part of the framework can be used independently. As a consequence, it is possible to combine different instantiations of *FrISCO*. Thus, one optimization can use multiple predictors for different aspects of dynamic program behavior, while on the other hand, one behavior predictor can be used by multiple optimizations.

To decide how to instantiate the framework, the typical starting point would be to select a speculative optimization that is to be performed (see Figure 4.13). This includes the derivation of a cost model, which is also dependent on the hardware (hardware features like size of the register set, cost of speculation).

---

[4]Of course, the framework can also be used for conservative optimizations.

96 A General Framework for Intelligent Speculative Optimizations

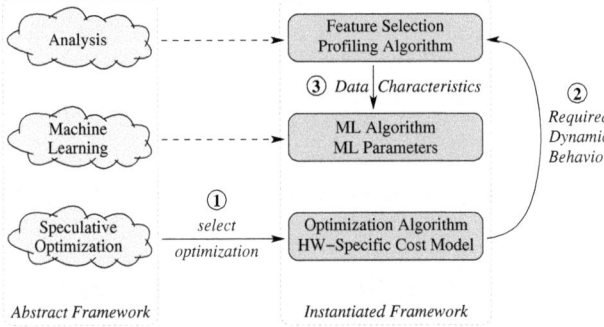

Figure 4.13: Instantiating *FrISCO*

Based on that, it can be determined which aspects of dynamic program behavior are relevant. This in turn concretizes the analysis phase, since it determines the abstraction level and which code features and which dynamic program behavior should be collected. While the second phase for machine learning is generic, it may also prove advantageous to tailor this phase to the chosen instantiation, since different learning algorithms and different learning parameters can be considered. It depends on the characteristics of the data which choice is best. In summary, the instantiation of the framework is done step by step: The instantiation of the optimization phase is followed by the instantiation of the analysis phase, which finally leads to the instantiation of the machine learning phase.

4.6 Summary

In this chapter, we have presented our general framework for intelligent speculative optimization. As central point, we propose to admit unsafe, but more precise information as the result of program analyses, which allows for the use of heuristics. This makes the optimizations using these results speculative. They have an increased optimization potential at their disposal, but at the same time have to perform a precise cost estimation, since misspeculation poses an additional run-time overhead. We presented a general concept for a speculative, greedy optimization scheme which efficiently explores the search space of all possible transformations and selects the best ones (w.r.t. the cost model). To obtain precise heuristics, we presented an approach which uses machine learning to automatically create heuristics from profiling data. By

4.6 Summary

grouping programs with similar behavior together in program classes, the precision of the heuristics is further increased. Finally, we sketched how the general framework can be applied and used in practice, and we gave various examples for that.

In Section 1.2, we defined six objectives to asses the quality of our general framework. We revisit each objective in turn and decide whether or not it is fulfilled.

- **Generality of the Optimization** In our framework, optimizations are modeled as a sequence of simpler transformations. By that, virtually all optimizations are covered, hence the generality of the optimization is fulfilled.

- **Generality of the Regarded Behavior** We impose no restrictions on the regarded behavior. The level, at which the behavior is observed, can be freely chosen. Also the kind of behavior is arbitrary. The only demand we make is that the behavior can be modeled as a discrete set of classes. This can be achieved for almost all kinds of behavior, hence, this criteria is fulfilled.

- **Modularity** The framework is modular. Various heuristics can be combined with arbitrary optimizations. This especially allows for re-using heuristics in different optimizations as well as for using many heuristics in one optimization to obtain a comprehensive view on the dynamic program behavior.

- **Scalability of the Heuristics** The heuristics are given by models that are trained by machine learning. It depends on the chosen machine learning algorithm to which extent the heuristics are scalable. However, there exist a wide range of algorithms which are precise and highly scalable, as, *e.g.*, decision tree learning. Hence, scalability is given.

- **Precision Measure** To assess the quality of the heuristics, a precision measure is required. Since we have comprehensive training data available, we can use cross-validation to obtain a realistic measure of the precision of the heuristics. The idea of cross-validation is to divide the training data into two parts: With one part, the models are trained. With the other, the precision of the models is assessed. This guarantees realistic results, since the obtained models are applied to new, previously unseen data.

- **Cost Model** Our general framework reflects the importance of the cost model. It is central in choosing which transformation to apply during the optimization. The heuristics automatically obtained by machine learning provide the cost model with a precise picture of the dynamic behavior of the program. From that, it can be expected that the cost model adequately models the performance gains of different transformations.

Thus, the general *FrISCO* framework we presented in this chapter fulfills all our objectives for conceptual frameworks for speculative optimizations. In the next chapter, we present an instantiation of the framework, which targets the optimization of memory accesses. Due to the phenomenon of the memory gap, this optimization problem is highly relevant to ensure high performance on modern architectures. The instantiation entails the development of the required analyses together with the corresponding optimizations.

5 Intelligent Speculative Optimization of Memory Accesses

In the introduction, we have illustrated that the performance of general purpose computers is severely jeopardized by the *memory gap*. As a consequence, the development of novel optimization techniques, together with the corresponding analyses, is heavily required, since it is not uncommon that memory-intensive programs stall up to 50% of their execution time waiting for data to be fetched from memory. The key to overcome this problem lies in the optimization of the load instructions. By issuing loads as early as possible, their latency can be partly if not completely hidden, such that their value is directly available when required. In doing so, memory dependencies amongst the instructions must be regarded to maintain program correctness. As we have seen in Section 2.1.3, conservative analyses have to over-approximate the behavior of programs. This over-approximation is especially severe for the analysis of memory dependencies (see Section 2.3.2). As a result, a huge number of memory dependencies amongst the instructions is reported, most of which are not present at run-time. These dependencies chain the instructions tightly together, and little optimization is possible. Speculating on data dependencies permits to break those chains and to fully exploit the available optimization potential. In the previous chapter, we have presented our ***Fr**amework for **I**ntelligent **S**peculative **C**ompiler **O**ptimizations (FrISCO)*. The framework overcomes the problem of limited optimization potential in conventional compilers due to overly conservative static analyses by introducing *unsafe* analyses together with *speculative optimizations* that can make use thereof (while ensuring program correctness). In the following, we consider an instantiation of the *FrISCO* framework which aims at the optimization of load instructions and the latencies introduced by them. Following the approach presented in

Section 4.5, we instantiate *FrISCO* as follows: First, we select the speculative optimization to be performed. This determines which information about the dynamic run-time behavior is required to build the cost model in the second step. Then, we can decide how to instantiate the first two phases of *FrISCO* to collect the required information.

5.1 Speculative Optimization of Memory Accesses

In the application of our general framework, we consider the speculative optimization of memory accesses. In the following, we first discuss the optimization problem that we have. This yields the information that is required to decide about the profitability of a given code transformation. Then, we discuss which abstraction level suits best our optimization problem. Finally, we describe in detail our optimization algorithm, which performs speculative code motion. We show how it can overcome all kinds of dependencies and how the corresponding recovery code is created.

5.1.1 Optimization Problem

The aim of the optimization is to reduce the amount of stalls due to memory loads at program run-time. Hence, the objective function is the amount of latency that could be hidden for a given load, which constitutes the *performance gain*. At the same time, we need to keep an eye on code size to avoid a substantial code growth. This could increase the amount of instruction cache misses and thereby degrade performance. Thus, we specify an upper bound on the maximally admitted *code growth*. The optimization problem is therefore to maximize the performance gain while obeying the restrictions on code growth.

As described in Section 4.4, we propose to perform the optimization iteratively and to use the cost model for guiding the optimization. This allows for developing a comparably simple algorithm, which relies on the cost model to perform the best transformation in each optimization step.

For cost estimation, several aspects of the expected dynamic run-time behavior of the considered program are relevant. It is first important to know which load instructions are expected to lead to a high load latency, since for those, optimization maximally pays off. During the code motion, the optimization speculates on data dependencies, *i.e.*, it ignores potential dependencies

5.1 Speculative Optimization of Memory Accesses

amongst memory accesses if they are considered unlikely. Thereby, the optimization potential is increased. This requires information about the likeliness of data dependencies amongst memory accesses (or their *dependence degree*). Finally, the optimization moves code across basic block boundaries, which also increases the optimization potential. To determine the costs of different code motion transformations, it is important to know the execution frequency of basic blocks as well as the probabilities of branches.

Besides, the cost model needs further information to derive the estimated gain. To determine by which amount the latency could be reduced by code motion, the distance in cycles between two positions in the code has to be known. To that end, the *issue cycle* of an instruction (relative to the surrounding basic block) has to be known for each instruction[1]. This information can be initially determined by the scheduler of the compiler, which assumes a fixed latency for each instruction[2]. While this is appropriate for most instructions, it is highly imprecise for load instructions, which may encounter latencies ranging between a few and a few hundred cycles. Hence, a precise prediction of load latencies is highly required. Additionally, this is also important to detect which loads are worth being optimized in the first place. During the optimization, as code motion proceeds, the issue cycles have to be correspondingly updated. Besides the issue cycle, the cost model requires information about the additional overhead caused by speculation, which depends on the considered target platform. This includes the cost caused by the check for successful speculation (validity check) and by the cost of recovery code execution in case of misspeculation.

To sum up, the optimization needs the following information to build the cost model:

- load latencies
- likeliness of memory dependencies
- branch probabilities and basic block frequencies
- relative issue cycle of instructions
- overhead of validity checks and of recovery code execution

While the first three items refer to information on the dynamic behavior of the program, the last two items are mainly static properties. To estimate the dynamic behavior, heuristics can be used. For branch probabilities and

---

[1] In case of parallel processors, multiple instructions can be executed at one cycle.
[2] More precisely, it is common to distinguish different types of produced and consumed data, respectively, and to specify a fixed latency for each combination of producer type and consumer type.

basic block frequencies, a highly scalable heuristics has been proposed by Wu et al. [WL94]. For predicting the latencies as well as the likeliness of dependencies, however, proposed heuristics lack either precision or scalability. Hence, in Section 5.3, we present our approach to use machine learning to yield two precise and scalable heuristics, which predict the latency of a load instruction and the likeliness of a dependency for a pair of memory instructions, respectively. The relative issue cycle of instructions can be precisely estimated at compile-time. Except for load instructions, most instructions have typically a fixed execution time, which depends on the target platform. From that, the relative issue cycle in a basic block can be determined. To deal with the varying latency of load instructions, the heuristics for load latencies can be used. The overhead of speculation depends on the hardware platform and can be seen as a parameter of the cost model.

The impact on code growth depends on whether or not speculation is supported by hardware, since this determines the amount of the required recovery code. For example, on the Itanium, one check instruction can detect misspeculation for an arbitrary number of intervening store instructions. Without hardware support, the number of required checks grows with the number of intervening stores. We consider both variants, with and without hardware support. As with the overhead of speculation, the information required to estimate code growth mainly depends on the regarded hardware platform.

5.1.2 Abstraction Level

The optimization we propose aims at reducing the latency of load instruction. As we have seen in Section 2.1, the IR passes different abstraction levels (from HIR to LIR). When developing a new optimization, the most adequate abstraction level has to be selected. Our optimization requires the following properties from the IR:

- It has been decided which data is held in memory and which in registers. Especially, this determines which data accesses require memory accesses.
- The abstract IR has been mapped to the concrete assembler level of the regarded target platform. This is important to determine the code size.
- We need a model of the regarded target platform to estimate the execution time of single instructions. This is vital for cost estimation.

5.1 Speculative Optimization of Memory Accesses

All requirements are fulfilled at the LIR level, *i.e.*, after code generation. In the LIR, the basic blocks of the CFG consist of sequences of simple, assembler-like instructions which operate on registers.

While we regard the IR at the LIR level, this does not mean that the rich information of HIR has become unavailable. Instead, we assume that each LIR construct has a link to the HIR construct it stems from. This combines the precision that we gain from the closeness to the target platform with the global view and the context information we have at the HIR level. Since we regard the IR at the LIR level, we have simple assembler-like instructions which operate on registers. The optimization moves load instructions upwards in the code. In doing so, data as well as control dependencies amongst the instructions must not be violated. This holds for data dependencies amongst registers as well as for those amongst memory locations. For register dependencies, output (*WAW, write-after-write*) and anti (*WAR, write-after-read*) dependencies are only caused by register shortage. Those dependencies can be overcome by register renaming. Hence, if we assume for now that we have an arbitrary number of registers available, we can safely neglect output and anti dependencies. Conversely, true dependencies amongst registers (*RAW read-after-write*) can never be ignored. Since we consider load instructions, true register dependencies from the load to previous instructions stem from address calculations (*e.g.*, for array accesses). Those instructions are required to determine the address that the load fetches data from and, hence, cannot be crossed. Concerning memory dependencies, as we consider load instructions, we need only to consider true dependencies (*RAW*), which can occur to preceding store instructions.

We assume that the code is *scheduled* and that for each instruction, its estimated issue cycle (relative to the surrounding basic block) is known. This is required to measure the number of cycles between the execution of two instructions, which is used to determine the amount of cycles by which a given load latency could be reduced.

5.1.3 Optimization Algorithm

As we have seen in Chapter 4, we consider an optimization that transforms the IR step-by-step. At each step, the cost model is used to rate different alternatives and to take the best one. Additionally, we determine the impact on code growth for each alternative and preclude transformations that exceed

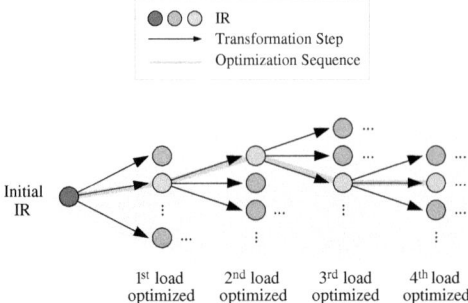

Figure 5.1: Tree of Transformation Sequences for Speculative Code Motion

a given limit. The optimization aims to reduce the effective latency of load instructions. To that end, we first build a list of candidates, namely loads with high expected load latencies, and then process each candidate in turn. The candidates are sorted by their latency in decreasing order such that we start with the most promising one. The idea is now to move the candidate upwards in the code, step-by-step. In the search tree of possible transformation sequences, we start with considering the first candidate. The alternatives are given by moving the candidate a different number of steps upwards. The cost model is used to rate each alternative. Then, at depth one in the tree, the best optimization for the first candidate was chosen, and we consider the second candidate. This process is repeated until we run out of candidates or until the limit for code growth is reached. Figure 5.1 shows the search tree. Note that the cost model is used to rate the benefits of a given transformation as well as to decide whether a given transformation is *admissible, i.e.,* whether it does not exceed a given code growth limit. This is important to limit the impact of the optimization on the instruction cache behavior. As another constraint, the amount of allowed speculation should be limited, since over-speculation also degrades performance. To that end, the fraction of speculative loads w.r.t. all loads is determined.

The resulting algorithm is shown in Figure 5.2. It is parametrized by the maximum allowed code growth as well as the maximum amount of allowed speculation. By these parameters, the algorithm can be tailored to the regarded target architecture. The vital parts of the algorithm are speculative code motion and the cost model. In the following, we describe speculative code motion in detail as well as the issue of recovery code generation. The cost model is described in detail in Section 5.2.

5.1 Speculative Optimization of Memory Accesses

---

1. build list of *optimization candidates* (loads with a high latency, sorted in decreasing order by latency)
2. process each candidate in turn
   - determine different optimization alternatives, for $k \in \{0..MAX_k\}$:
     - move the candidate k steps upwards
     - overcome dependencies by speculation
     - for each alternative, determine the *estimated optimization gain* and the *code growth* (based on the *cost model*)
   - take the best *admissible* solution
   - insert recovery code as required
   - proceed with next candidate, unless exit condition satisfied (*e.g.*, maximum code growth or maximum level of speculation)

Figure 5.2: Algorithm for Speculative Code Motion

Speculative Code Motion

When considering to move a load instruction upwards, different kinds of dependencies may be present to the preceding instruction. The kind of dependency determines by which means the dependency can be overcome and what the consequences for the optimization gain as well as for code size are. Note that the algorithm itself does not consider the advantage of a given transformation. It moves the load instruction stepwise upwards, coping with dependencies as required, and uses then the cost model to decide whether or not this solution leads to an improvement. In Section 2.4.1, we have seen how memory dependencies can be overcome by data speculation. Section 2.4.2 has shown how to deal with control dependencies by control speculation. The corresponding cost model, which is the crucial part of the optimization and which is used to decide whether or not a given transformation should be performed, is presented in Sections 5.2.2 and 5.2.3, respectively. In both cases, the load is marked as speculative, and at its original location, a special check instruction is inserted that detects misspeculation.

The only remaining kind of dependency not dealt with so far is a true register dependency. In that case, the result register of a previous instruction is used by the considered load as address register. In other words, the preceding

Figure 5.3: Construction of a LAC chain (a) True Data Dependency Prevents Code Motion (b) LAC chain Enables Further Code Motion

instruction performs *address calculation* for the regarded load. This is quite common in typical code, and address calculations are caused by, *e.g.*, array or struct accesses. Obviously, there is no way to move the load across that previous instruction. To still render optimization possible in that case, we group the load and the preceding instruction together to build a *Load Address Computation (LAC) chain*. Then, we can proceed with moving the whole LAC chain upwards. Of course, this step may be repeated, *i.e.*, if there is another instruction that is required for address computation, it is put in front of the LAC chain.

Figure 5.3 illustrates the construction of a LAC chain. On the left, we see that code motion of the load instruction cannot cross the add instruction, since it calculates the address the load refers to. This can be solved by building a LAC chain, as shown on the right: Both instructions are coupled together and can now be moved further upwards. Different from before, we now have to consider the dependencies from all instructions of the LAC chain to the preceding instructions during code motion. Note that the last instruction of a LAC chain is the originally targeted load instruction. Since a single load can be considered as a LAC chain of length one, from now on we use the term LAC chain.

The optimization transforms different load instructions in turn. Hence, when moving code upwards, we may encounter check instructions, which were inserted by a previous optimization of another load ld_{prev}. If there is no dependency between the LAC chain and the check instruction, it can be safely crossed without any further precautions. Otherwise, we have to take a closer look at the situation. We know that the check is preceded by a number of advanced loads. In case speculation is successful for ld_{prev}, the dependency actually holds between the LAC chain and the advanced loads, and we can cross the check instruction. Otherwise, if speculation fails for ld_{prev}, crossing the check is not allowed in general. However, if speculation fails, we know that

5.1 Speculative Optimization of Memory Accesses

the check will detect that and issue corresponding recovery code. Thus, if we add the currently regarded LAC chain to the recovery code of the encountered check, we can safely cross the check. By that, we can exploit the cycle distance created by the previous optimization to further reduce the latency of the currently optimized load.

With that, we can overcome all kinds of dependencies to preceding instructions. However, the transformation itself does not regard whether or not a given code motion step appears beneficial. It is due to the cost model to decide about that. The encountered kind of dependency determines the required code transformation to overcome the dependency as well as the corresponding cost model. In the following, we consider the kinds of dependencies that might occur and describe how they can be overcome. The corresponding cost models are described in detail in Section 5.2. From the regarded LAC chain to a preceding instruction ins, the following different kinds of dependencies may occur:

Memory dependency: If ins is a store that might alias with any instruction in the LAC chain, the dependency is speculatively ignored and the optimization proceeds. Similarly, if ins denotes a function call that might affect a value loaded within the LAC chain, the dependency is ignored speculatively.

Control dependency: If the beginning of a block is reached, control speculation renders moving the LAC chain to preceding blocks possible. This may require code duplication if the current block has multiple predecessors.

Register dependency: If there is a true register dependency from any instruction of the LAC chain to ins, as for address calculation, ins is put in front of the LAC chain. Note that ins is then either an arithmetic instruction (for offset calculation) or a load (for indirect accesses). As a special case, if ins is a check instruction of a previously speculatively optimized load ld_{prev} upon which ld depends (for indirect accesses), we can cross ins without updating the LAC chain if we append the LAC chain to the recovery code of ins.

In case of control speculation, $i.e.$, when the LAC chain is moved to another block, it has to be ensured that it is executed for each path leading to the original block. Thus, it may be necessary to duplicate the LAC chain and to insert it in multiple target blocks. In Section 2.1.2, we have seen how the concept of a *dominance front* can be used to decide whether it is admissible to move code from its original block *blk* to a certain set of target blocks *DomF*. If *DomF* constitutes a dominance front of *blk*, the transformation maintains correctness. In other words, in that case it is guaranteed that the code is executed before reaching the original block *blk*.

Recovery Code Generation

During the optimization, for each considered candidate, the appropriate recovery code is collected. Conceptually, the recovery code belongs to the check instruction, which is inserted at the original location of the considered load candidate when speculation is performed. At the beginning, after data or control speculation, the recovery code contains nothing but a copy of the original load instruction. When performing code motion across a check instruction (stemming from a previously optimized load) upon which a dependency occurs, the recovery code belonging to that check instruction is extended by the LAC chain of the currently optimized load. This is the only case that causes non-trivial recovery code. A detailed example is given in Section 5.2.5. When the optimization is finished, the recovery code has to be inserted into the program code. To avoid a perturbation of the instruction cache behavior, it should be placed at the end of the program. For each check, new recovery code is added, which contains the corresponding code as well as an instruction for jumping back just behind the check. Depending on the regarded target architecture, trivial recovery code might be implemented more efficiently. On the Intel Itanium processor, the check instruction can issue automatically a reload in case of data misspeculation. Hence, if the recovery code contains nothing but the reload, the recovery can be completely done by the check instruction.

5.2 Cost Model

In this section, we derive the cost model that determines the performance gain as well as the code growth for a given transformation, which is used to guide the optimization. We start with conservative code motion and then consider the different cases, namely data speculation, control speculation, building LAC chains, and dealing with previously optimized loads. We present a cost model for each case and give illustrative examples.

5.2 Cost Model

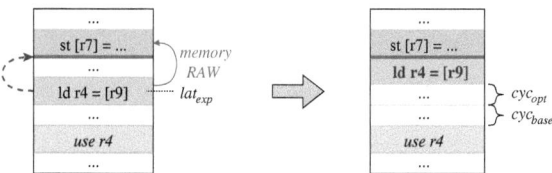

Figure 5.4: Conservative Code Motion

5.2.1 Conservative Code Motion

In the conservative case, code motion has to stop at any dependency. This makes it an intra-block optimization (*i.e.*, crossing basic block borders is not admissible). The regarded load *ld* is moved upwards as far as possible. If any data dependencies are present to a preceding instruction *ins*, the optimization has to stop. This kind of optimization is always safe.

Figure 5.4 shows an example. On the left, we see a basic block, which contains a load instruction that we want to optimize as well as an instruction that uses the loaded value. We assume that the load has latency of lat_{exp} cycles. Since loads can be issued in the background, this latency (or what remains thereof) only becomes visible when the loaded value is actually used. Hence, at the use site, the effective latency will be lower than the initial latency lat_{exp}. We also see a potential *read-after-write* memory dependency to a preceding store, which introduces a barrier for code motion (shown by the red line). On the right, we see how the load instruction was moved upwards up to the barrier. To determine the gain of this transformation, we compare the effective latency of the base version with that of the optimized version. To that end, we have to determine the distance (in terms of cycles) between the different instruction positions. Since we know for each instruction its issue cycle, the distance can be directly determined from that. In the figure, we see the distance between the original position of the load and its use (cyc_{base}) as well as the distance between the new position and the old position of the load (cyc_{opt}). For both the base and the optimized version, respectively, the distance between the corresponding load position and the use constitutes the amount of the load latency that could be *hidden* or *masked*. From that, we can compute the effective latency for the base and for the optimized version, respectively:

$$lat_{base} = lat_{exp} - cyc_{base} \tag{5.1}$$
$$lat_{opt} = lat_{exp} - cyc_{base} - cyc_{opt} \tag{5.2}$$

The gain of the optimization is given by the difference:

$$gain = lat_{base} - lat_{opt} = cyc_{opt} \tag{5.3}$$

This optimization has no effect on code size, hence the code growth is 0 (with and without hardware support for speculation):

$$code\_growth_{sw} = 0 \tag{5.4}$$
$$code\_growth_{hw} = 0 \tag{5.5}$$

Since the maximum optimization is achieved if lat_{base} is hidden completely, we assume that the distance by which a load is optimized never exceeds its latency. In other words, the effective latencies lat_{base} and lat_{opt} are always non-negative. This avoids unrealistic gains caused by a negative lat_{opt} (*e.g.*, if a load with a low latency is moved upwards by a long distance). In the optimization algorithm, this is realized as an exit condition in the optimization loop. Since *gain* is given by cyc_{opt}, this means that the further we move the load upwards, the higher the optimization gain (until $lat_{exp} = cyc_{base} + cyc_{opt}$). However, this does not hold for the general case, as we see in the following.

5.2.2 Data Speculation

In the previous section, we have presented the principle of code motion for the conservative case. As first extension, we now consider how data dependencies induced by memory accesses can be overcome to increase the optimization potential. As before, we move the load instruction upwards step-by-step. When we encounter a store instruction that might conflict with the load, speculation allows us to deliberately ignore that dependency and to optimize instead, *i.e.*, to move the load across the store. However, we have to decide whether or not speculation appears beneficial. As we will see in the following, the likeliness of the conflict can be used to decide whether or not to speculate.

5.2 Cost Model

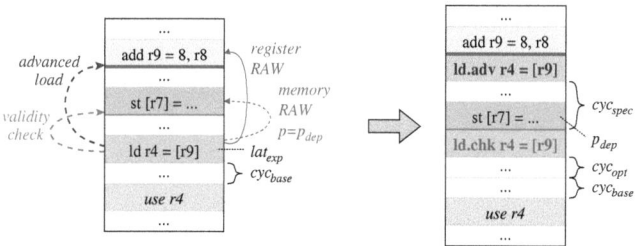

Figure 5.5: Data Speculative Code Motion

Figure 5.5 illustrates the case that we move the load across a potentially conflicting store[3]. On the left, we see the unoptimized code. A potential dependency (*memory RAW*) between the load and a preceding store is reported. We assume that we know the probability p_{dep} of that dependency. The figure also shows a true register dependency (*register RAW*) to a preceding instruction. As shown on the right, the load is moved upwards until the register dependency is reached, which cannot be overcome for now. This optimization is *unsafe*, or *speculative*, since a potential dependency is ignored. The load becomes an *advanced load*, which means that it is executed optimistically and that its value may be invalidated by the succeeding store. Additionally, we have to insert a *validity check* before the use, which detects if *conflicts* occurred (misspeculation), and corresponding *recovery code* that is executed in that case to restore the correct system state. The overhead or *penalty cycles* introduced by the check (cyc_{chk}) and, if necessary, by the execution of the recovery code (cyc_{rc}) depends on the way speculation is technically implemented. In case of hardware support, the check can be executed in constant time. The amount of cycles required to execute the recovery code is typically dominated by the latency of the regarded load (lat_{exp}), which has to be reloaded. However, due to the preceding advanced load, the loaded value may reside at a higher level in the cache hierarchy, which reduces its latency. cyc_{rc} denotes the additional number of cycles required by the two branches, which jump to the recovery code and back again, respectively.

We are free to insert the validity check anywhere between the last potentially conflicting store and the use of the loaded value. If speculation was successful, the position of the check does not matter. Otherwise, the check triggers the execution of recovery code to reload the invalidated value. In that

---

[3] We only consider stores which might conflict with the load. Stores that provably have no conflicts can be safely ignored.

case, the effective load latency is reduced by the distance from the check to the use site. Consequently, the check should be placed as early as possible, i.e., immediately behind the last possibly conflicting store, as shown in Figure 5.5. The amount of cycles that is hidden if speculation is successful is denoted as cyc_{spec}. The amount of cycles that is hidden in any case is given by $cyc_{base} + cyc_{opt}$. The overhead in case of misspeculation is given by the time required to execute the recovery code, $lat_{exp} + cyc_{rc}$. In any case, the overhead is cyc_{chk}. Speculation fails if the potential data dependency between load and store does occur, i.e., p_{dep} denotes the probability of misspeculation. From that, we can compute the effective latency achieved by the optimization:

$$lat_{opt} = lat_{exp} - cyc_{base} - cyc_{opt} + cyc_{chk} \\ - (1 - p_{dep}) \cdot cyc_{spec} + p_{dep} \cdot cyc_{rc} \qquad (5.6)$$

In the general case, multiple stores can be crossed by the speculative optimization. For each of the n stores, we know its corresponding conflict probability p_{dep}^i w.r.t. the optimized load instruction. Speculation fails if any of the dependencies does occur. The probability for that is given by:

$$p_{dep}^{any} = 1 - \prod_{1 \leq i \leq n} (1 - p_{dep}^i) \qquad (5.7)$$

To compute the effective latency of the optimized program, we use the same formula as above and replace p_{dep} by p_{dep}^{any}.

The overall optimization gain is then given by

$$gain = lat_{base} - lat_{opt} \\ = cyc_{opt} - cyc_{chk} + (1 - p_{dep}^{any}) \cdot cyc_{spec} - p_{dep}^{any} \cdot cyc_{rc} \qquad (5.8)$$

We see that p_{dep}^{any} is one central factor to decide about the profitability of speculation. Thus, it is clear that the more potential conflicting stores we cross, the higher gets p_{dep}^{any}, and the lower gets the optimization gain. This means that moving a load upwards as far as possible is certainly not the best solution. At the latest, optimization should stop if $(cyc_{base} + cyc_{opt} + cyc_{spec})$

5.2 Cost Model

exceed lat_{exp}, since then, no additional improvement can be gained and p_{dep}^{any} can only increase further. Without hardware support for speculation, the effect on code size depends on n, the number of stores that were crossed. In the worst case, for each store, a check and a conditional jump is required, plus the recovery code itself (a reload and a jump for branching back):

$$code\_growth_{sw} = 2 \cdot n + 2 \qquad (5.9)$$

For architectures with hardware support for speculation, one check instruction is sufficient, regardless how many store instructions were crossed. If the recovery code only consists of the reload, this can be automatically issued by the check instruction in case of misspeculation. Hence, we only need one additional check instruction:

$$code\_growth_{hw} = 1 \qquad (5.10)$$

As a special case of data speculation, a load can be moved across a function call. This requires the absence of register dependencies from the load to the call. cyc_{spec} and p_{dep}^{any} have to be computed from the code of the called function.

5.2.3 Control Speculation

With data speculation, as presented in the previous section, we are able to overcome unlikely memory dependencies from the regarded load to preceding store instructions. However, the optimization still has to stop at basic block borders. Given the typically small size of basic blocks, this drastically limits the optimization potential. However, without further precautions, loads cannot be moved to preceding blocks, since that might introduce an exception on another program path (*e.g.*, illegal address fault). With control speculation, exceptions are deferred, which makes code motion across basic block borders admissible. Generally, with control speculation, we are free to move the load to arbitrary basic blocks. It has to be guaranteed that the load has been executed before the original use site is reached. In other words, on all paths that lead to the original use site, the load has to be executed. This may require to perform code duplication. In the following, we assume that code motion moved code from its original basic block *blk* to a set of target blocks, denoted as *Tgts*. To ensure correctness of the optimization, *Tgts* has to constitute a *dominance front DomF* of *blk* (see Section 2.1.2).

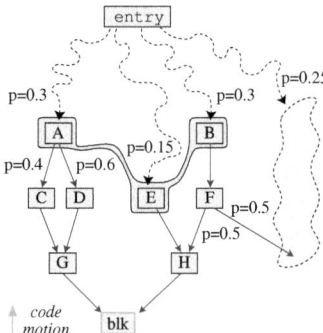

Figure 5.6: Control Speculation: Dominance Front and Branch Probabilities

As an example, Figure 5.6 shows an excerpt from a CFG. At each branch, the branch probability is annotated (unless $p = 1$). Additionally, since we only consider an excerpt of the CFG, the probabilities of the paths leading to A, B, and E, respectively, are shown. At the bottom, we have block blk, from which we want to perform upwards code motion. The optimization has decided to place the code in blocks A, B, and E, which form a dominance front for blk. Note that the probability of executing the dominance front needs not be 1. In the example, the probability of reaching A, B, or E is $0.3 + 0.15 + 0.3 = 0.75$. This needs not to be equal to the probability $P(blk)$ of reaching blk, which is $0.3 + 0.15 + (0.3 \cdot 0.5) = 0.6$ in the example. Not shown is the `exit` node, at which the control flow converges at the latest from left and right hand side of the shown CFG.

The optimization inserts a copy of the considered load in each block $t \in Tgts$ and replaces the original load in blk by a check instruction. To estimate the overall gain of the optimization, we first consider all possible paths leading from any node in $Tgts$ to blk. With that, we can determine the performance for each path and can obtain the overall gain by weighting each gain by the corresponding path probability. For a given $t \in Tgts$,

$$Paths_{blk}^t := PathsBetweenBlocks(t, blk)$$

contains all paths from t to blk. From the estimated branch probabilities, we can determine the relative probability of a path $\pi_{blk}^t \in Paths_{blk}^t$ by multiplying the probabilities of its control flow edges. This yields the conditional path probability $P(\pi_{blk}^t | t)$, given that t was reached. To obtain the overall performance gain for the considered optimization, the idea is now that we regard

5.2 Cost Model

each path π_{blk}^t from each $t \in \mathit{Tgts}$ to blk in turn, determine its performance gain, and sum up all gains, weighted by the corresponding path probability. To weight the incoming paths from one target $t \in \mathit{Tgts}$ to blk, we first need the probability of a path π_{blk}^t w.r.t. to blk, i.e., we need $P(\pi_{blk}^t|blk)$. An important property is $\sum_{t \in \mathit{Tgts}} \sum_{\pi_{blk}^t \in \mathit{Paths}_{blk}^t} P(\pi_{blk}^t|blk) = 1$, since all paths to blk contain one $t \in \mathit{Tgts}$ (remember that Tgts is a dominance front of blk). This is required for normalization when building the weighted sum of the performance gains of each path. We observe that for a path π_{blk}^t from a $t \in \mathit{Tgts}$ to blk,

$$P(\pi_{blk}^t|blk) \stackrel{(1)}{=} \frac{P(\pi_{blk}^t \cap blk)}{P(blk)} \stackrel{(2)}{=} \frac{P(\pi_{blk}^t)}{P(blk)} \stackrel{(3)}{=} \frac{P(\pi_{blk}^t \cap t)}{P(blk)} \stackrel{(4)}{=} \frac{P(\pi_{blk}^t|t) \cdot P(t)}{P(blk)}$$
(5.11)

Transformation (1) directly follows from the definition of conditional probability. For transformation (2), we observe that whenever π_{blk}^t occurs, we know that we have reached blk. Formally, $P(\pi_{blk}^t \cap blk) = P(\pi_{blk}^t) \cdot P(blk|\pi_{blk}^t) = P(\pi_{blk}^t) \cdot 1$. The same argument holds for π_{blk}^t and t in step (3). Transformation (4) again directly follows from the definition of conditional probability. Hence, since we already have the conditional path probability $P(\pi_{blk}^t|t)$, we need to determine the probabilities of reaching t and blk, respectively:

$$P(t) = \sum_{\pi \in \mathit{Paths}_t^{\mathrm{entry}}} P(\pi|\mathtt{entry}) \tag{5.12}$$

$$P(blk) = \sum_{\pi \in \mathit{Paths}_{blk}^{\mathrm{entry}}} P(\pi|\mathtt{entry}) \tag{5.13}$$

Note that $P(blk)$ may be below 1 if blk is conditionally executed (e.g., if Tgts and blk are part of a subgraph which is entered by a **then**-branch of an **if-then-else** construct). With that, we can determine $P(\pi_{blk}^t|blk)$ with equation (5.11). To determine the performance gain for a given path π_{blk}^t, the blocks of π_{blk}^t are considered as a straight line sequence of code. This yields cyc_{base}, cyc_{opt}, cyc_{spec} and p_{dep}^{any}. From that, using equation (5.8), we can compute the resulting gain for that path and denote the result as $PathGain(\pi_{blk}^t)$. Finally, we build the sum of those gains, weighted by the conditional probabilities of the corresponding paths:

116 Intelligent Speculative Optimization of Memory Accesses

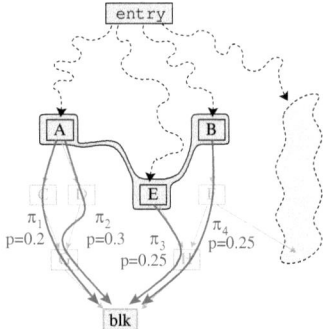

Figure 5.7: Control Speculation: Paths π_i leading to blk with Path Probabilities $P(\pi_i|blk)$

$$gain = \sum_{t \in Tgts} \sum_{\pi^t_{blk} \in Paths^t_{blk}} P(\pi^t_{blk}|blk) \cdot PathGain(\pi^t_{blk}) \quad (5.14)$$

Coming back to our example, Figure 5.7 shows all possible paths leading from the dominance front to blk, together with their conditional probabilities. For example, for path π_1, the probability is determined as follows: $P(\pi_1|blk) = P(\pi_1|A) \cdot P(A)/P(blk) = 0.4 \cdot 0.3/0.6 = 0.2$. As another example, for path π_4, we get $P(\pi_4|blk) = 0.5 \cdot 0.3/0.6 = 0.25$. Note that the sum of those conditional path probabilities is always 1. For each path, we can compute the gain achieved by the optimization. The weighted sum thereof yields the resulting gain.

Figure 5.8 gives an example how to compute the resulting gain. A load was moved from its original position in block 4 to its dominator, block 1. The figure also shows the branch probability at the control flow edges, the length of different code regions in cycles, and the dependence probability for the load and the store in block 2. There are two paths from block 1 to block 4, namely $1-2-4$ and $1-3-4$. For the first path, the probability is 0.8, and we have the following distances: $cyc_{base} = 0$, $cyc_{opt} = 5$, $cyc_{spec} = 35$. The probability for a conflict p_{dep} is 0.1. For an original latency lat_{exp} of 50 cycles, an additional recovery cost cyc_{rc} of 10 cycles, and a check overhead cyc_{chk} of 8 cycles, we can compute the expected gain $gain_1 = 5 - 8 + 0.9 \cdot 35 - 0.1 \cdot 10 = 27.5$. For the second path, the path probability is 0.2, and the distances are $cyc_{base} = 0$, $cyc_{opt} = 5$, $cyc_{spec} = 15$. The probability for a conflict p_{dep} is 0. Thus, $gain_2 = 5 - 8 + 1 \cdot 15 - 0 \cdot 10 = 12$. To obtain the overall estimated stall, we

5.2 Cost Model

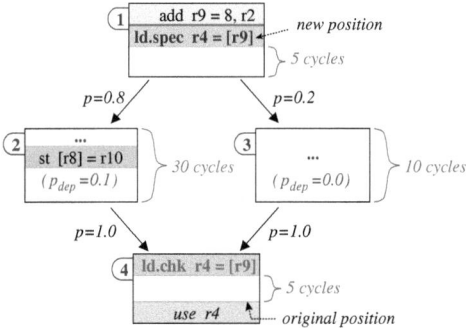

Figure 5.8: Control Speculative Code Motion

sum up the gains for each path weighted by the path probabilities and obtain a resulting performance gain of $0.8 \cdot 27.5 + 0.2 \cdot 12 = 24.4$ cycles.

To determine the impact on code growth, let n be the number of possibly conflicting store instructions that were crossed, and let $m = |Tgts|$ denote the number of blocks into which the load was speculatively moved. Then, the original load is replaced by m loads, which leads to (m-1) additional loads. Without hardware support for speculation, we need one check and one conditional jump for each possibly conflicting store, plus the recovery code itself (one reload and a jump for branching back). With hardware support, one check instruction is sufficient, and no recovery code is required, since the check automatically re-issues the load in case of misspeculation. This leads to the following code growth:

$$code\_growth_{sw} = (m-1) + 2 \cdot n + 2 = m + 2 \cdot n + 1 \qquad (5.15)$$
$$code\_growth_{hw} = (m-1) + 1 = m \qquad (5.16)$$

5.2.4 Load Address Computation Chains

In a previous example for data speculative code motion (see Section 5.2.2, Figure 5.5), we have seen that a true register dependency from the considered load to a preceding instruction has prevented further optimizations. Those dependencies are mostly caused by address calculations, which stem from, *e.g.*, array or struct references and are common in typical code. Hence, true dependencies from the register containing the load's address to preceding instructions are

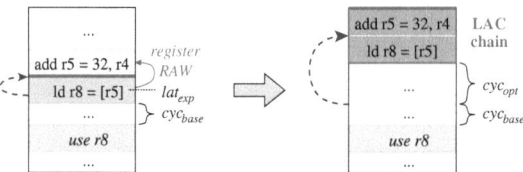

Figure 5.9: Code Motion with Load Instruction Chains

likely and therefore constitute a significant limitation of the optimization. As shown in Section 5.1.3, a solution to this problem is to include the instructions the load depends on in code motion. To that end, we build a *Load Address Computation (LAC) chain* by grouping together the load instruction and the instructions it depends on. Then, we perform code motion for the whole LAC chain. Unlike before, where we merely had to consider the dependencies from the regarded load to the preceding instructions, we now have to consider the dependencies from all instructions of the LAC chain.

Figure 5.9 gives an example. Since all extensions are orthogonal to each other and can freely be combined, for clarity, we do not consider data and control speculation in the example. On the left, we see that code motion has to stop at a true register dependency due to address calculation, which limits the optimization potential. On the right, we see how this problem can be overcome: Both instructions are grouped together to a LAC chain, which can be moved further upwards.

Address calculation typically consists of adding and multiplying. Thus, the corresponding instructions can be expected to have a low, constant latency, and moving the LAC chain together as a block is appropriate. For indirect references, however, address calculations may also contain load instructions. In that case, the latency is in general unpredictable, and scheduling the LAC chain together may cause additional stalls. Hence, loads should only be added to the LAC chain if their latency is expected to be low.

This extension merely increases the optimization potential and has no influence on the optimization gain. In case of code duplication due to control speculation, now the whole LAC chain has to be duplicated instead of the single load. Hence, the formulas to specify the code growth are as follows:

$$code\_growth_{sw} = (m-1) \cdot |LAC\ chain| + 2 \cdot n + 2 \qquad (5.17)$$

$$code\_growth_{hw} = (m-1) \cdot |LAC\ chain| + 1 \qquad (5.18)$$

5.2 Cost Model

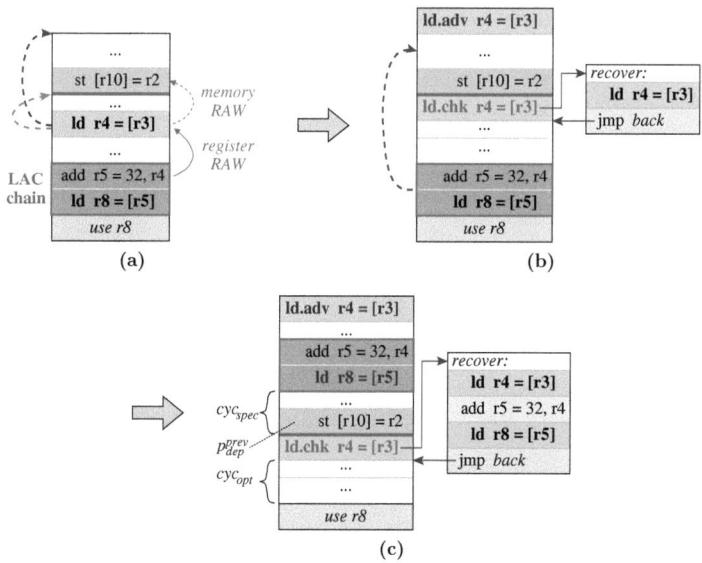

Figure 5.10: Code Motion across Check Instructions (a) Original Code (b) Optimization of First Load (c) Optimization of Second Load (with LAC chain)

5.2.5 Crossing Check Instructions

During code motion, we may encounter check instructions, which stem from a previous optimization of another load. Since the check instructions correspond to load instructions, the question is whether those checks can be crossed by code motion, and, if so, in which way. As an example, see Figure 5.10. In Figure 5.10a, we see two load instructions with a long latency. The figure also shows the true register dependency from the add instruction to the first load as well as the memory dependencies from the first load to the preceding store. Figure 5.10b shows how the first load is optimized, together with the corresponding recovery code, which simply reloads $r4$. Now the second load is optimized. First, the add instruction is added to its LAC chain, since it is required for address calculation. Then, during upwards code motion, the LAC chain reaches the check of the first load. As described above, the check can safely be crossed, given that the corresponding recovery code is updated. Figure 5.10c shows the result. The updated recovery code for the load from $r4$ now also executes the dependent instructions. In the example, neither a check instruction nor recovery code is required for $r8$ because the load from $r8$ itself was not speculatively optimized. Misspeculation can only occur for $r4$, and in that case, it is detected by the check for $r4$, and the load from $r8$ together with its LAC is re-executed.

Note that for this optimization, no speculation was performed. However, the gain depends on the previously performed speculation for another load. Thus, we need the probability of misspeculation p_{dep}^{prev} for the previously optimized load. Additionally, we need to determine cyc_{base}, cyc_{opt}, cyc_{spec}, cyc_{rc} for the regarded load as usual. (see Figure 5.10c for an example for cyc_{opt} and cyc_{spec}). To compute the effective latency, we have to distinguish whether or not speculation was successful for that previous load. If it was successful, we reduced the original latency by cyc_{spec} cycles. The probability for that case is $1 - p_{dep}^{prev}$. Otherwise, in case of misspeculation, we have to execute the recovery code. The overhead of executing the existing recovery code for the previous load were already reflected in the cost model. Hence, we only need to consider the additional costs we have, which is given by cyc_{rc}. In all cases, the original latency lat_{exp} is reduced by $cyc_{base} + cyc_{opt}$. Note that also the overhead induced by the check were already reflected previously when optimizing the corresponding load instruction. Thus, lat_{opt} can be computed as follows:

$$lat_{opt} = lat_{exp} - cyc_{base} - cyc_{opt} \\ - (1 - p_{dep}^{prev}) \cdot cyc_{spec} + p_{dep}^{prev} \cdot cyc_{rc} \quad (5.19)$$

The optimization gain is then given by

$$gain = lat_{base} - lat_{opt} \\ = cyc_{opt} + (1 - p_{dep}^{prev}) \cdot cyc_{spec} - p_{dep}^{prev} \cdot cyc_{rc} \quad (5.20)$$

Note that we have to ensure that the currently regarded load is not moved too closely to the previously optimized one. In other words, at the new position of the currently optimized load, the value loaded by the previous load has to be available. Otherwise, we would introduce a stall. Hence, we obtain the effective latency of the previously optimized load, lat_{opt}^{prev}, and we make sure that the distance between the previously optimized load and the regarded one does not fall below that value.

The code growth is given by the length of the LAC chain of the regarded load, since it is appended to the recovery code for the check instruction that is crossed. Hence:

$$code\_growth_{sw} = code\_growth_{hw} = |LAC\ chain| \qquad (5.21)$$

5.3 Learning the Memory Behavior of Programs

In the previous section, we have seen which information about the dynamic program behavior is required for a precise cost estimation, namely the latency of load instructions and the probability of dependencies amongst memory instructions. In this section, we describe how to use machine learning to automatically generate heuristics for those dynamic properties. As we have seen in Section 2.5, machine learning requires a set of observations (the training data), containing for each observation its features and its class. The model, which is automatically constructed, represents the relationship between features and the corresponding class. Hence, if we take static code features as features and if we model the dynamic program behavior as categorical class, we can use the model to yield a heuristics, which predicts the dynamic behavior based on static information. The training data is collected in the first step. To increase the precision of the predictors, we perform program classification, which allows us to use specific predictors tailored to a certain kind of programs instead of using one general predictor. Hence, in the second step, we describe how we use cluster analysis to automatically derive program classes. Finally, based on the identified program classes, the repository of predictors is built. This constitutes the third step. In the following, we consider each step in turn.

5.3.1 Collection of Training Data

For machine learning, we need static features plus the corresponding classes, derived from the dynamic program behavior. In Section 4.2, we have seen that the regarded dynamic behavior determines the level at which the behavior is observed, which defines the entity domain $\mathcal{E}$. Then, we need to decide which static features to collect ($\mathcal{F}_{code}, \pi_{cfeat}$) and how the regarded behavior can be collected via profiling (π_{beh}). For feature collection, the regarded compiler framework can be extended by an appropriate, typically simple static analysis to collect the static features. For profiling, the program suite is executed on typical input data, and the regarded behavior is observed. Note that we have to bring static and dynamic information together, *i.e.*, each dynamic observation has to be mapped to its corresponding static features. Since we consider classification learning, we also have to specify how the behavior can be mapped to a discrete set of classes (which defines the mapping I). Furthermore, for program classification, we have to specify which static program features should be collected (π_{pfeat}). This can also be realized as an analysis step in the regarded compiler framework. In the considered instantiation of the general *FrISCO* framework, we need predictors for load latency and for memory dependence degrees. In the first case, the entity domain $\mathcal{E}_{lat}$ is constituted by load instructions. Hence, we collect features of load instructions. For predicting memory dependence degrees, the regarded entity domain $\mathcal{E}_{dep}$ is constituted by pairs of memory accesses. Hence, we collect features for each memory instruction and combine them appropriately. The features together with the corresponding behavior for load latencies and memory dependence degrees, respectively, yield the two training sets we regard. Additionally, since we consider program classification, we have as another training set the set of programs, together with their static program features.

In the following, we first consider the collection of static features required for both regarded kinds of program behavior as well as for program classification. Then, we describe how to collect the corresponding classes by profiling, again for load latencies and for memory dependence degrees. Finally, we regard how to obtain the predictors from the training data.

Static Feature Analysis

We have three different kinds of training sets to predict load latencies, memory dependence degrees, and program classes, respectively. In general, all features are collected in the compiler by a special analysis phase.

Code Features: Load Latencies To predict the latency of a load, we need to collect static code features for load instructions. Since we are at the LIR level, a load corresponds to an assembler-like instruction. However, as we have the back link into the HIR, we can also collect context information. For machine learning, the set of available features is crucial to obtain precise models. Hence, it is best to collect as many features as possible. Later on, there exist techniques for feature selection, which help to keep only the most relevant

5.3 Learning the Memory Behavior of Programs

features. For a load instruction, the inherent features refer to the load itself, *i.e.*, *data type, size of the data type, size of the enclosing data type (*e.g., *an array), level of indirection (for pointers)*. Since we are at LIR, we can also collect information like *number of references to the stack-pointer, number of arithmetic instructions for address calculation* (add's, shl's, mul's). Finally, looking at the broader context, we can collect information like *if/loop nesting depth, block execution frequency, number of (load/store) instructions in the enclosing basic block/loop body*. As a result, for each load instruction, we obtain a feature vector containing static properties of that load and its context.

Code Features: Dependence Degrees A memory dependency occurs between a pair of memory instructions (loads or stores). Hence, we need static features for a pair of memory instructions. The features collected for load instructions can also be collected for store instructions. Thus, to obtain the features for a pair of memory instructions, we first collect the feature vector for each instruction and concatenate both vectors. Then, we add combined features, which compare the corresponding features of both instructions. For example, *is the data type equal?*, *is the level of indirection equal?*. As a result, for each pair of memory instructions, we obtain a feature vector which combines the features of both instructions.

Program Features For program classification, we need static features of the whole program, which cover its characteristics. Hence, we collect the fraction of load and store instructions and the fractions of the different types of variable accesses (int, float, array, struct, ...). We also collect information about the complexity of the program, like *program size (number of functions/blocks/instructions), amount of branching (average number of successors of a basic block), average number of points-to targets*. This yields a feature vector which contains the characteristics of the program.

Profiling and Class Derivation

The dynamic behavior of programs can be collected by profiling. This requires representative input data to run the programs. In the following, we first describe how to obtain load latencies by profiling. Then we regard how to use profiling to collect the dependence degrees amongst memory instructions.

Load Latencies For modern processors, information about dynamic behavior like load latencies can be collected using so-called *performance monitoring counters* during profiling. Due to the vast amount of information, sampling has to be performed, since otherwise, the program behavior could change due to the overhead of monitoring. Hence, experiments should be repeated multiple times to ensure that the profiling data covers most of the load instructions of the program. Profiling yields for each load instruction a list of experienced latencies. To obtain a class from that, as required for machine learning, we first build the mean value for each load. Then, we form 11 latency classes, representing a latency of $0, 10, 20, \cdots, 100$ cycles, respectively, and map each mean value to the class it is closest to. Load instructions for which no latency is reported during profiling are not included in the training set. This may happen either due to sampling, which is incomplete, or due to the fact that not all instructions may be executed for a given input set.

Dependence Degrees We collect the dependencies empirically for the programs in the training set using profiling. During execution, we collect the referenced addresses for all memory accesses. This gives us for every memory instruction the list of accessed addresses. Based on that, we can determine the dependence degree for each pair of instructions. Because we do not perform sampling, the information we collect is complete w.r.t. the training set.

When deciding about dependency amongst memory references, care has to be taken to distinguish different life ranges of addresses. For example, the stack resides in a fixed memory area, and if a function returns, its stack frame is re-used for the next called function. Similarly, memory that is allocated dynamically on the heap is re-used after de-allocation. To cope with the first problem, we monitor all function entry and exit points and maintain a list that contains the addresses of the currently valid stack-frames, annotated with a unique number. Similarly, we track all heap allocation and de-allocation sites of the program and maintain a list of currently allocated heap areas, together with a unique number. The unique numbers can be considered as a version number of a address range in the memory. When an access refers to a physical address, we first check whether it goes to an allocated heap area. If so, we obtain its version number. Otherwise, we check whether it accesses the stack. Again, if this is the case, we determine the corresponding stack frame and obtain its version. Otherwise, global data is accessed, which has a distinct (fixed) version number. Two memory accesses are only equivalent if they refer two the same address and if their version numbers coincide. By

5.3 Learning the Memory Behavior of Programs

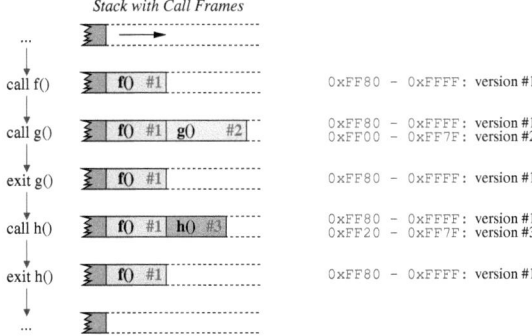

Figure 5.11: Distinguishing Different Versions of the Stack

that, we can distinguish different versions of memory areas and thus avoid false dependencies.

Figure 5.11 gives an example. We see a sequence of function calls and function returns, which changes the stack of call frames. Especially, we see that local variables of function g and of function h, respectively, partly share the same memory area. However, with our approach, each address range in the memory receives its own version. Thereby, we can distinguish a local variable of function g from a local variable of function h that reside both at 0xFF00 by their version number.

We are interested in determining the dependence degree for each pair of instructions. Intuitively, if all accesses go to the same address, the degree should be 1, if all are different, 0. For the general case, we have two instructions ins_1 and ins_2, and the following functions to represent the profiling results: $Targets(ins)$ denotes the accessed addresses of ins, $Count(ins)$ the number of all accesses and $TgtCount(ins, tgt)$ the number of accesses to a target tgt. For normalization, we calculate the fraction of all accesses from ins to a given target tgt, $TgtFrac(ins, tgt) = TgtCount(ins, tgt)/Count(ins)$. For ins_1 and ins_2, we consider every common target tgt in turn and compare the fractions that the instructions point to tgt respectively. It is obvious that *both* instructions have to refer to tgt if they should overlap. Hence, for each tgt, we take the minimum of both fractions. Note that a multiplication of both fractions would not be appropriate, since the fractions do not represent independent probabilities. The resulting degree is the sum thereof for all common targets tgt:

Instr 1	Instr 2	DepDegree
10 20 30 40	10 10 20 20	$min\{\frac{1}{2},\frac{1}{4}\} + min\{\frac{1}{2},\frac{1}{4}\} = \frac{1}{2} = 0.5$
10 20 30 40	40 50 60 70	$min\{\frac{1}{4},\frac{1}{4}\} = \frac{1}{4} = 0.25$
10 20 30 40	10 10 10	$min\{\frac{1}{4},1\} = \frac{1}{4} = 0.25$
10 10 20 40	10 20	$min\{\frac{1}{2},\frac{1}{2}\} + min\{\frac{1}{4},\frac{1}{2}\} = \frac{3}{4} = 0.75$

Table 5.1: Calculation of the Dependence Degree

$$DepDegree(ins_1, ins_2) = \sum_{tgt \in \bigcap_{k=1,2} Targets(ins_k)} \min_{k=1,2} TgtFrac(ins_k, tgt) \quad (5.22)$$

Clearly, *DepDegree* returns a value in [0..1]. As example, Table 5.1 shows four pairs of memory accesses, together with their accessed addresses, and their resulting *DepDegree*. For simplicity, we omit the version number.

Note that the dependence degree is an over-approximation. It does not regard the order of accesses. For example, if two instructions iterate over the same array in opposite directions, the analysis returns a dependence degree of 1. However, we consider the degree as a measure of the inherent dependency of two instructions, rather than the actual dependency. And, clearly, two instructions that refer to the same array have a dependency among them. Besides, code optimizations may change the iteration order and the actual dependencies, while the dependence degree as defined above remains stable.

5.3.2 Identification of Program Classes

Machine learning allows for the automatic construction of models from the collected training data, which represent the relationship between features and classes. Various learning algorithms are available to construct the models (see Section 2.5.1). We are interested in models with an explicit and concise representation, which allow for building highly scalable predictors. To obtain precise predictors, different learning algorithms can be evaluated to find the algorithm which suits best. From the model, we can automatically generate executable code (*e.g.*, C code), which can be used as a heuristic function. It receives static features from the compiler and returns the predicted class.

5.3 Learning the Memory Behavior of Programs

From the collected training data, predictors are constructed via machine learning. In our case, these predictors can be used to respectively predict the expected latency of a load and the estimated dependence degree of a pair of memory instructions. Since there are different kinds of programs, one universal predictor cannot be expected to yield precise predictions for all programs. Hence, we propose to identify groups of programs with similar behavior and to learn one specialized behavior for each program class. This yields a repository of predictors instead of one single universal predictor. Since we consider two different kinds of dynamic behavior, namely load latencies and memory dependence degrees, we obtain one classification for each behavior. In the following, we consider the case of learning memory dependence degrees. The procedure is analogous for learning load latencies.

Through program classification, we want to automatically group programs together that are similar to each other. This requires a *distance measure* on programs. For a given set of programs, the distance measure can be represented as a distance matrix, which contains the distance for each pair of programs. Based on that, a program classification can be obtained by clustering algorithms. The algorithm is called *unsupervised*, since the correct result (*i.e.*, the correct clustering) is unknown. The clustering algorithm aims at achieving two goals, namely to find a clustering such that the inner-cluster distance is minimized and that the between-cluster distance is maximized. In our case, the first goal is important, while the second can be neglected. There are two kinds of clustering algorithms: partitioning clustering yields a given number of classes, while hierarchical clustering yields a hierarchy of clusters, from which an arbitrary number of clusters can be created. However, in both cases, we can regard the cluster analysis as a function, which receives the distance matrix as well as the number of classes that should be identified. Then, for a different number of classes, the corresponding clusterings can be determined and the best one can be selected. Once the clustering is obtained, each program of the representative program suite is assigned to a program class. From that, the program class predictor can be trained. It learns the relationship between static program features and the corresponding program class and can be used to predict the program classes for previously unseen programs. Finally, the repository of behavior predictors is built. It contains one specialized predictor for each program class (see Section 5.3.3). When a program is to be optimized, first its program class is determined by the program class predictor, then the corresponding behavior predictor is selected from the repository.

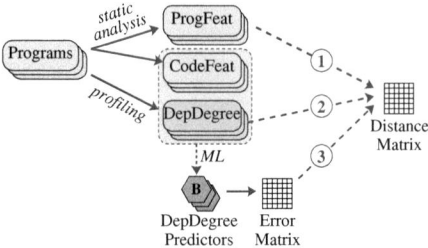

Figure 5.12: Obtaining the Distance Matrix

Distance Measure

The distance matrix is vital for clustering, since it defines the similarity of programs. In Section 4.3.2, we have seen how the distance matrix can be obtained. Figure 5.12 shows that either the static code features (①), the memory behavior (dependence degree, see ②), or the capability of programs to explain each other (expressed by the error matrix, see ③) can be used to derive the distance measure. In the following, we consider each case in turn.

Program Features The program features contain representative information about a whole program, like the relative frequency of different kinds of instructions or the distribution of different data types. Based on that, the distance matrix can be obtained by first normalizing each entry of the feature vector and by using a common distance measure like the euclidean distance. This yields a normalized distance. Normalization is important because otherwise, features with a wide value range would dominate the resulting distance. One exemplary program classification could, e.g., contain one class C_1={*programs that operate mostly on integer data*} and C_2={*programs that operate mostly on floating-point data*}. However, the program features do not depend on the considered memory behavior, which is one disadvantage of this alternative. Solely relying on static features is not sufficient to obtain program classes that group programs together that have a similar memory behavior.

Memory Behavior (Dependence Degree) The second alternative defines similarity with help of the dynamic behavior of programs, as collected by profiling. Since the behavior is expressed by a finite number n of classes, the behavior of each program can be summarized by the histogram of its behavior. This yields a vector of length n, which contains the number of corresponding

5.3 Learning the Memory Behavior of Programs

observations for each class. This vector can again be normalized such that the sum of its elements is 1. Then, the euclidean distance can be used to obtain the distance matrix. The advantage of this variant is that it actually allows for grouping programs together which behave similarly. As an example, we could obtain the following three classes: $C_1=\{programs\ with\ mostly\ low\ dependence\ degrees\}$, $C_2=\{programs\ with\ mostly\ high\ dependence\ degrees\}$, $C_3=\{other\ programs\}$.

Prediction Accuracy (Error Matrix) The aim of program classification is to obtain one predictor for each program class. Hence, the programs in one class should be able to predict each other. This motivates the third alternative: Using mutual prediction accuracy as similarity measure. The idea is that for each program, one predictor for memory dependence degrees is trained. Then, it is applied to each other program of the representative training suite. The comparison of the predicted classes with the correct ones yields the prediction error. There are different possibilities to perform the comparison. One way is to calculate the mean absolute error of the predictions. Another way is to determine the correlation between the predicted and the correct classes, respectively. The prediction error can be directly used as distance matrix. The advantage of this alternative over the other two is that it actually allows for grouping programs together that predict each other precisely. By that, more accurate predictions can be expected.

Cluster Analysis

Once the distance matrix has been constructed, clustering can be performed. The idea is to group the programs into clusters such that the inner-cluster error is low. Conceptually, this can be thought of as permuting the rows and cells of the distance matrix simultaneously until quadratic blocks form along the diagonal. Figure 5.13 gives an example for a program suite containing 10 programs. On the left, we see an exemplary distance matrix, together with the corresponding program numbers. For the sake of clarity, we only distinguish three different distances: none (shown as white box), low (green), high (yellow). Since each program has maximal similarity (or minimal distance) with itself, the diagonal contains only white boxes. For the remaining matrix, we see that green and yellow boxes appear to be scattered randomly. In the next step, a simultaneous permutation of rows and columns is performed to bring programs with low distance together (note that the program numbers

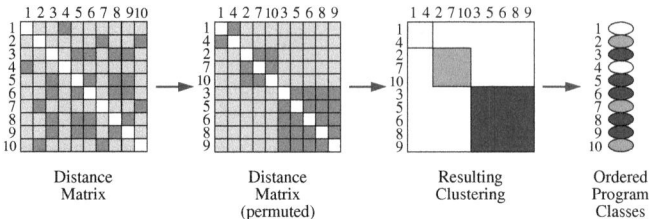

Figure 5.13: Cluster Analysis Based on the Distance Matrix

have also been permuted correspondingly). We see that three clusters have manifested themselves, of size 2, 3, and 5, respectively. From that, we can derive the corresponding classes, as shown in the final step. This is used in the following to train the program class predictor, as described in Section 4.3.3. The program class predictor is constructed from the static program features and the corresponding program classes. For each regarded dynamic property, a separate program class predictor is created. Finally, for each identified program class, a specialized behavior predictor is trained from the training data of the corresponding programs. This yields the repository of behavior predictors.

5.3.3 Repository of Predictors

As a result from clustering, we obtain a set of classes. To obtain the predictor repository, one specialized behavior predictor is trained for each program class. In other words, we have to construct one predictor from the training data of multiple programs. In Section 4.3.4, we have presented different techniques to establish that goal. We can either first combine the training data sets and train one predictor with that or first train a set of predictors and combine those to one predictor. In the latter case, we have again different options for combination. We can take the most frequent result returned by the predictors or, if applicable, we can determine the mean value of all results. This requires that the classes representing the dynamic behavior are quantitative, which is the case for the dependence degree as well as for load latencies.

5.3.4 Combination with Alias Analyses

As mentioned before (compare Figure 4.8), the overall precision can be increased if we combine the heuristics with a conventional static alias analysis.

Whenever the analysis reports *no* or *yes* for a dependency amongst memory accesses, we use that value and interpret it as a probability of $p = 0$ and $p = 1$, respectively. When the analysis reports *maybe*, which can be expected to be the common case, we consult our heuristics. By that, we obtain exact information when available and approximate precisely with our machine learned heuristics, otherwise.

5.4 Summary

In this chapter, we have described the application of the general *FrISCO* framework to the optimization of memory accesses. At the beginning, we discussed the regarded optimization problem in detail and identified the information about the dynamic run-time behavior that is required by the cost model. With that, we instantiated each of the three phases of *FrISCO* in turn. We started by presenting our algorithm for speculative code motion. Especially, the algorithm can overcome all kinds of dependencies with the help of speculation. The algorithm relies on the cost model to decide which transformation to apply. For each of kind of transformation performed by the optimization algorithm, we showed how the corresponding performance gain is precisely modeled. After that, we have shown how machine learning can be used to obtain the heuristics required by the cost model. The regarded dynamic behavior, in our case the latency of load instructions and the dependence degree amongst memory instructions, respectively, determines at which level the behavior is observed. From that, it follows which static code features should be collected and how the corresponding profiling data can be collected. We further described how to discretize the behavior to classes, as required by classification learning. With that, we have all required information for the training phase. Then, machine learning algorithms can be used to automatically generate predictors from the training data. We use our proposed concept of program classification to group similar programs together and to have one specialized predictor for each program class. As a result, for each regarded dynamic behavior, we have a set of heuristics, which can be used by the cost model to perform a precise cost estimation. This enables the optimization to perform those transformations which are expected to yield the highest optimization gain.

In Section 1.2, we defined three criteria to rate the quality of an application of our general framework. We revisit each criterion in turn and discuss whether or not it is fulfilled by our instantiated framework.

- **Precision of the Heuristics** The concept of program classification we propose achieves highly precise heuristics. This is shown in Section 7.1, where we present an empirical evaluation of the precision of the heuristics and discuss the results.

- **Correctness** The algorithm for speculative code motion can overcome all kinds of dependencies. For each kind, we presented a transformation which guarantees correctness in all cases. In case of misspeculation, special recovery code is executed to reconstruct the correct system state.

- **Optimization Gain** We presented a comprehensive cost model, which models the expected performance gain for each possible code transformation. It draws information from the heuristics, which estimate the dynamic memory behavior of the program under compilation. With that, it can be expected that the optimization gain of given transformations is precisely modeled. In our experiments described in Section 7.2, we can show that the optimization achieves a significant optimization gain.

6 Implementation

In this chapter, we describe the implementation of the instantiated FrISCO framework, which targets the optimization of memory accesses. As a result, we obtained a complete experimental compiler platform, which supports the full C language and which can cope with huge software like, *e.g.*, the GNU gcc within reasonable time. In the following, we first sketch the tools we used for our implementation. Then, we show a specialized version of the general framework, which shows how its abstract parts were mapped to implementation modules. After that, we consider each module in turn and describe notable aspects of its implementation.

6.1 Overview

An overview of the implementation of the FrISCO framework, instantiated for the optimization of memory accesses, is shown in Figure 6.1. The diagram corresponds to the overview of the general FrISCO framework (compare Figure 4.3, page 82) and illustrates how the abstract components were specialized and implemented. The main parts correspond to the three phases of the abstract framework. The acquisition of the training data (*i.e.*, static features plus profiled behavior) is performed in the *analysis phase*. We use the $CoSy^©$ compiler framework for the feature collection. Since the optimization operates at LIR level, the features are collected after the IR was lowered to the LIR by our Itanium backend. For profiling, we use the tools *Pin*[Int07] and *pfmon*[HP04]. Additionally, we developed tools for trace analysis in C++ to post-process the profiled dependencies. The *machine learning* phase is entirely implemented within the *R Project*[RCT08]. The data acquired in the analysis phase is used to identify similar programs to perform program classification. This is done for

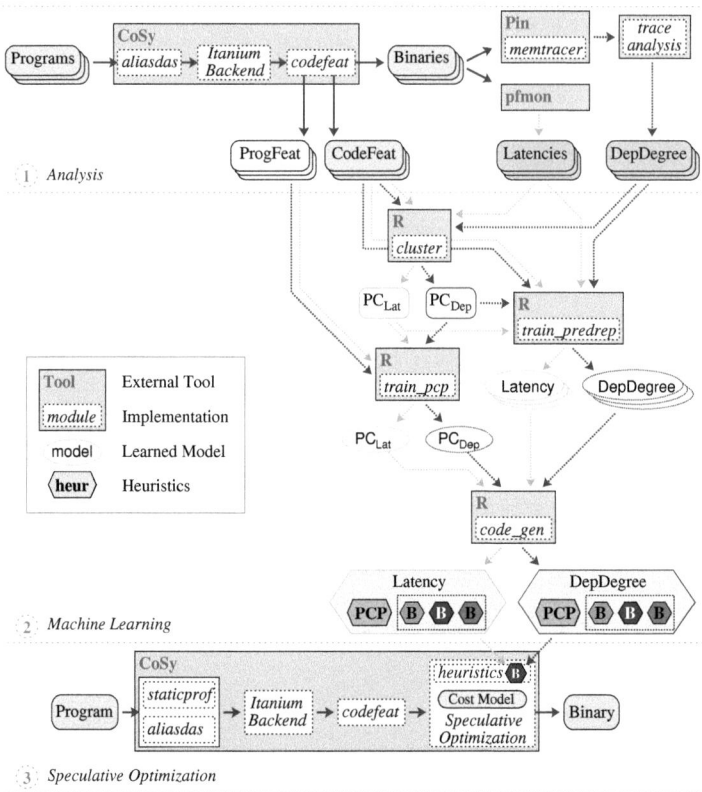

Figure 6.1: Implementation of *FrISCO*

each considered program behavior, namely, for load latencies and for memory dependence degrees. With that information, a predictor is built that predicts the class of a program based on its features as well as a repository containing one behavior predictor per program class that predicts program behavior based on the corresponding code features – again, this is performed once for each of the two considered program behaviors. Finally, code generation is performed to generate executable heuristics from the predictors, written in C. The *speculative optimization* phase is completely implemented within the *CoSy* compiler framework. First, we perform a state-of-the-art static branch prediction to obtain the probabilities of branches (*staticprof*). Then, a state-of-the-art alias analysis is performed (*aliasdas*). While alias analyses are imprecise in case of reported *maybe* dependencies, in the opposite case (*no* dependency), their results are safe and the heuristics for dependence degrees needs not be con-

6.1 Overview

sulted. Next, code generation is performed by our Itanium backend, and the IR is transformed into LIR. This is required because the heuristics as well as the optimization operates at LIR level. Feature extraction is done by the *codefeat* engine, which considers both IR and LIR (*i.e.*, high-level and low-level IR) and annotates the LIR with the corresponding code features. The features are required by the machine learned heuristics to precisely predict the dynamic program behavior, namely, load latencies and dependence degrees. Based upon the heuristics, the cost model is built, and the code is speculatively optimized. Finally, the resulting assembler code is emitted, which is translated to the executable binary. In the following, we first briefly introduce the external tools we used. Then, we consider each of the three phases in turn and describe in detail peculiarities of our implementation.

External Tools

CoSy As compiler platform, we use the *CoSy* compiler development system by ACE[ACE]. The *CoSy* system is a modular compiler, which contains over 50 state-of-the-art program analyses and optimizations, which are termed as *engines*. The C front end translates the source code into the *Common CoSy Medium-level Intermediate Representation (CCMIR)*, upon which all analyses and optimizations operate in turn. After high-level, machine-independent analyses and optimizations have been performed, the CCMIR is transformed by a rule-based code-generator to obtain the *Low-level Intermediate Representation (LIR)*, which represents the assembler instructions of the target architecture. On the LIR, low-level analyses and optimizations can be performed before the final code is emitted. To target *CoSy* to a new hardware platform, a specification for the considered platform has to be developed. This includes a specification of the register file, of the functional units of the processor, of their latencies, and of code selection rules that map the abstract CCMIR to the corresponding assembly language instructions. Additionally, further technical details have to be programmed manually in C. This includes the *calling conventions*, which specify how arguments and return values are passed between functions, the *memory model*, the *data representation*, and *stack frame construction*. The platform is highly modular and allows the developer to add custom analyses and optimizations to the system. *CoSy* offers various data structures (*e.g.*, lists, trees, hash sets, hash maps) and CCMIR walkers to ease the development of new engines. Within that platform, we did the following implementations:

- a state-of-the-art alias analysis (engine *aliasdas*, following Das [Das00])
- a state-of-the-art static branch predictor (engine *staticprof*, following Wu et al. [WL94]
- a complete backend for the Intel Itanium2 processor
- the *codefeat* engine for feature collection (both code features and program features)
- the *speculation* engine for the speculative optimization (together with the cost model)

The third phase of the framework, speculative optimization, was fully implemented in the compiler platform.

pfmon, Pin, C++ The training data, which is collected in the analysis phase, contains information about the code features and the corresponding dynamic behavior. To collect the dynamic behavior information, we used the profiling tools *pfmon*[HP04] and *Pin*[LCM+05, Int07]. *pfmon* allows for directly collecting latencies of load instructions during program execution. The dynamic binary instrumentation tool *Pin* allows for monitoring specific instructions, which we used to observe the accessed addresses for all memory instructions. To process the collected raw data to obtain the dependence degrees for each pair of memory instructions, we developed utility programs in C++.

R Project The second phase of the framework, machine learning, was entirely implemented within the *R Project* for statistical computing [RCT08]. All regarded algorithms for classification learning as well as for clustering were already provided with *R* or were drawn from the *Comprehensive R Archive Network*. *R* defines a script-like, functional language, in which we implemented the algorithms of the machine learning phase of the FrISCO framework. For classification learning, we use the *rpart* package, which is based on Breiman et al. [BFOS84]. It implements an algorithm to build a *decision tree* by performing *recursive partitioning* of the data. For cluster analysis, we use the *hclust* package (Murtagh [Mur85]), which performs hierarchical, agglomerative clustering based on a distance matrix.

6.2 Analysis Phase

In the analysis phase, the training data is acquired for a suite of representative programs. Based on that, the predictors are built in the next phase. This requires as a prerequisite to compose a program suite, which covers a wide bandwidth of applications. The data acquisition consists of the collection of static features as well as in profiling the regarded behavior. Feature collection is done per program as well as per instruction to yield program and code features, respectively. As a result, we obtain feature tables (rows: programs/entities, columns: features). We save the tables in the *comma-separated value (CSV)* file format. Profiling is performed to collect load latencies as well as dependence degrees. Finally, we bring the collected features and the profiling data together, *i.e.*, we establish the link from the profiled behavior to the corresponding feature vector. In the following, we regard each task of data acquisition in turn.

6.2.1 Suite of Representative Programs

Since the generated heuristics should be generally applicable to all kinds of programs, it is important to build the training data from a set of programs that covers a wide bandwidth of behavior. The CPU benchmark suites proposed by the *Standard Performance Evaluation Company (SPEC)*[SPEC] pursue exactly that aim. Hence, we used the programs from their program suites SPEC CPU1995, CPU2000, and CPU2006. Each program of the program suite comes with different sets of input data, which we used for profiling. The programs are written in Fortran, C, and C++. We translated Fortran programs to C programs via *f2c* (Feldman [Fel90]). For our representative program suite, we took all C and all translated Fortran programs. Additionally, we added programs from the *Pointer-Intensive Benchmark Suite*[PIBS95], which are written in C and which also come with typical program inputs. Altogether, our program suite contains 39 programs.

6.2.2 Static Program Features

We developed the *CoSy* engine *codefeat* to collect significant and representative features of a whole program as well as of instructions. For a program, we collect data-centric features, which reflect which data types are used in the program, as well as structural features, which reflect characteristics of the IR. For the data-centric features, we determine the relative frequency of types of variable usages. We distinguish between the following types: integer, floating-point, pointer, integer array, floating-point array, composite (*e.g.*, struct), recursive composite (*e.g.*, linked list). To determine the relative frequencies, we consider each access to a variable and classify its type. With that, we count the number of accesses for each type and normalize it by the number of all accesses. To take the execution frequency of instructions and the size of data types into account, we use four different weighting schemes to count the accesses:

1. each access has the weight 1
2. each access is weighted by its (statically estimated) execution frequency
3. each access is weighted by the size of its data type
4. each access is weighted by its size and its frequency

Since we distinguish 7 type categories, this yields 7 relative frequencies (which sum up to 1) for each weighting scheme. In addition to those data-centric features, we also collect features to capture the structure of the CFG. We count the number of referenced variables, expressions, basic blocks, and basic block successors, respectively. Additionally, we add up the size of the points-to sets, as reported by a static alias analysis we implemented (for more details, see Section 6.4.3). From that, we determine derived features like *average number of expressions per basic block*. We use two different weighting schemes: Use the same weight for all entities, or weight each entity by its execution frequency. With that, we build one feature vector per CFG (*i.e.*, per function). To obtain the resulting whole-program feature vector, we cumulate over all CFGs in turn and determine the average values. Altogether, this yields $4 \cdot 7 + 2 \cdot 8 = 44$ features. The feature vector is shown in Table 6.1. Internally, the feature vector is kept within a C *struct* termed *s_progfeat*. As a result of the collection of program features, we obtain one feature vector per program.

6.2.3 Static Code Features

To build predictors, machine learning requires a feature vector for each regarded entity. For load latencies, the entity is given by load instructions. For dependence degrees, the entity is given by a pair of memory instructions. Hence, we collect features for each memory instruction. From that, the features for a pair of memory instructions can be obtained by combining the

6.2 Analysis Phase

Data-centric Features	
(relative frequencies, sum is 1; four sets of features: unweighted, weighted by frequency, by size, by frequency and size)	
reg	integral integer variables
ptr	integral pointer variables
freg	integral floating-point variables
arr	integer arrays
farr	floating-point arrays
rec	composite data structures
rrec	composite data structures with self-referential members
Structural Features	
(two sets of features: unweighted, weighted by frequency)	
obj	number of variable references
expr	number of expressions
blk	number of basic blocks
nxt	number of basic block successors
ptsz	number of points-to targets
expr_blk	expressions per basic block
next_blk	successors per basic block
avg_ptsize	average points-to targets per reference

Table 6.1: Static Program Features

corresponding two feature vectors. We developed a *CoSy* engine to collect significant and representative features per memory instruction. The features reflect properties of the memory reference itself as well as inherited properties of preceding instructions that calculate the referenced address. Additionally, we collect information about the context of the instruction, namely its surrounding basic block and, if applicable, its surrounding loop. For the basic block context, we count the number of all instructions as well as the number of special types of instructions (memory instructions, loads, stores, calls). With that, we can determine the relevance of the corresponding instruction type. We also collect information about the CFG (number of predecessors/successors, block frequencies, and, if applicable, the if-nesting depth). If the instruction is part of a loop, we determine the loop body and collect statistic features (number of blocks, number of different types of instructions). Because the loop body may contain further loops, which have a higher execution frequency, we additionally collect weighted statistic features (each occurrence of an instruction is weighted by the execution frequency of its basic block). Altogether, this yields 80 features per memory instruction. The resulting feature vector is used to learn load latencies. To obtain the resulting feature vector for an instruction pair, as required to learn dependence degrees, we concatenate the feature vectors of both instructions. Additionally, we automatically construct combined features as follows: Are the corresponding features of both instructions equal, both zero, both non-zero. This yields altogether 230 features. The components of the feature vector are shown in Table 6.2. Internally, the feature vector is kept within a C *struct* termed *s_codefeat*.

6.2.4 Profiling Load Latencies

Modern processors offer special *performance monitoring counters*, which can be used to monitor special events during program execution like cache misses. We used the *pfmon*[HP04] tool to collect the load latencies on the Itanium. We monitored the "Data Cache Level 1 – Miss" event and collected the address of the corresponding instruction as well as its experienced latency. Since *pfmon* performs sampling, we repeated each program run 30 times. As a result, we have a list of instruction addresses and corresponding latencies. If multiple latencies are reported for an instruction, we calculate the average value. Since classification learning requires the behavior to be encoded as discrete values, we discretize the latency by the following function:

$$d : \mathbb{N} \to \mathcal{C}_{lat}, d(x) = min\{\lfloor \frac{x}{10} + 0.5 \rfloor, 10\}.$$

This yields 11 classes $\mathcal{C}_{lat} = \{0, 1, .., 10\}$. The latency is divided by 10 and rounded to the next integer, which constitutes the corresponding class. Any latencies above 100 are mapped to the highest class 10. This mapping represents a trade-off between precision of the classes on the one hand and precision of the predictors on the other. With more classes, the behavior is more precisely modeled, but the predictors can be expected to be less precise. On the other hand, with fewer classes, the predictors perform better, but the behavior is modeled less precise.

6.2.5 Profiling Memory Dependence Degrees

To collect the addresses that are accessed by memory instructions, we use the profiling tool Pin[Int07]. It provides an *Application Programming Interface*

6.2 Analysis Phase

Features of the referenced object	
ref_size	size
ref_supsize	size of the surrounding structure if appropriate
ref_num_obj	number of objects
ref_num_cont	number of de-references
ref_num_ptr	number of references to pointers
ref_num_sp_rel	number of references to the stack pointer
ref_num_gp_rel	number of references to the global data pointer
ref_num_add	number of additions
ref_num_mul	number of multiplications
ref_is_glob	is the referenced object a global?
ref_is_loc	is it a local variable?
ref_is_par	is it a function parameter?
ref_is_arr	is it an array?
ref_is_rec	is it a record?
ref_is_union	is it a union?
ref_is_recrec	is it a recursive record?
ref_ptsize	number of points-to targets of the reference
Features of the indirectly referenced objects	
all features listed above; boolean features become count features (e.g., how many indirect references to arrays)	
Totaled features	
sum of direct and indirect features	
Features of the surrounding basic block	
blk_preds	number of block predecessors
blk_succs	number of block successors
blk_sum_ins	number of instructions
blk_sum_memins	number of memory instructions
blk_sum_ld	number of loads
blk_sum_st	number of stores
blk_sum_call	number of calls
blk_freq	frequency of the block (statically predicted)
blk_if_depth	if nesting depth
Features of the surrounding loop (if appropriate)	
loop_depth	number of surrounding loops
inner_loops	number of contained loops
loop_sum_bb	number of blocks (+ weighted by frequency)
loop_sum_ins	number of instructions (+ weighted)
loop_sum_memins	number of memory instructions (+ weighted)
loop_sum_ld	number of loads (+ weighted)
loop_sum_st	number of stores (+ weighted)
loop_sum_call	number of calls (+ weighted)

Table 6.2: Static Code Features per Memory Instruction

(API) to monitor program execution at the desired abstraction level. In our case, we monitor instructions of a program. In Section 5.3.1, we have described how the dependencies amongst memory accesses can be determined via profiling data. First, we record for each memory access the referenced address as well as the address of the corresponding instruction. As we have seen previously, certain physical addresses may be re-used. This is the case for local data, which resides in a procedure's stack frame, as well as for data on the heap, which may be re-allocated after de-allocation. Hence, for the corresponding memory ranges, the corresponding version number has to be determined. To that end, we additionally track each function call and function return and annotate the appropriate version number at the corresponding stack frame. Besides, we also track function calls which refer to memory management (malloc, calloc, free) and again assign the appropriate version number at the corresponding address range. By that, we can determine a version number for each physical address. If an address is neither within a stack frame nor within an allocated heap region, it refers to global data, and we used a fixed, distinct version number to express that case. Thus, for each memory access in the program, we record the accessed physical address, its version number, and the address of the corresponding instruction.

The result from profiling is a log file that contains the collected data for each executed memory access. For each memory access *ins*, we have the number of accesses for a given target *tgt*, *TgtCount(ins,tgt)*, which can be used to determine the total number of accesses performed by *ins*, *Count(ins)*. From that, we can calculate the dependence degree for two instructions ins_1, ins_2 (with *TgtFrac(ins,tgt)* = *TgtCount(ins,tgt)/Count(ins)*; see also equation (5.22)):

$$DepDegree(ins_1, ins_2) = \sum_{tgt \in \bigcap_{k=1,2} Targets(ins_k)} \min_{k=1,2} TgtFrac(ins_k, tgt), \quad (6.1)$$

Since most instructions are executed multiple times due to loops, the log file is very huge (typically several gigabyte). Especially, the whole file cannot be held in memory for further processing. To make the huge data manageable, we observe that equation (6.1) is *modular*, *i.e.*, the degree is determined by considering each common target independently. For each target, we can determine the fraction it constitutes for the corresponding instruction and use the minimum of both fractions for cumulation. Hence, it is possible to consider each occurring target in turn, determine the involved instruction pairs, determine their fractions, and update the corresponding DepDegree value. For that

6.2 Analysis Phase

technique, it is only required to hold all accesses to a given target at once in the memory, which is much less than the whole log file. We implemented the corresponding algorithm in a C++ tool that performs *trace analysis*. Initially, the log file is sorted by the accessed targets. This is done via merge sort, which allows for sorting files of arbitrary size. First the log file is partitioned into smaller chunks that fit into main memory. Then, each chunk is sorted. Finally, the sorted chunks are merged together. Next, the dependence degree is calculated. To that end, the sorted log file is iterated twice. In the first iteration, the number of referenced addresses *Count(ins)* is determined for each instruction *ins* by summing up the counts for each target *tgt*, *TgtCount(ins,tgt)*. In the second iteration, the overlap is determined for each instruction pair ins_1, ins_2 by summing up the overlaps for each common target. The current overlap for each instruction pair is stored in a two-dimensional array *DepDegree*. The log file is processed, and for each target *tgt* and for each instruction pair ins_1, ins_2, the corresponding overlap is given by the minimum of *TgtFrac(ins_1,tgt)* and *TgtFrac(ins_2,tgt)*. The overlaps are cumulated as appropriate in the array *DepDegree* (see equation (6.1)). Note that *TgtCount(ins_i,tgt)* is 0 if there is no reference from ins_i to *tgt*. As the result of our trace analysis, the array *DepDegree* contains the dependence degree for each instruction pair.

The dependence degree calculated so far is a value $dep \in \mathbb{Q}_{[0..1]}$. Since we use classification learning, we have to discretize the dependence degrees and encode them as discrete values. We use the following function:

$$d : \mathbb{Q}_{[0..1]} \to \mathcal{C}_{dep}, d(x) = \lfloor 10 \cdot x + 0.5 \rfloor.$$

This yields 11 classes $\mathcal{C}_{dep} = \{0, 1, .., 10\}$. The dependence degree is multiplied by 10 and rounded to the next integer, which constitutes the corresponding class. As before, this mapping represents a trade-off between precision of the classes on the one hand and precision of the predictors on the other.

6.2.6 Combination of Code Features and Profiling Data

So far, we have described how to collect the code features and the profiling data. Both kinds of data were collected separately and, hence, have to be brought together to be usable for machine learning. This means that for each entity for that we have collected the dynamic behavior, we have to find the corresponding code features. First, we consider how to match the features and the profiling data for the case of load latencies. Profiling yields a list of instructions together with their experienced load latency. An instruction is given by its instruction address. With that, we can identify the corresponding memory instruction in the executed binary. However, during feature collection in the compiler, the addresses of instructions are not yet available. To still make the link from instruction address to the corresponding feature vector, we use the relative position of an instruction with respect to the function it belongs to. For each memory instruction, we determine the function it resides in as well as its relative position within that function. During feature collection, we determine the relative positions of instructions by a virtual emit phase: For each function, we process its basic blocks in the same order as for code generation. By that, we can obtain the relative position of each instruction. The feature vector contains special fields that contain the function and the relative position of an instruction. Those fields are not used for machine learning, they are merely used to establish the link between the profiled information and the corresponding feature vector.

For the case of dependence degrees, *i.e.*, to link the profiling data with the corresponding code features for instruction pairs, we proceed similarly. Profiling yields the dependence degree for an instruction pair, which is given by two instruction addresses. For each address, we determine the corresponding feature vector as described above. Then, both vectors are combined by concatenating their values and by building combined features.

As a result of the data acquisition, the training data is ready to be used for machine learning in the next phase. For each program, we have a table which contains static features as well as experienced latency for each load instruction, as well as another table which contains static features as well as the corresponding dependence degree for each pair of memory instructions.

6.3 Machine Learning

The aim of the machine learning phase is to construct behavior predictors that predict load latencies as well as memory dependence degrees. This phase is entirely implemented within the *R Project*[RCT08], using its script-like, functional language *R*. All classification and clustering algorithms we used were provided by the *R Project* or by the *Comprehensive R Archive Network*. We started first investigations on using machine learning for predicting dependence degrees in the diploma thesis [Hee07], and we performed an empirical study on how to obtain good clusterings in the diploma thesis [Rol09]. For the implementation of the machine learning phase, we wrote functions in *R* that

6.3 Machine Learning

bring the training data collected in the previous phase into R and preprocess it for normalization, invoke the provided functions appropriately to perform clustering and machine learning, and generate executable C code from the predictors. The core tasks of this phase are the construction of a distance matrix on programs, the program classification, the construction of the program class predictor, and the construction of the behavior predictor repository. The whole phase is performed twice, once for each considered memory behavior (*i.e.*, load latencies and memory dependence degrees). In the following, we consider each subtask in turn and convey the central ideas.

6.3.1 Data Preparation

The training data collected in the previous phase is given as a set of CSV files, one per program of the program suite and per considered memory behavior. Those files can be read into *R* and are represented as a list of tables. The rows correspond to the observations, the columns to the features and, as a special column, to the observed behavior. The features are named and can be accessed by name within *R*. The number of observations per program depends on the program and on the input data it was executed with. To make learning feasible, we define a fixed upper bound for the number of observations. When a table contains more than 3000 observations, we randomly select 3000 observations and disregard the rest. Next, we process the features. Depending on the considered program behavior, we may have up to 230 features per observation. We perform *feature selection* to keep only the most important ones. To that end, we determine the correlation between each feature and the observed behavior. Then, we select the 25 features with the highest correlation. The correlation is averaged for all training data. Especially, for each table, the same features are selected. As a result, for each program, we have a table with at most 3000 rows (the observations) and with 26 columns (25 features plus the observed behavior). Additionally, for program classification, we have another table which contains the program features. The rows correspond to the programs and the columns to their features.

6.3.2 Predictor Construction

A predictor can be directly build from a table. It models the relationship between the *features* and the observed behavior, which is termed as *response*. We use the *rpart* package within the *R Project*, which constructs a decision tree to

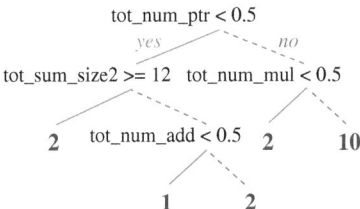

Figure 6.2: Learned Decision Tree

model the relationship. The decision tree is a binary tree which has conditions at its inner nodes and class values at its leaves. The aim is to partition the feature space into orthogonal hyper-boxes such that the observations within a hyper-box mostly share the same behavior. The tree is iteratively built. At each step, a feature F and a threshold value val are selected and the currently considered hyperspace is divided into two partitions $F <= val$ and $F > val$. F and val are chosen such that the partitioning groups observations with similar behavior together as best as possible. Then, for each partition, the partitioning is repeated. At the same time, the decision tree is built. Each partitioning adds another node to it. The process stops if all observations of a partition have the same behavior or if the number of observations of a partition falls below a fixed threshold. As a result, the built classification tree models the relationship between features and response. It can be used to make predictions for new data. An example is shown in Figure 6.2. We see a tree which partitions the feature space into 5 hyper-boxes using 4 conditions. To make a prediction, we start at the root. Iteratively, the condition of the currently regarded node is evaluated, and the result determines whether we continue with the left child or with the right. When we reach a leaf, we report the annotated class value as prediction. For example, if $tot\_num\_ptr=1$ and $tot\_num\_mul=2$, the exemplary tree would return a dependence degree of 10.

6.3.3 Program Classification

To increase the precision of the predictors, we perform program classification and group similar programs together. This is done by cluster analysis, based on a distance matrix. We use the *hclust* package within the *R Project*. The cluster analysis starts with all programs being in a separate cluster. Then, iteratively, the two clusters that are closest to each other (with respect to the distance matrix) are merged together. This is repeated until all programs belong to the

6.3 Machine Learning

```
cluster_programs <- function(tablist) {
  # tablist: list of tables, one per program
  models = sapply(tablist, function(tab) {
              rpart(behav ~ ., tab)
           });
  # models: list of predictive models (decision trees)
  errmat = sapply(models, function(model) {
              sapply(tablist, function(tab) {
                 mean(abs(predict(model,tab) - tab$behav))
              })
           });
  # errmat: distance matrix
  cutreee(hclust(errmat),3);
}
```

Figure 6.3: Program Classification via Hierarchical Clustering

same cluster. The result of clustering is given by a *dendrogram*. A dendrogram is a binary tree which represents all intermediate clusterings obtained during the cluster analysis. In other words, for each k between 1 and n (n being the number of programs), a clustering with k clusters can be determined from the dendrogram. To obtain sensible clusterings, we state a lower bound for cluster size and an upper bound for the number of clusters to avoid over-fitting. A cluster should contain at least 5 programs, and the number of clusters should not exceed 6.

To obtain the distance matrix, we build one predictor for each program. Then, we apply each predictor to all programs and compare the predicted behavior with the correct behavior to derive the *mean absolute error*. Since we have 11 classes to model the program behavior, the mean deviation error ranges from 0 to 10. As a result of the cluster analysis, we have a list that assigns each program to its cluster number. The corresponding R code is shown in Figure 6.3. The function *cluster_programs* expects the list of tables containing the training data. First, the relationship between the features and the response variable (termed *behav*) is learned for each table. This is done via the *rpart* function, which expects a *formula* and a table. The formula denotes which relationship should be learned, in our case, the relationship between response variable *behav* and all other features (indicated by the dot). To obtain predictive models for all tables, the *sapply* function is used, which resembles the *map* function of typical functional languages. Then, based on that models, the distance matrix *errmat* is built. For each model and for each table, the model is used to predict the behavior for that table, and the predictions are compared with the correct response (*tab$behav* selects the response from the table *tab*). Since the 11 classes can be mapped to the numbers 0 to 10, the difference can be determined for each prediction. Then, the absolute value thereof is taken, and the mean value is derived. This yields the mean deviation prediction error. Overall, the result is a matrix. Upon that matrix, hierarchical clustering is performed and yields the dendrogram. From that, a clustering which yields 3 clusters is selected and returned.

Clustering yields for each program the number of the program class it belongs to. This constitutes the response variable and can be used together with the static program features to build a program class predictor.

6.3.4 Construction of the Behavior Predictor Repository

With the information from program classification, we can build a repository of specialized behavior predictors. For each program class, one behavior predictor is built. As we have described in Section 4.3.4, we consider various ways of combining the training data of the programs of a program class to obtain one predictor. The first alternative is to merge the feature tables of all programs of the regarded program class. If the number of observations exceeds our limit of 3000, we again perform sampling. Then, we use *rpart* to build a decision tree. The second alternative is to build a set of predictors via *rpart*, one per program within the program class, and to make predictions by consulting all predictors and by combining their votes. Here again, we consider different alternatives. We either take the majority vote and break ties by taking the lowest or the highest class, respectively, or we compute the arithmetic mean of all votes and round it to the nearest class value. The latter case is admissible, since the behavior is represented by quantitative classes. With that, we have one composite predictor per program class. It contains the predictors for each program of the program class and combines their votes to make a prediction. In the evaluation, we compare the precision of the different combination schemes against each other. As result, we have a repository of predictors, one for each program class.

Overall, we obtain a two-stage behavior predictor from the training data, which contains the program class predictor and the repository of behavior predictors. To make predictions about the memory behavior, first the program class of the regarded program is determined based on its static code features.

```
if (tot_num_ptr <0.5)
  if (tot_sum_size2 >=12)
    return 2;
  else
    if (tot_num_mul <0.5)
      return 1;
    else return 2;
else
  if (tot_num_add <0.5)
    return 2;
  else return 10;
```

Figure 6.4: Code Generation from Decision Trees

Second, the corresponding predictor is selected from the repository, and it is used to predict the memory behavior, based on the static code features of the considered instruction or instruction pair.

6.3.5 Generation of Executable Code from the Predictors

The *rpart* algorithm builds predictors in form of decision trees. Within R, those predictors can be used to make predictions for new data. However, we require the predictors to be applicable outside of R, namely, within our compiler framework. To that end, we developed a code generator in R, which takes in a decision tree and generates C code from that, which implements the decision tree. A decision tree can be implemented by nested *if-then-else* constructs. For each inner node, we create an *if-then-else* construct that checks the annotated condition. For the *then*-branch, we recursively generate code for the left child of the node. For the *else*-branch, we take the right child. Whenever we reach a leaf, we report the annotated class label as prediction. Figure 6.4 shows the C code that was generated by our function from the decision tree shown in Figure 6.2.

While the function to predict program classes is directly given by the code generated from the corresponding decision tree, the function for a behavior predictor may correspond to multiple decision trees if the predictors were combined by voting. In that case, the function of the behavior predictor first evaluates all decision trees of the corresponding program class and then combines their votes appropriately. Based on those functions, the code for the overall behavior predictor can be generated. First, the program class is determined. Then, the function of the corresponding behavior predictor is consulted to obtain the resulting prediction. The program features and the code features are passed to the functions as appropriate using the C *struct*s *s_progfeat* and *s_codefeat*, respectively. Those *struct*s were defined within the *codefeat* engine, which performs the feature collection.

As a result of the machine learning phase, one heuristics for predicting load latencies and one heuristics for predicting memory dependence degrees are generated. The heuristics are written in C and use the data structures that were defined in our *CoSy* engine *codefeat*. Hence, the heuristics can be used in the compiler to predict the memory behavior. This only requires an additional analysis step that determines the static features of the program and of each memory instruction, which is done by *codefeat*.

6.4 Speculative Optimization

In the preceding phase for machine learning, heuristics for predicting the memory behavior of programs were generated. In the phase of speculative optimization, this information is used to guide a speculative optimization of memory accesses, performing upwards code motion. This phase was entirely implemented within the *CoSy* system. For the implementation, we first needed to establish our compiler platform for the Intel Itanium2, which mainly consisted in developing a backend for the Itanium2 processor. Then, we implemented a state-of-the-art static branch predictor to obtain branch probabilities as well as a state-of-the-art alias analysis to make our heuristics more precise. Finally, we implemented the algorithm for speculative upwards code motion (described in Section 5.1.3) as well as the cost model (see Section 5.2). In the following, we consider each task in turn.

6.4.1 Itanium Backend

The *CoSy* system provides a highly modular compiler framework, which comprises many state-of-the-art optimizations and which facilitates retargeting to new target hardware platforms by using the rule-based code generator *BEG* (backend generator; based on bottom-up rewrite systems, see Emmelmann et al. [ESL89]). To establish a compiler framework with the Intel Itanium2 processor as target architecture, the main task was to develop a backend within the *CoSy* system. The vital parts can be described by a backend specification.

6.4 Speculative Optimization

However, peculiarities like calling conventions (how are values passed to and returned from functions) require manual C programming.

The backend specification describes the register file, the functional units of the processor together with latencies amongst them, and, mainly, how to map the abstract CCMIR to the concrete assembler language of the target architecture. The specification of register file and functional units is straightforward. The derivation of rules requires more effort, since every construct of the CCMIR has to be mapped to assembler code. Altogether, the specification contains 229 code selection rules. To complete the backend, we had to manually program specific parts. The major tasks were the following:

- specify whether a given data type fits in a register (and if so, in which kind of register)
- generate the required data directives for global data
- specify how parameters are passed to functions (which fit in a register, which should be passed on the stack, which registers to use)
- regard the alignment of data as demanded by the target architecture

All required information was taken from the official technical specifications of the Itanium2 processor by Intel [Int06b, Int06c, Int06d, Int01]. As a result, we obtained a compiler platform that compiles arbitrary C programs and generates assembler code for the Intel Itanium2. Based on the specification of the functional units and the latencies amongst them, scheduling is performed during compilation. As a result, each instruction receives the cycle at which it is executed (relative to the surrounding basic block). To generate executable binaries from the assembler files, we use Intel's Itanium assembler (which is part of Intel's *icc* compiler [Int06a]).

6.4.2 Static Branch Predictor

To determine branch probabilities statically, we implemented the heuristics presented by Wu et al. [WL94]. For each branch, the probability is determined as follows: For the condition the branch depends on as well as for both branch targets, certain characteristics are determined. Based on that information, a set of simple heuristics decides whether or not the branch is taken. Each heuristics has an associated weight, which expresses the relevance of that heuristics. Finally, all predictions are combined to yield the probability that the branch is taken. Additionally, from that information, the frequencies of basic blocks can be derived. This topic was investigated in the diploma theses [Tet07]. We implemented the static branch predictor (or static profiler) in the *CoSy* engine *staticprof*.

6.4.3 Alias Analysis

The idea of our framework is to use heuristics to overcome the imprecision of static analyses. However, we can also benefit from that part of information returned by static analyses that *is* precise. Whenever alias analyses report a memory dependency to be absent, this information is exact. Only for the other case, when a dependency is reported as *potentially present*, alias analyses are highly imprecise. Hence, we combine our heuristics for dependence degrees with a state-of-the-art alias analysis. Whenever we want to determine the dependence degree for an instruction pair, we first consult the alias analysis. If it returns no dependency, we know that this information is exact and return a dependence probability of 0. Otherwise, we consult our heuristics and return the predicted probability (see also Figure 4.8). Thus, we implemented the one-level flow alias analysis proposed by Das [Das00]. The analysis is scalable and was empirically proved to outperform other static analyses in terms of precision (see Mock et al. [MDCE01]). We developed a *CoSy* engine *aliasdas*, which performs the alias analysis and annotates the results in the CCMIR. We performed initial investigations on that topic in the diploma thesis [Opp07].

6.4.4 Speculative Upwards Code Motion

We implemented the algorithm for speculative upwards code motion as *CoSy* engine (see Figure 5.2 for the algorithm). This includes the implementation of the cost model as well as of the actual upwards code motion, which can overcome all kinds of dependency. As we have seen in Section 5.1.1, the cost model needs information about the dynamic program behavior as well as about the target architecture. In the following, we revisit the different kinds of required information and state by which parts of the implementation they are collected.

- **load latencies, likeliness of memory dependencies:** yielded by our generated heuristics
- **branch probabilities, basic block frequencies:** yielded by the implemented static branch predictor

6.4 Speculative Optimization

- **relative issue cycle of instructions:** yielded by the generic scheduler, which is part of *CoSy*

- **overhead of validity checks and of recovery code execution:** from the documentation of the Intel Itanium2 architecture [Int04, p.33]

We implemented the algorithm for speculative code motion as described in Section 5.1.3, Figure 5.2. The optimization operates on the LIR level and processes the program function by function. We initially investigated the algorithm in the diploma thesis [Sch07] and developed the full version based on this experience. First, a list of optimization candidates is built. We identify all load instructions, predict their latency with our heuristics and subtract the cycle distance to obtain the effective latency. The instruction that uses the loaded value can be determined by analyzing the register dependencies. The distance is determined by inspecting the relative issue cycles of the instructions. The candidate list is sorted by effective latencies in decreasing order to ensure that optimization starts with promising candidates. Each candidate is processed in turn. It is iteratively moved upwards step-by-step, and after each transformation, the resulting effective latency is determined via the cost model. Each transformation is actually performed on the code. During code motion, the best encountered code configuration is saved. Code motion stops when a maximum number of transformations has been performed. Of all transformations, the code with the highest optimization gain (*i.e.*, with the lowest effective load latency) is kept. For each code configuration, the code size is determined. This allows for limiting the impact of the optimization on code growth. During code motion, dependencies are overcome as described in Section 5.1.3. Memory dependencies can be ignored with data speculation. Control dependencies can be overcome with control speculation. Opposed to the general algorithm we presented in the previous chapter, we do not perform code duplication. For code motion across basic block borders, we consider only dominator blocks of the currently regarded blocks, which makes code duplication needless. Still, as described for the general algorithm, we consider each possible path from the target block to the original basic block, determine its optimization gain and sum up all gains, weighted by the corresponding conditional path probabilities. True register dependencies are overcome by *LAC* chain construction. We rename all registers that are only internally used within a *LAC* to virtual registers. By that, we circumvent output and anti dependencies on registers.

When a function call is crossed during code motion, it is considered as a possibly conflicting store in the cost model. The probability is determined by

Parameter	Default	Explanation
max_freq_ratio	2.0	maximally admitted ratio between the frequencies of the target block and of the original block for control speculation
max_lac_length	6	maximally admitted length of the LAC
max_lac_loads	2	maximally admitted number of load instructions in LAC
max_cand_abs	3	maximally admitted number of optimization candidates per function
max_cand_rel	0.005	maximally admitted fraction of optimization candidates per function (w.r.t. number of instructions of the function)
max_code_growth	0.05	maximally allowed fraction of code growth

Table 6.3: Parameters of Speculative Code Motion

considering the dependence probabilities between the currently optimized load and each store instruction of the called function and by choosing the highest probability thereof. The costs of speculation were taken from the technical specification of the Intel Itanium2 processor. Because the Itanium supports speculation by hardware, the cost of the validity check is constant and does not depend on the number of stores that were speculatively crossed. The cost model reflects a peculiarity of the implementation of speculation on the Itanium: When an effective latency is only partially reduced by speculative code motion, *i.e.*, when the loaded value is not yet available when reaching the check instruction, the Itanium reports a misspeculation. This makes speculative code motion only profitable if the distance between advanced load and check instruction amounts at least to the load latency.

The algorithm can be fine-tuned by a number of parameters (see Table 6.3). Code motion across basic block borders is controlled by the parameter *max_freq_ratio*, which avoids that code gets moved into blocks with a higher frequency. This would impair program performance. The construction of LAC chains ensures that the upper bound for the number of (load) instructions, specified by *max_lac_length* (*max_lac_loads*), is not exceeded. The Itanium uses a special hardware table (ALAT) to decide whether a speculatively loaded value is still valid. This table is of very limited size (32 entries). Hence, to avoid over-speculation, the parameters *max_cand_abs* and *max_cand_rel* specify the number of candidates that may be optimized per function. The first parame-

SLOC	Language	Module
418	C++	*Pin: memtracer*
4342	C++	*Trace Analysis*
7829	R	*Generation of Predictors, Experimental Evaluation, Code Generation*
2981	C	*CoSy: aliasdas*
1938	C	*CoSy: staticprof*
1450	C	*CoSy: codefeat*
4808	C	*CoSy: Speculative Optimization*
4618	C	*CoSy: Itanium Backend*
7694	CGD	*CoSy: Itanium Backend* – Backend Specification
36078		Total

Table 6.4: Source Lines of Code (SLOC) of the Implementation Modules

ter specifies an absolute value, the second a relative value w.r.t. the number of instructions in the regarded function. The maximum value of both parameters is used as an upper bound on the number of optimized loads. The parameter *max_code_growth* specifies which amount of code growth is admissible. The shown default parameters have led to the best performance results.

6.5 Summary

In this chapter, we described how we implemented the instantiated FriSCO framework, targeting the optimization of memory instructions. The analysis phase was implemented using CoSy for feature collection and *pfmon* and *Pin* for profiling. The machine learning phase was entirely implemented within the *R Project* and yields executable heuristics, written in C, to predict memory dependence degrees and memory latencies. In the speculative optimization phase, which was fully implemented within CoSy, those heuristics were integrated and are accessible from our speculative optimization. Table 6.4 lists the number of source lines of code (SLOC) for each module we implemented (comments and empty lines were not counted). As a result, we obtain an executable compiler that accepts the full C language, speculatively optimizes memory accesses, and generates executable binaries for the Itanium architecture,

7 Experimental Results

In this chapter, we describe the results of our experiments with the implementation of the instantiated *FrISCO* framework. First, we evaluate the automatically generated predictors. Second, we investigate the optimization gain that our optimization achieves using those predictors.

7.1 Evaluation of the Predictors

As initial experiment, we determine the general applicability of decision tree learning to predict both regarded kinds of memory behavior. This entails two steps: First, we perform *self-validation* to see whether the relationship between features and behavior can be identified. Second, we use *cross-validation* to get a first impression whether the learned models can be transferred from one program to another. We solely use the training set of programs for that first experiment. After that, we present our main experiment, which evaluates the precision of the obtained predictors for the validation set of programs. To that end, we initially perform self-validation on the validation set. This yields an upper bound for the predictor precision, against which we can compare the other results. Then, we train one general predictor from the training set of programs and assess its precision for the validation set. After that, we perform program classification and train a set of specialized predictors using the training set, and we evaluate their precision for the validation set. In both cases, we also compare the 4 different schemes to combine data sets (merge, vote-min, vote-max, vote-average, see Section 4.3.4) against each other.

In the following, we first describe the validation methods we use, namely self-validation and cross-validation. Then, we present the program suite that we use for our experiments. After that, we describe our experiments.

7.1.1 Validation Methods

In Section 2.5.3, we have presented different error measures to evaluate the precision of a predictor for a given data set, for which the correct classes are known. On top of that, there are different validation methods, which decide which data to use for training and which for validation. In the following, we describe self-validation and cross-validation.

For *self-validation*, training data and validation data are identical, *i.e.*, the predictor is applied to the data it was trained with. The comparison of predicted and actual classes of the data yields the prediction error. The error can not be considered as a realistic estimate, since the model was trained to minimize this error in the first place. Hence, this error can be expected to be very low. However, self-validation can be used to analyze whether a relationship can be learned in principle. If self-validation yields bad results, the learning scenario has to be modified, *e.g.*, by adding more features or by changing the classification of the data. In case of *cross-validation*, a predictor is trained with one part of the training data, and it is validated with another part. Because the predictor is validated with new data, cross-validation yields a more realistic estimate of the predictor precision. If we have m training data sets, we have $m \times (m-1)$ combinations of two data sets, upon which *pairwise cross-validation* can be performed. If we have a means of aggregating data sets together, we can also perform *leave-one-out cross-validation*: For every data set in turn, a predictor is trained with all other data sets but the regarded one, and the resulting predictor is then validated with the omitted data.

We use both self-validation and cross-validation to assess the general applicability of machine learning for our training data. For the main experiment, we use neither of those methods. However, the setting can be compared with that of cross-validation. Because the training set and the validation set are disjoint, the obtained results yield realistic error estimates. To estimate the predictor precision for a given pair of predicted and correct classes, we use the mean absolute error together with the correlation. Additionally, to investigate the general applicability of machine learning, we consult the Δk-accuracy.

7.1.2 Program Suite

We want to use machine learning to identify the relationship between static code features and program behavior. This requires a representative program

7.1 Evaluation of the Predictors 159

suite to obtain usable predictors. Furthermore, to get a realistic impression of the predictor precision, it is important to apply it to new data. In other words, the training set and the validation set must be disjoint. We use programs from the SPEC CPU benchmark suites[SPEC], which were designed to cover a wide range of typical program behavior. Each program is provided with three sets of input data, which are of increasing complexity: *test*, *train*, and *ref*. The first SPEC benchmark suite was presented 1992. Since then, new suites have been released in 1995, 2000, and 2006 to reflect the continuous development of new software. Especially, the complexity of the contained programs increased with every release (for a comparison of Spec'00 and Spec'06, see Agaram et al. [AKLM06]). To obtain a sufficiently comprehensive program suite, we use three SPEC benchmark suites: SPEC CPU1995, SPEC CPU2000, and SPEC CPU2006. We use programs from Spec'95 and Spec'00 for the training set, and Spec'06 as validation set. Some programs are part of multiple benchmark suites (in different versions). For example, *bzip2* is contained in Spec'00 as well as in Spec'06. To ensure that training set and validation set are disjoint, we exclude programs from the training set that are also contained in the validation set, and add them to the validation set. This concerns 4 programs: Spec'95: *perl*, Spec'00: *bzip2*, *perlbmk*, *mcf*[1]. Our chosen program sets for training and validation, respectively, ensure realistic validation results, since both sets are disjoint. Additionally, the chosen setting adds another challenge to our approach: Compared to the current Spec'06 suite, the programs of the preceding suites are less complex. Hence, we try to predict the behavior of today's programs with those of yesterday. If we are successful with that, we have evidence that we obtained generally applicable predictors.

We performed the experiments for both regarded memory behaviors, dependence degrees and load latencies, separately. The training and validation sets for one behavior differ slightly from those for the other behavior, mainly because the profiling to obtain the dependence degrees is highly expensive both in terms of time and memory. Table 7.1 and Table 7.2 show the training and validation sets for dependence degrees and load latencies, respectively, together with the used input set. More details on the programs can be found in [SPEC].

For each program, we performed profiling to obtain the regarded behavior, which we classified in 11 classes (0-10). To get a first impression of the characteristics of the programs, we determined the distribution of the behavior w.r.t. the classes. For the dependence degree (see Figure 7.1), we observe that

---

[1]Note that the program *go* from Spec'95 is not an older version of *gobmk* from Spec'06.

Experimental Results

Dependence Degrees	
Training (28 Programs)	*Spec'95 (test)*: applu apsi fpppp hydro2d mgrid su2cor swim tomcatv turb3d wave5 compress go li m88ksim
	Spec'00 (test) : ammp applu apsi art equake mesa sixtrack swim
	Spec'00 (train): crafty gap gzip parser twolf vpr
Validation (10 Programs)	*Spec'00 (train)*: bzip2 mcf perlbmk
	Spec'06 (test): bzip2 gobmk hmmer mcf perlbench sjeng sphinx

Table 7.1: Dependence Degrees: Training and Validation Sets of Programs (together with the chosen input data set)

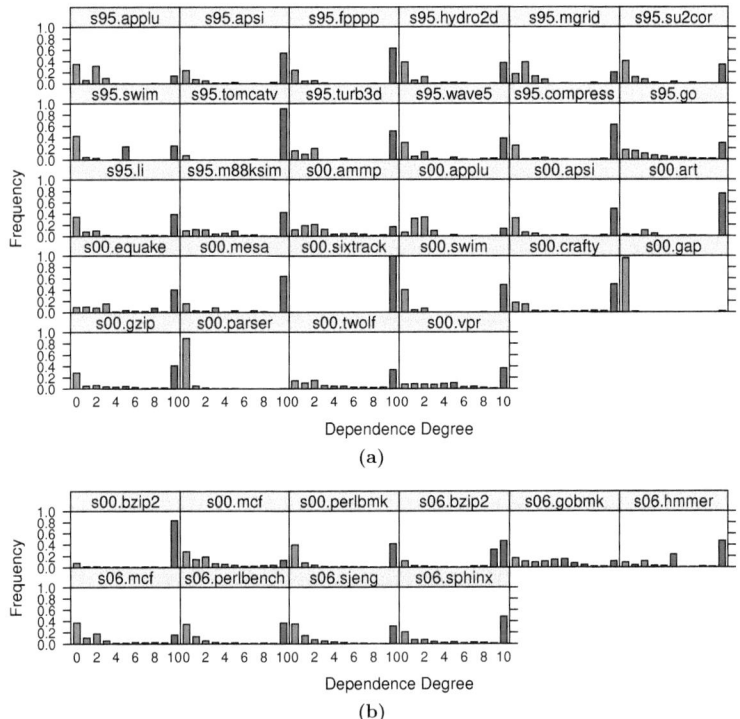

Figure 7.1: Distribution of Dependence Degrees (a) Training Set (b) Validation Set

7.1 Evaluation of the Predictors 161

the distribution varies significantly from program to program. We can identify different kinds of distribution:

1. distributions, in which almost all dependencies are highly likely,
2. distributions, in which almost all dependencies are highly unlikely,
3. distributions with a peak for both highly unlikely and likely dependencies, and
4. the rest.

The distributions for load latencies are shown in Figure 7.2. Opposed to dependence degrees, the distributions are similar to each other. They have a high peak in the lower classes. For most programs, almost all loads were classified in the first three classes (0-2). There are only a few programs that have a different distribution. For example, for the *mcf* programs, the distribution is more balanced.

7.1.3 General Applicability of Machine Learning

To assess the general applicability of decision tree learning to obtain behavior predictors, we performed self-validation as well as cross-validation on the training set of programs. For self-validation, we considered each program of the training set in turn, built one predictor and used it to predict the regarded program. We assessed the precision of each predictor and averaged the results. We proceeded similarly for cross-validation. We considered all pairs of programs that contain two different programs, trained a predictor with the first program and validated it with the second. Again, the precision was determined and averaged over all pairs. To interpret the results, we used the results of random predictors as reference. With that, we can identify the amount of information that was extracted by machine learning. We used two random predictors: *random* randomly predicts one of the classes. *random-prob* first determines the distribution of the classes of the training set and then predicts a class based on that distribution. We used the second predictor to decide whether the decision tree predictor has actually identified a relationship between features and classes, or whether it only has found the most frequent classes, which may happen for training data with a highly skewed class distribution.

Dependence Degrees For dependence degrees, the results of self-validation are shown in Figure 7.3 for each of the considered prediction algorithm. On the

Load Latencies	
Training (26 Programs)	*Spec'95 (train)*: hydro2d swim tomcatv turb3d wave5 compress go ijpeg li m88ksim *Spec'00 (train)*: ammp applu apsi art equake mesa mgrid swim wupwise crafty gap gzip parser twolf vortex vpr
Validation (13 Programs)	*Spec'95 (train)*: perl *Spec'00 (train)*: bzip2 mcf perlbmk *Spec'06 (train)*: bzip2 gobmk h264ref hmmer mcf milc perlbench sjeng sphinx

Table 7.2: Load Latencies: Training and Validation Sets of Programs (together with the chosen input data set)

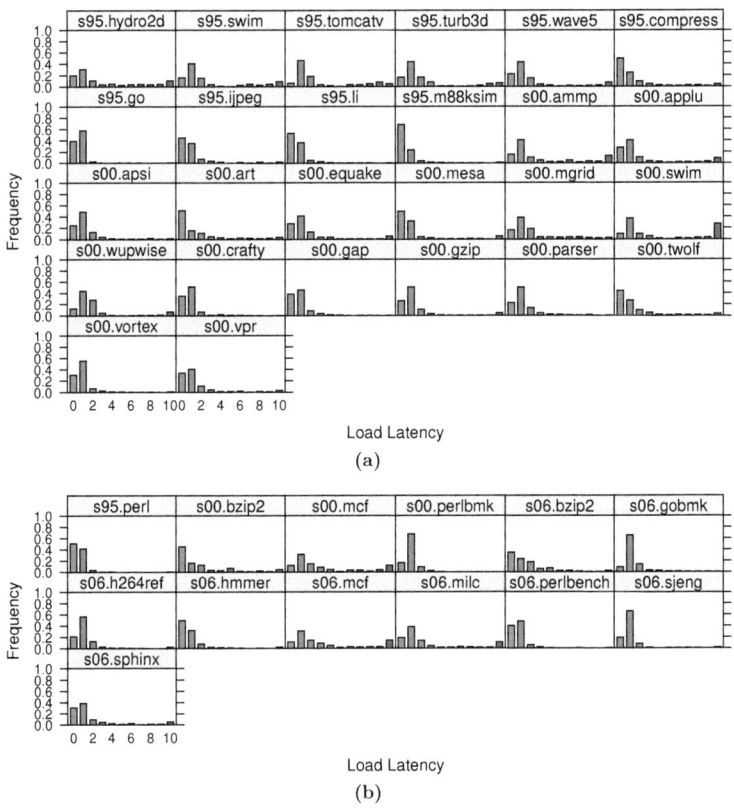

Figure 7.2: Distribution of Load Latencies (a) Training Set (b) Validation Set

7.1 Evaluation of the Predictors

left, we see the mean absolute error (MAE) together with the correlation. The bars indicate the standard deviation. The *random* predictors err on average by 4.33 classes, and the correlation is almost zero (0.01). The *random-prob* performs slightly better (MAE 3.75, Cor 0.01), which is an evidence that the distribution of the dependence degrees is not uniform. However, due to its randomness, the correlation remains unchanged. The *rpart* predictor has a low error (0.99) and a high correlation (0.79). This shows that *rpart* could successfully identify the relationship between features and classes for a given program. On the right, the Δk-accuracy is shown (the MAE is indicated by the abscissa of the star). For the *random* predictors, it starts low and grows almost linearly. For the *random-prob* predictors, the performance is slightly better, but still, about 40% of the predictions have an absolute error above 4 classes (the $\Delta 4$-accuracy is about 60%). Again, *rpart* performs drastically better. It starts high and has a steep curve. For example, 70% of the predictions are exactly correct, and almost 90% have an error of at most 2 classes. While the results for the *rpart* predictors are excellent, they merely show that the relationship is in principle learnable. They cannot be considered as realistic estimates of the predictor precision for new data. For a more realistic impression, we perform cross-validation on the training set of programs. The results are shown in Figure 7.4. We see that *random-prob* (4.84, Cor 0.01) performs even worse than *random* (4.75, Cor 0.01), which is an evidence for the fact that the distributions of the dependence degrees differ amongst the programs. As before, we see that *rpart* performs best. The error is higher than for self-validation (3.25), but still, we have a high correlation (0.43). For the Δk-accuracy, the predictors perform similarly to self-validation, with the difference that the curves for the *random-prob* and *rpart* predictors, respectively, have been moved downwards. For *rpart*, two third of the predictions have an error of at most 2.

Load Latencies The results of self-validation for load latencies are shown in Figure 7.5. As before, we see that the random predictors perform worse than *rpart*. However, the error of *random-prob* (MAE 2.75, Cor 0.03) is significantly below that of *random* (MAE 3.48, Cor 0.03). This is caused by the fact that the distribution of load latencies is highly skewed (see Figure 7.2). Still, it is evident that *rpart* has identified a relationship between features and latencies for each program (MAE 1.22, Cor 0.46), which is especially shown by the high correlation. The Δk-accuracy gives more evidence for the skewness of the distribution of the latencies. For the random predictors, the curves are

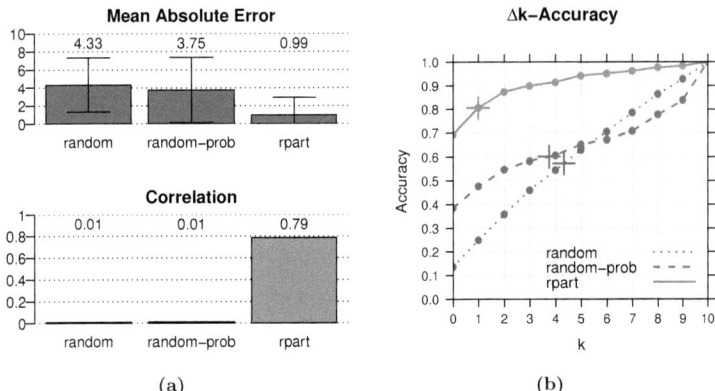

Figure 7.3: Dependence Degrees: Self-Validation on the Training Set (a) Mean Absolute Error and Correlation (b) Δk-Accuracy

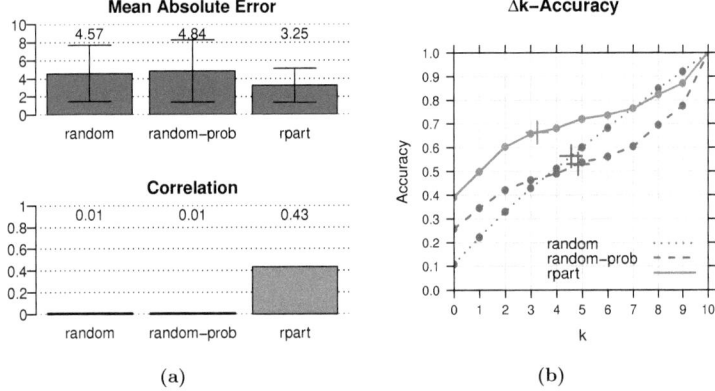

Figure 7.4: Dependence Degrees: Cross-Validation on the Training Set (a) Mean Absolute Error and Correlation (b) Δk-Accuracy

7.1 Evaluation of the Predictors

comparatively steep. For *rpart*, almost 60% of the predictions are correct, and for about 80%, the error is below 2 classes. The results from self-validation show that the relationship between features and latencies is in principle learnable. However, the high skewness of the distribution of the latencies makes learning a harder task. The training data contains more examples for certain classes, hence, the resulting predictor will be specialized for those classes. The results from cross-validation (shown in Figure 7.6) further give evidence for that assumption. While the error for *random* (3.46, Cor 0.03) and *random-prob* (2.96, Cor 0.03) is hardly changed, the error for *rpart* is doubled (2.60), leaving little room between the results of *random-prob* and *rpart*. However, the correlation still shows that *rpart* could extract information (0.11 *vs.* 0.03). The Δk-accuracy illustrates the similar performance of all predictors.

The results show that decision tree learning is applicable to model the program behavior we consider. For dependence degrees, we have a low absolute error together with a high correlation, which shows that the relationship between features and behavior could be well learned. For load latencies, we also have a low absolute error. The correlation is not as high as for dependence degrees, but still significantly greater than the correlation of the random predictors. Hence, also for load latencies, a relationship between features and latencies could be learned. From the results, we see that both kinds of regarded memory behavior, dependence degrees and load latencies, can be learned via machine learning. With that, the initial experiment is successfully finished, and we continue with the machine learning phase.

7.1.4 Program Classification

The first step of the machine learning phase of *FrISCO* is to perform program classification of the programs in the training set. To that end, we use cluster analysis. For the distance matrix, which is required by the cluster analysis, we used the results from pairwise cross validation collected in the initial experiment. We trained a predictor for each program and applied it to every program. With that, we obtained for each pair of programs the mean absolute error, which is used as distance measure. With hierarchical clustering, the programs of the training set were automatically grouped together. Hierarchical clustering yields a hierarchy of different clusterings, which have 1 to m (the number of programs in the training set) clusters. We selected the clustering with the lowest average inner-cluster error. If clustering yields k clusters, the result of the cluster analysis can be seen as a classification of the programs

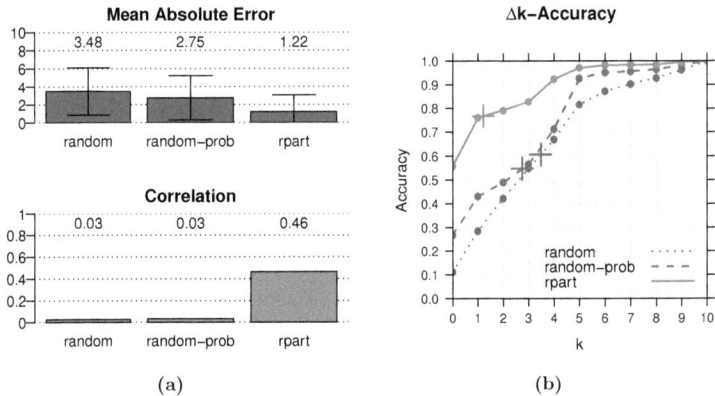

Figure 7.5: Load Latencies: Self-Validation on the Training Set (a) Mean Absolute Error and Correlation (b) Δk-Accuracy

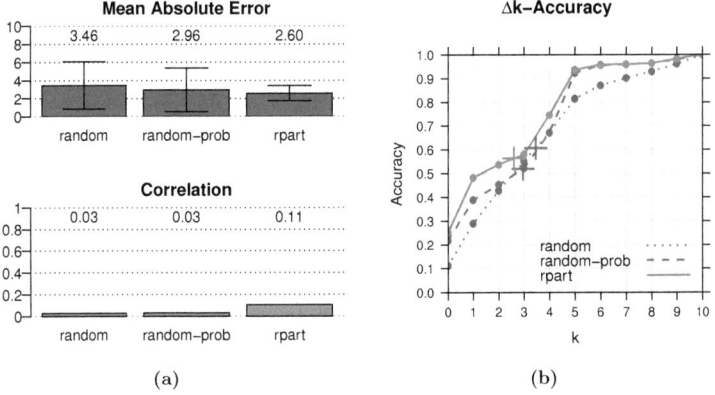

Figure 7.6: Load Latencies: Cross-Validation on the Training Set (a) Mean Absolute Error and Correlation (b) Δk-Accuracy

7.1 Evaluation of the Predictors

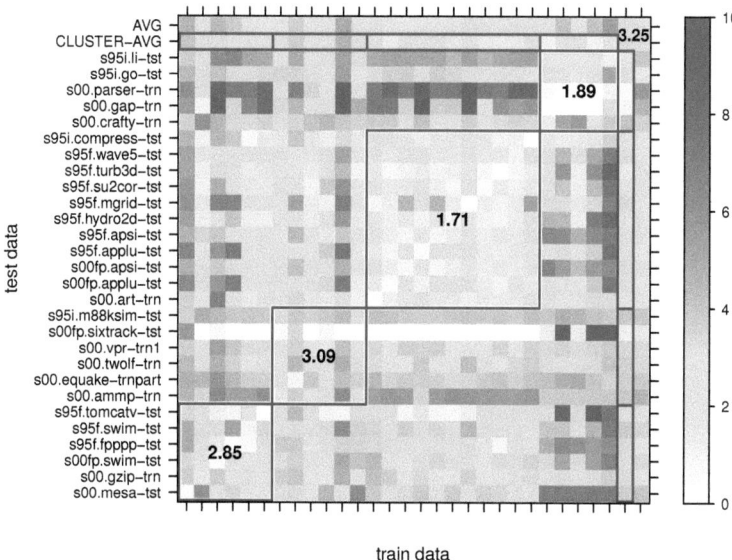

Figure 7.7: Dependence Degrees: Distance Matrix for the Training Set

in the training set into k classes. From the static program features and those classes, we trained the program class predictor. That predictor was used to determine the classes of the programs in the validation set. In the following, we consider both regarded behaviors, namely dependence degrees and load latencies, in turn. We show the obtained distance matrix together with the resulting clustering, present the obtained program class predictor, and show the resulting classification of the programs of the validation set.

Dependence Degrees

The resulting distance matrix for the prediction of dependence degrees on the training set of programs is shown in Figure 7.7. For a given cell of the matrix, the column denotes the program the predictor was trained with and the row denotes the program that was validated with the predictor (columns and rows are sorted identically). Since we have 11 classes, the error ranges between 0 and 10. It is color coded, as shown in the legend on the right. In the first row/last column, the average error of the corresponding column/row is shown. The average error of the whole matrix (disregarding the diagonal, as its cells correspond to self-validation) is 3.25. With that distance matrix, we

Class	Programs (Training Set)	MAE	Cor
1	*Spec'00*: swim mesa gzip *Spec'95*: fpppp swim tomcatv	2.85 (±1.30)	0.44
2	*Spec'00*: sixtrack ammp equake twolf vpr *Spec'95*: m88ksim	3.09 (±1.36)	0.27
3	*Spec'00*: applu apsi art *Spec'95*: compress applu apsi hydro2d mgrid su2cor turb3d wave5	1.71 (±0.76)	0.79
4	*Spec'00*: crafty gap parser *Spec'95*: go li	1.89 (±1.75)	0.62
1–4	**Weighted Average Values**	**2.28 (±1.18)**	**0.51**
	Overall Average Values (no program classes)	**3.25 (±1.89)**	**0.43**

Table 7.3: Dependence Degrees: Identified Program Classes for the Training Set

performed the cluster analysis. Intuitively speaking, the aim of clustering is to group programs together, such that cells with a low error are within clusters and cells with a high error are put outside. The result is also shown in the figure (the columns/rows of the matrix were permuted according to the clustering). We obtained 4 program classes, indicated by the black squares. The error within each class is also shown (again without considering the corresponding diagonals). In the second row/second last column, the average error for the column/row of the corresponding cluster is shown. We see that clustering achieved to reduce the error: Within each class, the error is below the overall mean error, and in most cases, the error reduction is significant. We also see that the within-cluster row/column means are always below the overall row/column means (compare the first and second rows/columns).

The resulting classes are shown in Table 7.3. For each class, we see the induced mean absolute error (together with the standard deviation) and the correlation, as yielded by inner-class pairwise cross-validation. In other words, the values are obtained by computing the average values of the corresponding sub-matrices of the distance matrix (that are induced by the program classification), as indicated by the four black squares in Figure 7.7. Again, the values on the diagonals are ignored. Additionally, we see the average of the cluster errors, weighted by the corresponding cluster size. As reference, the overall error and the correlation, as obtained without program classes, are shown. In all but in class 2, the correlation increases and the MAE (together with the standard deviation) is reduced significantly. In class 2, the MAE (together with

7.1 Evaluation of the Predictors

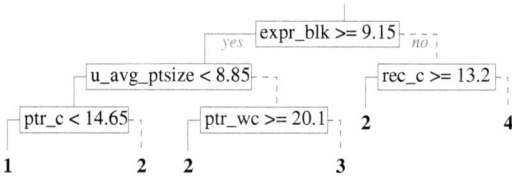

Figure 7.8: Dependence Degrees: Decision Tree of the Program Class Predictor

the standard deviation) is reduced but also the correlation decreases. Overall, for our distance matrix, the MAE could be reduced from 3.25 to 2.28. Note that all those results were computed solely from the distance matrix.

From the obtained clustering together with the static program features (listed in Table 6.1, p.139), we trained a predictor using *rpart*. The resulting decision tree is shown in Figure 7.8. Each inner node contains a condition with regard to the program features, and the result of that condition determines whether we branch to the left (condition was fulfilled) or right (otherwise). The leaf nodes are annotated with a class label, which constitutes the resulting prediction. For a given program feature vector, we start at the root and traverse the tree iteratively until we arrive at a leaf. The annotated class is reported as result. There may be multiple paths (from the root to a leaf) that report the same class. The figure illustrates the advantages of the decision tree learning algorithm: Its result is directly readable by the human user, and it can be interpreted to gain insights into the problem domain. From the tree, we can interpret the four classes and identify characteristics of the contained programs as follows:

- **Class 1:** larger basic blocks, few pointers, few points-to targets
- **Class 2:** larger basic blocks and significant pointer usage, or significant usage of structured variables
- **Class 3:** larger basic blocks, some pointers, more points-to targets
- **Class 4:** small basic blocks, few structured variables

This means that classes 1 and 3 have characteristics of floating-point intensive applications, with the difference that class 3 has more pointer usage, which cannot be analyzed precisely by alias analyses. Class 4 contains control-intensive programs. For class 2, the results are not as uniform as for the other classes. It contains programs that are pointer-intensive or that are control-

Class	Programs (Validation Set)
1	*Spec'06*: bzip2
2	*Spec'06*: sphinx
3	*Spec'00*: bzip2 *Spec'06*: hmmer
4	*Spec'00*: mcf perlbmk *Spec'06*: gobmk mcf perlbench sjeng

Table 7.4: Dependence Degrees: Predicted Program Classes for the Validation Set

intensive and make significant use of structured variables. We applied the program class predictor to the program features of the programs in the validation set. Table 7.4 shows the result. Remember that the validation set for dependence degrees contains 3 Spec'00 programs and 7 Spec'06 programs, three of which are more recent versions of the 3 Spec'00 programs. *mcf* and *perlbench/perlbmk* reside in the same class. The two versions of *bzip2*, however, are put into classes 1 and 3, respectively. Hence, the features of the program must have slightly changed. Comparing both versions of *bzip2*, from Spec'00 to Spec'06, the number of lines of code grew from 3227 to 5114, and the number of C files also grew from 2 to 9. However, while the program complexity appears to have increased, the pointer behavior appears to have become slightly less complex for *bzip2*.

Load Latencies

For load latencies, we also performed pairwise cross-validation to obtain the distance matrix. The result is shown in Figure 7.9, together with the resulting clustering. The overall mean average error amounts to 2.60. Clustering yields 5 program classes, and the within-cluster error is notably below that overall error. The resulting classes are shown in detail in Table 7.5, together with the average error for the clustering and with the overall error. For the per-class results, we see that in all but one case, the error (together with the standard deviation) is reduced significantly and the correlation is increased. In the one remaining case, for class 1, the error is slightly reduced (together with the standard deviation), but the correlation also is decreased. Overall, if we consider the average performance of the program classification, we see that the MAE could be reduced from 2.60 to 2.03, and also the correlation improves from 0.11 to 0.18.

7.1 Evaluation of the Predictors

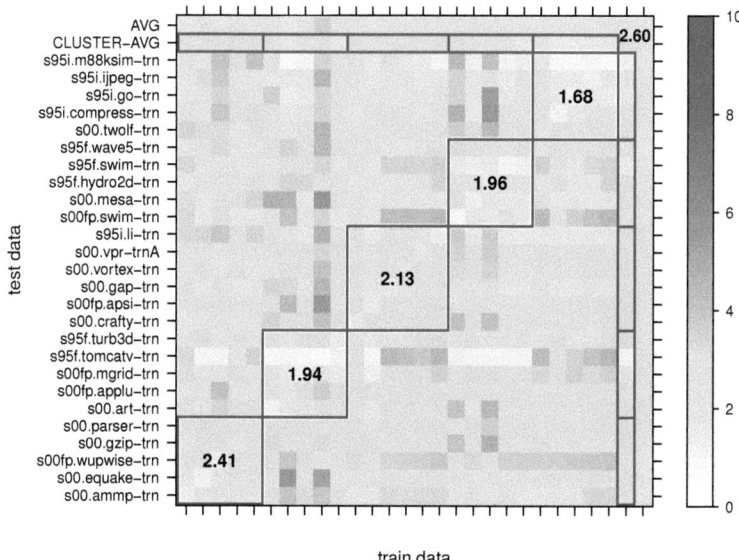

Figure 7.9: Load Latencies: Distance Matrix for the Training Set

Class	Programs (Training Set)	MAE	Cor
1	*Spec'00*: wupwise ammp equake gzip parser	2.41 (±0.27)	0.06
2	*Spec'95*: tomcatv turb3d *Spec'00*: applu mgrid art	1.94 (±0.82)	0.31
3	*Spec'95*: li *Spec'00*: apsi crafty gap vortex vpr	2.13 (±0.28)	0.14
4	*Spec'95*: hydro2d swim wave5 *Spec'00*: mesa swim	1.96 (±0.58)	0.26
5	*Spec'95*: compress go ijpeg m88ksim *Spec'00*: twolf	1.68 (±0.42)	0.11
1–5	**Weighted Average Values**	**2.03 (±0.47)**	**0.18**
	Overall Average Values (no program classes)	**2.60 (±0.83)**	**0.11**

Table 7.5: Load Latencies: Identified Program Classes for the Training Set

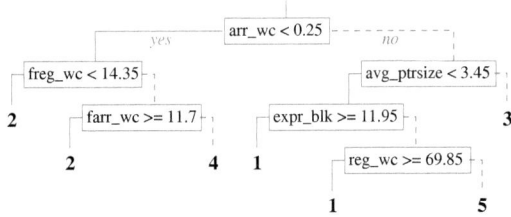

Figure 7.10: Load Latencies: Decision Tree of the Program Class Predictor

With that program classification, we trained a program class predictor. The resulting decision tree is shown in Figure 7.10. By means of the tree, we can interpret the characteristics of the programs of each program class as follows:

- **Class 1:** few points-to targets, larger basic blocks or mainly variables of integral type
- **Class 2:** hardly integer arrays, few variables of floating-point type or some floating-point arrays
- **Class 3:** more points-to targets
- **Class 4:** hardly integer arrays, some variables of floating-point type, few floating-point arrays
- **Class 5:** few points-to targets, smaller basic blocks, variables not mainly of integral type

This means that Classes 2 and 4 resemble floating-point applications, with the difference being the relevance of floating-point arrays. Class 3 contains programs with hardly predictable pointers. Classes 1 and 5 may be characterized as programs with a transparent pointer behavior, the difference being that in class 1, basic blocks tend to be larger. We applied the predictor to the programs of the validation set. The resulting classes are shown in Table 7.6. Remember that the validation set contains 1 Spec'95 program, 3 Spec'00 programs, and 9 Spec'06 programs. For the 4 programs from the older benchmarks, more recent versions are contained in Spec'06. We see that both versions of *mcf* as well as all three perl variants *perl/perlbmk/perlbench* were put into the same class. Again, as for dependence degrees, the two versions of *bzip2* reside in different classes (classes 3 and 5, respectively). And again, the difference appears to be the more complex pointer behavior of Spec'00 *bzip2*.

7.1 Evaluation of the Predictors 173

Class	Programs (Validation Set)
1	*Spec'06*: hmmer sphinx
2	*Spec'06*: milc
3	*Spec'95*: perl *Spec'00*: bzip2 mcf perlbmk *Spec'06*: mcf sphinx perlbench
4	–
5	*Spec'06*: bzip2 gobmk h264ref sjeng

Table 7.6: Load Latencies: Predicted Program Classes for the Validation Set

7.1.5 Predictor Precision for the Validation Set

From the obtained program classification, we built a set of specialized heuristics, one per program class. Together with the program class predictor that we trained, this yields a composite heuristics that can be applied to the validation set. For each program in the validation set, we determined its program class and selected the corresponding specialized heuristics to predict the program behavior. We performed a set of experiments on the validation set of programs. First, as a limit study, we performed self-validation. That is, from each program of the validation set, we trained a predictor and used it to predict the data it was trained with. This experiment is the only one that uses the validation set to train predictors. While the results of self-validation are not realistic, they can be used to define an upper bound on predictor precision. Next, we performed different experiments without program classification to have a baseline, against which we can compare the results with program classification. To train one predictor from a set of programs, the corresponding data sets have to be combined. In Section 4.3.4 (p. 89), we have presented two alternatives to that end: The data sets can be either merged, or we can train a set of predictors, one from each data set, and combine there votes. In the latter case, we distinguish three different schemes how to combine the votes: We either take the majority vote and break ties by taking the minimal/maximal class, or we take the mean value of the votes and map it back to a class. All these schemes require the classes to be quantitative, which is the case for our scenario. Altogether, this yields four different combination techniques. For each technique, we construct one predictor and apply it to the validation set of programs. Next, we perform the same experiments *with* program classification. For each combination technique, we build a composite heuristics and apply it to the validation set of programs. In total, this yields

174 Experimental Results

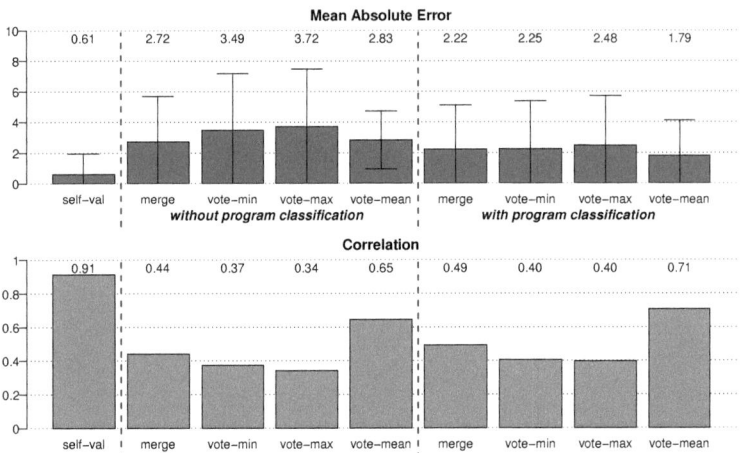

Figure 7.11: Dependence Degrees: Predictor Precision for the Validation Set

9 experiments: self-validation and four combination techniques without and with program classification, respectively. For each experiment, we determined the mean absolute error as well as the correlation. In the following, we present the results for dependence degrees and for load latencies in turn.

Dependence Degrees The results for dependence degrees are shown in Figure 7.11. On the left, we see the result of self-validation. As expected, the error is very low, and the correlation is near to 1. Next, we see the different experiments performed without program classification. We see at first glance that the *merge* and the *vote-mean* combination technique performs best, both in terms of the error as well as of correlation. For *vote-mean*, the error (2.83) is slightly above the error of *merge* (2.72). However, the standard deviation of the error is significantly lower (1.89 *vs.* 2.96), and also the correlation is higher (0.65 *vs.* 0.44). Hence, for the experiments without program classification, *vote-mean* is the best combination technique. For the results with program classification, we see that all predictors perform better (only *merge* experiences a lower correlation). Especially, we see that for *vote-mean*, we have highly precise results: The error is reduced to 1.79 (best result without program classification: 2.72), and correlation goes up to 0.71 (*vs.*0.65). Also, the standard deviation is low. Hence, program classification could reduce the mean absolute error by almost 1 class. The detailed results for each of the pro-

7.1 Evaluation of the Predictors

	Program	without PC		with PC		
		Err	Cor	Class	Err	Cor
Spec'00	bzip2	1.06	0.85	3	0.64	0.87
	mcf	2.92	0.49	4	2.38	0.43
	perlbmk	3.46	0.76	4	1.36	0.82
Spec'06	bzip2	3.20	0.74	1	1.39	0.83
	gobmk	2.58	0.36	4	2.31	0.40
	hmmer	2.42	0.66	3	2.05	0.64
	mcf	3.54	0.28	4	2.43	0.54
	perlbench	3.56	0.76	4	1.37	0.84
	sjeng	2.94	0.75	4	2.18	0.75
	sphinx	2.67	0.81	2	1.82	0.92
	mean value	2.83	0.65		1.79	0.71

Table 7.7: Dependence Degrees: Detailed Results of the Predictor Precision for the Validation Set (for the *vote-mean* combination technique)

grams of the training set are shown in Table 7.7. We see the results without and with program classification, using the *vote-mean* combination technique.

Load Latencies The results for load latencies are shown in Figure 7.12. While the error for self-validation is low, the correlation is significantly lower than for dependence degrees (0.48 *vs.* 0.91 for dependence degrees). As we have discussed earlier, this is caused by the fact that the distributions of the load latencies are highly skewed towards lower latencies. For the experiments without program classification, the results are similar. However, as before, the *vote-mean* predictor performs best (lowest error, lowest standard deviation, highest correlation). For the experiments with program classification, we see that the precision of the predictors is improved. Again, the *vote-mean* predictor with program classification performs best. It reaches a mean absolute error of 1.99, which is close the the error of self-validation (1.23). Also, the correlation is significantly higher than in all other cases (0.18 *vs.* 0.09) and is comparatively high, considering the 0.48 of self-validation. Hence, we see that also for load latencies, program classification has a significant positive effect on the predictor precision. As before, the *vote-mean* predictor performs best. The detailed results for the programs of the validation set are shown in Table 7.8.

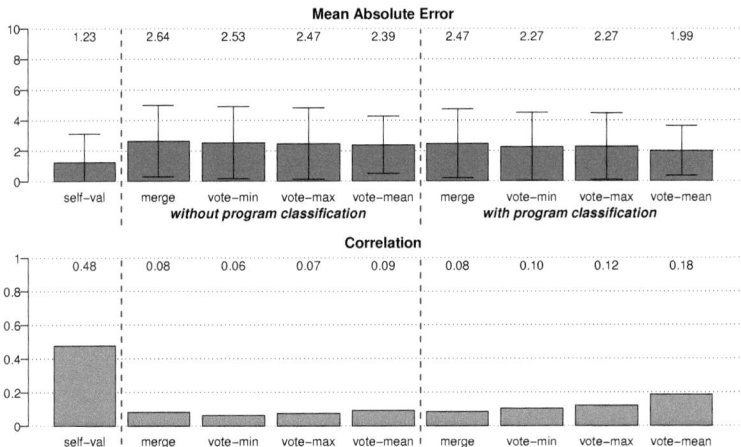

Figure 7.12: Load Latencies: Predictor Precision for the Validation Set

Program		without PC		with PC		
		Err	Cor	Class	Err	Cor
Spec'95	perl	1.69	0.12	3	1.19	0.10
Spec'00	bzip2	2.49	0.16	3	2.16	0.28
	mcf	2.88	0.06	3	2.25	0.24
	perlbmk	2.11	0.12	3	1.97	0.15
Spec'06	bzip2	2.58	0.04	5	2.07	0.34
	gobmk	2.44	0.04	5	1.98	0.01
	h264ref	2.17	0.13	5	2.15	0.06
	hmmer	2.23	0.09	1	1.67	0.32
	mcf	2.91	0.07	3	2.23	0.22
	milc	2.73	0.10	2	1.93	0.27
	perlbench	1.98	0.12	3	1.84	0.12
	sjeng	2.57	0.01	5	2.38	0.19
	sphinx	2.24	0.11	1	2.03	0.09
mean value		2.39	0.09		1.99	0.18

Table 7.8: Load Latencies: Detailed Results of the Predictor Precision for the Validation Set (for the *vote-mean* combination technique)

7.2 Optimization

In the previous section, we have presented experiments with the machine learned predictors, and we have seen that precise predictors could be trained from the training set of programs. In this section, we present our run-time experiments, which we performed to assess the actual performance improvement that could be achieved with our approach. To that end, we use the implementation of our proposed speculative optimization of memory accesses, together with heuristics that were automatically generated from the trained predictors. We first describe the experimental setup and present then the results.

7.2.1 Experimental Setup

We measured the run-time performance for the 11 C programs of the SPEC CPU2006 benchmark suite[2]. As target platform, we used the Intel Itanium2 processor. We compiled each program in a base version and in an optimized version. For the base version, we optimized each program with -O4, which performs over 50 state-of-the-art analyses and optimizations provided with CoSy on the program. We also performed our implementation of a state-of-the-art alias analysis for the base version. For the optimized version, we additionally performed our speculative optimization. The generated heuristics did not increase the compilation time notably. Our speculative optimization was typically finished within less than one minute, except for very huge programs like the *gcc*. In that case, the optimization took a few minutes, compared to an overall compilation time of over an hour. We used the *ref* data provided with the SPEC benchmarks as input data for all experiments. The program performance was measured with the *pfmon*[HP04] tool. We ran each program three times and chose the median values. The aim of our optimization is to improve program performance. Hence, we measured the required execution time for each program. In order to explain the effect our optimization has on the execution time, we furthermore measured the number of stall cycles for different kinds of stalls, using the performance counters of the Itanium. We also measured the amount and the kind of speculation that was performed at run-time. In the following, we consider both tasks, measuring stalls and measuring the degree of speculation, in turn.

---

[2] We had to exclude the C program 462.libquantum, which is part of SPEC CPU2006, because the CoSy front end is not fully C99 compliant.

Our optimization aims at reducing cache stalls. Hence, we measured the amount of stalls caused by integer loads and by floating-point loads. The former lead to data cache (D-$Cache$) stalls, the latter to floating point unit (FPU) stalls. Possibly negative effects of our optimization are an increased code size and an increased register pressure. To cope with the first, we measure the amount of integer cache (I-$Cache$) stalls. For the second, we measure stalls caused by the Itanium's *Register Stack Engine (RSE)*. The Itanium provides an automatic register-windowing mechanism that is invisible to the programmer. Each function can allocate as many local registers as it needs (up to 96 registers). The *RSE* works in the background and swaps parts of the register file to a backing store and back again, whenever necessary. The more registers a function needs, the higher the overhead of the RSE. Hence, an increased amount of *RSE* stall cycles indicates an increased register pressure. For each of the 4 considered types of stalls, we determine the fraction it constitutes w.r.t. the original program execution time as well as how much it could be improved by our optimization. Additionally, we determine how many instructions could be effectively executed per cycle. This value expresses the parallelism that was available during run-time. We can use the instructions per cycles (IPC) count to determine to which extent our optimization increased the available parallelism.

To measure the degree of speculation that was performed, we first collected statistics during the optimization. Additionally, we compared the binaries of the base and of the optimized version, respectively, to determine the code growth. Then, we executed the programs and measured how frequently certain kinds of instructions were executed dynamically. We observed load instructions as well as speculative load and check instructions. To that end, we used the performance counters of the Itanium.

7.2.2 Results

The static optimization statistics for the programs are shown in Table 7.9. For each program, we collected the static count of loads, the amount thereof that our optimization considered as optimization candidates, and the amount of the candidates that were actually optimized. Additionally, the table shows the code growth. The static load count differs from program to program, ranging from a few hundred to over a hundred thousand. In most cases, many of the load instructions are considered as expensive and become optimization

7.2 Optimization

program	load instructions			code growth
	count	candidates	optimized	
bzip2	4141	32.5%	7.1%	0.8%
gcc	149711	10.2%	29.2%	1.2%
gobmk	38475	32.4%	30.9%	1.8%
h264ref	63222	80.4%	10.3%	8.2%
hmmer	16095	94.1%	22.3%	8.3%
lbm	556	38.7%	92.1%	0.4%
mcf	713	47.1%	64.0%	10.3%
milc	7508	69.2%	26.8%	4.9%
perlbench	63949	4.2 %	17.2%	0.7%
sjeng	6254	1.1 %	20.0%	0.6%
sphinx	7563	88.8%	9.6%	4.5%

Table 7.9: Static Optimization Statistics

candidates. For most programs, about one forth of the candidates are selected for optimization. The resulting code growth is in all but three cases below 5%.

The run-time results are shown in Figure 7.13. We see that for 5 programs, run-time could be reduced significantly by up to 3.75%. For the remaining programs, there are 4 programs with marginal improvement, and two programs for which the optimization had hardly an effect. Detailed results are shown in Table 7.10. For each program, the table lists the improvement with respect to execution time (ET) and to the available parallelism (instructions per cycle, IPC). Next to these improvements, we show the effect of our optimization with respect to four different kinds of stalls, namely D-cache stalls (for integer loads), FPU stalls (for floating-point loads), I-cache stalls, and RSE stalls (captures

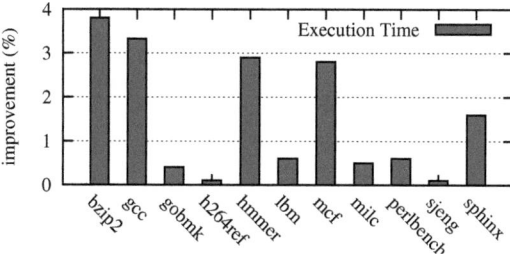

Figure 7.13: Run-Time Results

	ET	IPC	D-Cache		FPU		I-Cache		RSE	
program	impr	impr	frac	impr	frac	impr	frac	impr	frac	impr
bzip2	3.75	4.34	30.6	12.0	0.0	13.7	0.0	4.0	0.0	13.0
gcc	3.32	2.33	48.2	4.6	1.3	1.9	2.2	−6.6	0.9	19.7
gobmk	0.36	1.87	0.1	−1.3	3.0	0.7	0.1	3.1	1.0	22.8
h264ref	0.07	0.06	10.5	0.4	0.7	0.2	1.3	−2.2	0.7	21.7
hmmer	2.86	3.15	8.9	−1.6	1.4	11.1	0.2	7.1	0.0	1.7
lbm	0.55	0.42	45.2	0.2	24.0	1.7	0.2	9.7	0.0	0.7
mcf	2.75	11.86	86.8	3.4	0.0	0.5	0.1	0.5	0.0	2.2
milc	0.45	-0.27	22.1	−0.7	53.6	0.6	0.0	4.6	0.0	−1.5
perlbench	0.60	0.00	14.0	1.2	0.1	0.1	3.0	3.7	4.1	0.1
sjeng	0.14	-1.08	9.0	−6.1	1.1	1.5	5.1	27.8	1.4	7.3
sphinx	1.59	2.93	17.1	2.2	33.6	1.0	0.2	3.6	0.6	12.2
average	1.49	2.33	26.59	1.30	10.80	3.00	1.12	5.03	0.78	9.08

Table 7.10: Impact on the Stall Behavior (all values in %)

register pressure). For each kind of stall, we show the fraction it constitutes in the base version as well as how much it could be improved by our optimization. All values are given as percent. We see that the IPC improvement correlates with the ET improvement. In the following, we regard the 5 programs with the highest improvement in turn. For *bzip2* and *gcc*, the improvements were mainly caused by a reduction of integer load stalls. In case of *hmmer*, the effects on the stall behavior is negligible. The improvement is caused by the increased IPC, which was achieved by our optimization by the increased code motion opportunities. For *mcf*, the improvement is due to a reduction of integer load stalls. For *sphinx*, the reduction of integer as well as floating-point loads together with an increased IPC are the reasons for the improvement. The results for the I-cache stalls show that our optimization did not introduce additional stalls due to code growth. There are only two programs that have an increased number of I-cache stalls (*gcc* and *h264ref*). However, in both cases, the I-cache stalls constitute less than 2.2% of the execution time. Especially, we see that for the two programs with the highest code growth, *mcf*, *hmmer*, and *h264ref* (see Table 7.9), I-cache stalls are not an issue. Similarly, the register pressure was not increased by our optimization. There is only one benchmark that has an increased amount of RSE stalls (*milc*). For that benchmarks, the fraction the RSE stalls constitute is hardly measurable. Overall, we see that the optimization could improve the run-time performance significantly in many cases, while avoiding performance degradation in all cases.

7.2 Optimization

program	regular loads	speculative loads			checks	
		data	ctrl	both	data	ctrl
bzip2	99.31	–	1.36	–	–	0.68
gcc	98.20	0.08	4.17	0.13	0.08	1.86
gobmk	96.87	0.58	4.09	0.54	0.72	1.89
h264ref	99.51	0.05	0.49	0.05	0.17	0.26
hmmer	96.91	0.00	3.12	0.00	0.00	3.08
lbm	100.00	–	–	–	–	0.00
mcf	85.14	–	32.51	–	–	15.34
milc	96.77	–	0.88	–	–	0.81
perlbench	99.98	–	0.14	0.00	0.00	0.02
sjeng	100.00	–	–	–	–	0.00
sphinx	99.24	0.00	6.16	–	0.00	0.74

Table 7.11: Dynamic Instruction Count for Loads and Speculative Instructions (with respect to the dynamic load count of the base version, in %)

To determine the actual amount of speculation that was performed at runtime, we used the performance counters to count the number of load and of speculative instructions during execution time. Table 7.11 shows the results. We see the amount of the different kinds of instructions with respect to the number of load instructions in the original program. All values are given as percent. A value of 0.00 represents some small fraction, whereas '–' states the complete absence of the corresponding instruction. We see that control speculation prevails over data speculation. The speculative instructions amount to a few percent of the number of original loads in all but one case: For *mcf*, speculation was heavily performed. From Table 7.10, we see that *mcf* is the program with the highest amount of D-cache stalls. Hence, there are many opportunities for speculation. Data speculation is less frequently performed than control speculation. The reason lies in the hardware implementation of data speculation on the Itanium processor. If the latency of a load could only be partially hidden by speculation, the program experiences a full stall at run-time. The reason is that data speculation uses the ALAT table, and a corresponding entry is only added when the load was successfully finished. The check instruction consults the ALAT table and reports misspeculation if no matching entry is found. Hence, data speculation is only advantageous if the latency can be completely hidden. Given that the latency can amount to hundreds of cycles, this cannot be achieved in most cases. Conversely, control speculation uses a special *Not a Thing (NaT)* bit, which is annotated at each register. Whether or not a load yields an exception is decided before the

Latency	Optimized Candidates		Improvement of
	Only Full Hiding	*Partial Hiding Admitted*	**Performance Gain**
1 – 4	31.2%	2.2%	-18.7%
5 – 9	24.3%	18.6%	23.6%
10–19	17.1%	61.6%	68.5%
20–29	8.6%	42.3%	77.9%
30–39	12.7%	70.2%	49.3%
40–49	19.4%	79.3%	46.5%
50–	6.7%	73.6%	158.8%
All	23.6%	7.0%	35.6%

Table 7.12: Fraction of Optimized Loads with respect to Candidates

actual value is loaded. Hence, a check instruction for control speculation can decide whether or not a load raises an exception before the load is finished. Thus, control speculation can be performed also if the original latency could only partially be hidden. As a consequence, the optimization mostly performs control speculation.

We expect better results for architectures that have better support for speculation than the Itanium. As mentioned, we throttled the optimization such that it only makes an optimization if the latency of a given load can be completely hidden. To get an impression of the effect of this limitation, we regard the fraction of optimized loads w.r.t. all optimization candidates, differentiated by the expected original latency. Additionally, in another run, we performed the optimization and enabled the partial hiding of a load latency. The results are shown in Table 7.12.

For the throttled version that only admits full hiding of the latency, as we used in the run-time experiments, 23.6% of the candidates are selected for optimization on average. The table shows that mostly candidates with a low latency are chosen. For loads with a latency below 10 cycles, the fraction of chosen candidates is above average, while for the remaining cases, the fraction is below average. Especially, only 6.7% of load instructions with an latency of at least 50 cycles were optimized. This is caused by the fact that the higher the latency of a load, the harder it is to hide it completely. If we drop the restriction that the latency has to be fully hidden, the results are completely different, as shown in the right column of Table 7.12. On average, 7.0% of the candidates were chosen for optimization. While this may appear surprising at first because one would expect that the optimization performs more optimization in that case, the table shows that it is more efficient. The algorithm selects candidates with higher latencies, such that optimization pays more off. The fraction of the candidates that were optimized grows as latency increases. From the candidates with a latency above 30 cycles, over 70% were selected for optimization. We also compared the optimization gain that is achieved in the throttled version with that that would be achieved with the partial-hiding variant. The last column of Table 7.12 shows that the gain increases significantly. Especially, for loads with latencies above 50 cycles, the optimization gain is increased by 158.8%. On average, it increases by 35.6%. Note that the partial-hiding variant obtains more improvement while choosing only one third as many candidates for optimization compared to the throttled version. These results show that on the Intel Itanium architecture, many candidates with a high latency are not selected for optimization, which leads to significant limitations on the achieved optimization gain. We also see that the optimization will achieve considerably more performance improvements on architectures without the limitations of the Itanium.

7.3 Summary

In this chapter, we have presented the results of the experiments that we performed to investigate the improvement caused by our *FrISCO* framework, instantiated to the optimization of memory accesses. First, we analyzed the machine learning phase. We could show that for both learning domains, namely dependence degrees as well as load latencies, the relationship between features and behavior is in principle learnable. Then, we performed program classification as foundation for building a set of specialized predictors. We performed a set of experiments on the validation set of programs to empirically determine the best combination technique, which is required to obtain one predictor from multiple programs' training data, as well as to assess the improvement caused by our concept of program classification. We could show that the *vote-mean* combination technique performs best in all cases (with and without program classification and for both regarded program behaviors). Due to program classification, the predictor precision increased significantly. For dependence degrees, the mean absolute error could be reduced from 2.72 to 1.79 classes (correlation: from 0.65 to 0.71). For load latencies, the error went down from 2.39 to 1.99 classes (correlation: from 0.09 to 0.18). With our runtime experiments, we could show that our speculative optimization, together with the machine learned heuristics, could significantly improve program performance in most cases. For the SPEC CPU2006 benchmark, the execution time could be reduced by up to 3.75% (average: 1.49%). At the same time, the amount of instruction cache stalls or of stalls due to increased register pressure did not increase notably. This shows that our cost model could effectively identify advantageous optimizations while at the same time avoiding additional overhead. We could show that the optimization would achieve notably better optimization results on a platform that implements speculation better than the Itanium. Overall, we could show that the regarded memory behavior, namely dependence degrees and load latencies, can be learned to automatically yield precise heuristics, and that those heuristics together with our speculative optimization significantly improve the run-time behavior.

8 Conclusion

In this chapter, we summarize the central results of this thesis. With that, we revisit the criteria we defined in the introduction and discuss whether we succeeded in meeting these criteria. Finally, we outline and discuss directions for future work.

8.1 Results

In this thesis, we have presented our conceptual *Framework for Intelligent Speculative Compiler Optimizations (FrISCO)*. The framework aims at providing compilers with knowledge about the run-time behavior of programs to bridge the gap between static program analyses on the one hand and dynamic program behavior on the other. This solves the problem of over-approximation, which is inherent to static program analyses, and increases the optimization potential.

The principal idea of our framework is to admit unsafe, yet more precise program analyses within the compiler and to use their results in speculative optimizations, which use the information to derive precise cost models. In our approach, we use heuristics to predict the dynamic program behavior. We presented a method to generate such heuristics automatically in a one-off training phase from profiling data via machine learning. Due to our concept of program classification, the heuristics are not restricted to a certain kind of programs. Instead, they yield precise results for arbitrary programs (given that the representative program suite used in training the heuristics was chosen thoroughly). The obtained heuristics are highly scalable and can be automatically translated to executable code to be used within the compiler.

With the heuristics, the compiler can predict the dynamic program behavior solely based on static information about the code. These predictions are used in compiler optimizations, which become speculative, since the predictions are unsafe. We presented a general optimization algorithm, onto which most existing optimizations can be mapped. The algorithm transforms the programs iteratively and greedily explores the search space of all possible transformations, using a cost model that is evaluated with the help of the heuristics. Of course, the optimization ensures that the program behavior is not changed in case of misspeculation. The admission of unsafe information together with speculative optimization allows for exploiting far more optimization potential because the drastic over-approximation of conservative analyses can be overcome. At the same time, the cost model benefits from the precise predictions to rate each possible program transformation w.r.t. the expected optimization gain and thereby selects the best transformation.

The conceptual framework is applicable to a wide range of program behavior and program optimizations. We have presented a set of possible applications and have described the steps required to instantiate the general framework. In the second part of this thesis, we have shown the application of the framework to the optimization of memory accesses, which is a highly important optimization problem due to the *memory gap*. For the applied framework, we have presented a novel optimization algorithm that iteratively performs speculative code motion to reduce the effective latency of load instructions. The idea is to execute expensive loads earlier to hide their latency. During code motion, the algorithm overcomes memory dependencies, register dependencies, and control dependencies, and it maintains a precise cost model which captures the effect of the performed transformation on the latency of the optimized load. By that, different applicable transformations are rated and the best is selected. We presented a cost model that captures the benefit of each different kind of speculative transformation as well as the combined benefit. The cost model relies on information about the memory behavior of a program, namely the probability of memory dependencies and load latencies. We have presented how to build heuristics for that via machine learning.

We fully implemented the instantiated framework. As target architecture, we chose the Intel Itanium2 processor, a modern VLIW processor that offers hardware support for speculation. In our experiments, we could first show that the heuristics predict the memory behavior precisely. Especially, we could show that our concept of program classification improves the precision significantly. The mean absolute error was reduced from 2.72 to 1.79 classes for dependence degrees and from 2.39 to 1.99 classes for load latencies. Second, we could demonstrate with run-time experiments that our speculative optimization significantly improves program performance and avoids performance degradation due to the cost model. The execution time of programs was reduced by up to 3.75% (on average by 1.49%), while an increase in stalls due to code growth or increased register pressure could be avoided in all cases. By applying the conceptual framework to the optimization of memory accesses, we have shown the practical applicability of our framework and have made a contribution to an important optimization problem.

8.2 Discussion

In the introducing chapter, we have defined objectives to assess the quality of the general framework as well as of the applied framework. In the following, we revisit the criteria in turn and discuss whether or not they are met by our approach. In the general framework, the only assumption on the optimization algorithm is that it transforms the program step-wise. As every optimization can be expressed iteratively, the *generality of the optimization* is given. We do not put any restrictions on the regarded dynamic behavior, as long as it can be observed via profiling. Hence, also the *generality of the regarded behavior* is given. Our concept of program classification allows for obtaining a predictor that yields precise results for all kinds of programs. By this, we achieve the *generality of the analyses*. The three phases of the conceptual framework have clear interfaces and can be combined freely. Any observed run-time behavior can be used to train arbitrary heuristics, which can be used by any speculative optimizations. Therefore, the *modularity* criterion is fulfilled. For machine learning, we propose to use algorithms with a concise representation (*e.g.*, decision trees). The obtained representations are instructive to the compiler developer and can be efficiently implemented to guarantee the *scalability of the heuristics*. We have described a methodology to assess the precision of the obtained heuristics. Since we perform cross-validation, the obtained results can be considered as a realistic *precision measure* for the heuristics. In the optimization phase of our general framework, we integrated the *cost model* explicitly as part of the optimization. By that, the cost model can be used to assess each applicable transformation during the optimization. Thereby, we ensure that the best transformations are selected. For the application of the conceptual framework, we could experimentally demonstrate the high *precision of the heuristics* for a wide range of different applications. This is especially due to our concept of program classification. The optimization algorithm ensures *program correctness* for each kind of speculation by adding the appropriate recovery code. In our run-time experiments, we could show a significant *optimization gain* for the SPEC CPU2006 benchmark suite. Therefore, we could show that all imposed objectives are met by our approach. We think that many existing approaches can benefit from our conceptual framework by using automatically generated heuristics as well as a precise cost model.

With the presented application of the framework, we have first shown how to automatically generate a precise, highly scalable heuristics for the memory behavior of programs. Second, we have presented an optimization that uses the heuristics for precise cost estimation. In our experiments on the Intel Itanium, we achieved significant performance improvements (up to 3.75%). We have also shown that the optimization can lead to notably more performance improvements on other architectures that have better support for speculation than the Intel Itanium[1]. Additionally, the presented heuristics for memory behavior is a result of its own and can be used directly in other existing speculative optimizations to increase the performance gain.

8.3 Outlook

In this thesis, we presented a conceptual framework to increase the optimization potential in static compilers on the one hand and to exploit it by speculative optimizations on the other. Furthermore, we presented how we applied the conceptual framework to the optimization of memory accesses, and we implemented that instantiated framework within our compiler infrastructure targeting the Intel Itanium processor. With our experimental results, we could prove the practical applicability of our framework. Still, there are some useful extensions conceivable, and our work also raised some open questions which are to be investigated by future research. In the following, we start by considering extensions of the instantiated framework. Then, we discuss future research building upon the conceptual framework, and we end by looking beyond the approach presented in this thesis.

---

[1]Concerning speculation, the Intel Itanium architecture has one major drawback: If the latency of a speculatively optimized load is not completely hidden, the hardware reports misspeculation for that load. As a consequence, a partial reduction of the effective load latency has no positive effect on run-time performance (see also Section 6.4.4, page 154).

8.3 Outlook

Our implementation of the speculative optimization does not consider code duplication, as it is the case for our conceptual algorithm. It would be interesting to extend the implementation by that aspect and to assess the improvement caused by that. Another extension could also be to investigate other target platforms, as the implementation of speculation on the Itanium has its drawbacks. It would also be interesting to evaluate the benefit of speculation when done solely by software, which renders the optimization presented in this thesis applicable to all target platforms. For the training of the heuristics, we also would like to investigate the effects of increasing the size of the representative program suite significantly. We expect that this would lead to even clearer program classes and would furthermore increase the precision of the heuristics.

For the conceptual framework, we have given a number of possible application scenarios. It would be interesting to select another scenario from that list and to investigate the benefit the investigation of our framework would cause. The conceptual framework presented in this thesis assumes that the phases machine learning (train the heuristics), compiler optimization (using the heuristics), and finally program execution are strictly separated. However, those phases may also be integrated together, as in *iterative compilation* (initially proposed by Bodin et al. [BKK+98], current approaches are, *e.g.*, Agakov et al. [ABC+06] and Pingjing et al. [LCW08]). By that, parameters of the cost model could be automatically fine-tuned to different kinds of programs. Going beyond that, the idea of our conceptual framework could also be applied to *dynamic* or *continuous compilation* (*e.g.*, Childers et al. [CDS03] and Christophe et al. [BC07]), in which case the programs are executed within a dynamic run-time system. This allows the optimizations to dynamically adjust to the program behavior during run-time.

On an even more general level, we consider machine learning techniques an indispensable tool to assist optimizations, especially for application areas that are very complex and not yet completely explored. Representing the cost model explicitly as part of the optimization, which is one central idea of this thesis, on the one hand allows for trading off performance gains with additional overhead of a transformation and on the other hand makes the optimization less machine dependent, as the cost model can contain architectural parameters. One application scenario, to which the ideas of this thesis could be transferred, is the *Multiprocessor System-on-Chip (MPSoC)* paradigm. For MPSoC, it is still an open question how to best distribute an application to the network of processors. The hardly predictable amount of communications between the processors severely limits run-time performance. This problem is similar to the implications of the memory gap, yet it adds complexity at another level. Therefore, we think that our experience from building a cost model for optimizing memory accesses can be used as a foundation to model the communication cost for MPSoCs. Another important parameter for performing a good task allocation in MPSoCs is the estimated execution time of tasks. Again, our results can be used as a starting point to model that problem. We think that the development of a combined model for both problems, communication costs and task scheduling, based upon our results, is very promising to achieve a better efficiency with MPSoCs than with today's methods.

As short-term goal, other instantiations of our conceptual framework appear interesting (see Table 4.1, page 95 for some suggestions). For the long-term, looking at the promising results of this thesis, we are convinced that machine learning can be successfully used in other domains to make the compiler more intelligent, thereby bridging the gap between static compilation and dynamic program behavior.

List of Figures

1.1	The Memory Gap	18
1.2	Covered Fields of Research	20
2.1	Architecture of a Compiler	24
2.2	Compiler IR	26
2.3	C code and resulting CFG	27
2.4	Data Dependencies for Registers	29
2.5	Dominator Tree of a Control Flow Graph	30
2.6	Dominance Front	31
2.7	Tree of Possible Transformation Sequences	35
2.8	Aliasing and Points-To Table	42
2.9	Data Speculation	46
2.10	Control Speculation	47
2.11	Speculation with Recovery Code	48
2.12	Speculation with and without Hardware Support	50
2.13	Machine Learning	54
2.14	Decision Trees	58
2.15	Discriminant Analysis	58
2.16	k-nearest Neighbors	59
2.17	Δk-Accuracy	63
3.1	C code and Resulting Points-To Graphs	70

4.1	Extending Compiler Frameworks with *FrISCO*	80
4.2	Phases in *FrISCO*	81
4.3	*FrISCO*: Extended Framework with Program Classes	82
4.4	Combination of Predictors	86
4.5	Three Ways to Identify Program Classes	87
4.6	Construction of the Program Class Predictor	89
4.7	Construction of Behavior Predictors	89
4.8	Combining Program Analyses and Heuristics	90
4.9	Black-box View of Compiler Optimizations	91
4.10	Optimization Step for Conservative Optimizations	92
4.11	Optimization Step for Speculative Optimizations	93
4.12	Optimization Step in *FrISCO*	94
4.13	Instantiating *FrISCO*	96
5.1	Tree of Transformation Sequences for Speculative Code Motion	104
5.2	Algorithm for Speculative Code Motion	105
5.3	Construction of a LAC chain	106
5.4	Conservative Code Motion	109
5.5	Data Speculative Code Motion	111
5.6	Control Speculation: Dominance Front	114
5.7	Control Speculation: Path Probabilities	116
5.8	Control Speculative Code Motion	117
5.9	Code Motion with Load Instruction Chains	118
5.10	Code Motion across Check Instructions	119
5.11	Distinguishing Different Versions of the Stack	125
5.12	Obtaining the Distance Matrix	128
5.13	Cluster Analysis Based on the Distance Matrix	130
6.1	Implementation of *FrISCO*	134
6.2	Learned Decision Tree	146
6.3	Program Classification via Hierarchical Clustering	147
6.4	Code Generation from Decision Trees	149

7.1	Distribution of Dependence Degrees	160
7.2	Distribution of Load Latencies	162
7.3	Dependence Degrees: Self-Validation on the Training Set	164
7.4	Dependence Degrees: Cross-Validation on the Training Set	164
7.5	Load Latencies: Self-Validation on the Training Set	166
7.6	Load Latencies: Cross-Validation on the Training Set	166
7.7	Dependence Degrees: Distance Matrix for the Training Set	167
7.8	Dependence Degrees: Decision Tree of the PC Predictor	169
7.9	Load Latencies: Distance Matrix for the Training Set	171
7.10	Load Latencies: Decision Tree of the PC Predictor	172
7.11	Dependence Degrees: Predictor Precision for the Validation Set	174
7.12	Load Latencies: Predictor Precision for the Validation Set	176
7.13	Run-Time Results	179

List of Tables

2.1	Categorization of Program Analyses	32
2.2	Types of Statements	43
2.3	Configuration of the Intel Itanium2 McKinley Processor	52
4.1	Exemplary Instantiations of *FrISCO*	95
5.1	Calculation of the Dependence Degree	126
6.1	Static Program Features	139
6.2	Static Code Features per Memory Instruction	141
6.3	Parameters of Speculative Code Motion	154
6.4	Source Lines of Code of the Implementation Modules	155
7.1	Dependence Degrees: Training and Validation Sets of Programs	160
7.2	Load Latencies: Training and Validation Sets of Programs	162
7.3	Dependence Degrees: Program Classes for the Training Set	168
7.4	Dependence Degrees: Program Classes for the Validation Set	170
7.5	Load Latencies: Program Classes for the Training Set	171
7.6	Load Latencies: Program Classes for the Validation Set	173
7.7	Dependence Degrees: Detailed Results of the Predictor Precision	175
7.8	Load Latencies: Detailed Results of the Predictor Precision	176
7.9	Static Optimization Statistics	179
7.10	Impact on the Stall Behavior	180
7.11	Dynamic Instruction Count for Speculative Instructions	181

7.12 Fraction of Optimized Loads with respect to Candidates 182

Bibliography

[ABC+06] Felix Agakov, Edwin Bonilla, John Cavazos, Björn Franke, Grigori Fursin, Michael F.P. O'Boyle, John Thomson, Marc Toussaint, and Christopher K.I. Williams. Using machine learning to focus iterative optimization. In *Fourth IEEE/ACM International Symposium on Code Generation and Optimization (CGO 2006)*, pages 295–305, Washington, DC, USA, 2006. IEEE Computer Society.

[ACE] Associated Compiler Experts bv., Amsterdam, The Netherlands. http://www.ace.nl.

[ACG+04] Lelac Almagor, Keith D. Cooper, Alexander Grosul, Timothy J. Harvey, Steven W. Reeves, Devika Subramanian, Linda Torczon, and Todd Waterman. Finding effective compilation sequences. In *ACM SIGPLAN/SIGBED Conference on Languages, Compilers, and Tools for Embedded Systems (LCTES'04)*, pages 231–239. ACM Press, 2004.

[ACM+98] David I. August, Daniel A. Connors, Scott A. Mahlke, John W. Sias, Kevin M. Crozier, Ben-Chung Cheng, Patrick R. Eaton, Qudus B. Olaniran, and Wen-Mei W. Hwu. Integrated predicated and speculative execution in the impact epic architecture. In *25th Annual International Symposium on Computer Architecture (ISCA 1998)*, pages 227–237. IEEE Computer Society, 1998.

[AG09] Lars Alvincz and Sabine Glesner. Breaking the curse of static analyses: Making compiler intelligent via machine learning. In *3rd Workshop on Statistical and Machine learning approaches to ARchitectures and compilaTion (SMART'09)*, January 2009.

[AKLM06] Kartik K. Agaram, Stephen W. Keckler, Calvin Lin, and

Kathryn S. McKinley. The memory behavior of data structures in C SPEC CPU2000 benchmarks. In *SPEC Benchmark Workshop*, 2006.

[And94] Lars Ole Andersen. *Program Analysis and Specialization for the C Programming Language*. PhD thesis, DIKU, University of Copenhagen, May 1994.

[AR94] Santosh Abraham and Bantwal Ramakrishna Rau. Predicting load latencies using cache profiling. Technical Report HPL-94-110, HP Labs, 1994.

[BC07] Jean Christophe Beyler and Philippe Clauss. Performance driven data cache prefetching in a dynamic software optimization system. In *Proceedings of the 21st annual international conference on Supercomputing (ICS '07)*, pages 202–209, New York, NY, USA, 2007. ACM.

[BFOS84] Leo Breiman, Jerome Friedman, Richard A. Olshen, and Charles J. Stone. *Classification and Regression Trees*. Wadsworth and Brooks, Monterey, CA, 1984.

[BKK$^+$98] Francois Bodin, Toru Kisuki, Peter M.W. Knijnenburg, Michael F.P. O'Boyle, and Erven Rohou. Iterative compilation in a non-linear optimisation space. In *Proceedings of the Workshop on Profile and Feedback-Directed Compilation*, October 1998.

[BL94] Thomas Ball and James R. Larus. Optimally profiling and tracing programs. *ACM Transactions on Programming Languages and Systems (TOPLAS)*, 16(4):1319–1360, 1994.

[BL96] Thomas Ball and James R. Larus. Efficient path profiling. In *29th Annual ACM/IEEE International Symposium on Microarchitecture (MICRO-28 1996)*, pages 46–57. IEEE Computer Society, 1996.

[BMH$^+$93] Roger A. Bringmann, Scott A. Mahlke, Richard E. Hank, John C. Gyllenhaal, and Wen-Mei W. Hwu. Speculative execution exception recovery using write-back suppression. In *26th Annual International Symposium on Microarchitecture (MICRO-26 1993)*, pages 214–223, Los Alamitos, CA, USA, 1993. IEEE Computer Society Press.

[Bre01] Leo Breiman. Random forests. *Machine Learning*, 45(1):5–32,

2001.

[CCL+96] Fred C. Chow, Sun Chan, Shin-Ming Liu, Raymond Lo, and Mark Streich. Effective representation of aliases and indirect memory operations in ssa form. In *6th International Conference on Compiler Construction (CC'96)*, pages 253–267. Springer-Verlag, 1996.

[CDS03] Bruce Childers, Jack W. Davidson, and Mary Lou Soffa. Continuous compilation: A new approach to aggressive and adaptive code transformation. In *17th International Parallel and Distributed Processing Symposium (IPDPS 2003)*, page 205. IEEE Computer Society, 2003.

[CFA+07] John Cavazos, Grigori Fursin, Felix Agakov, Edwin Bonilla, Michael F.P. O'Boyle, and Olivier Temam. Rapidly selecting good compiler optimizations using performance counter. In *Fifth International Symposium on Code Generation and Optimization (CGO 2007)*. IEEE Computer Society, 2007.

[CFR+91] Ron K. Cytron, Jeanne Ferrante, Barry K. Rosen, Mark N. Wegman, and F. Kenneth Zadeck. Efficiently computing static single assignment form and the control dependence graph. *ACM Transactions on Programming Languages and Systems (TOPLAS)*, 13(4):451–490, 1991.

[CHJL04] Peng-Sheng Chen, Yuan-Shin Hwang, Roy Dz-Ching Ju, and Jenq Kuen Lee. Interprocedural probabilistic pointer analysis. *IEEE Transactions on Parallel and Distributed Systems*, 15(10):893–907, 2004.

[CLD+04] Tong Chen, Jin Lin, Xiaoru Dai, Wei-Chung Hsu, and Pen-Chung Yew. Data dependence profiling for speculative optimizations. In Evelyn Duesterwald, editor, *13th International Conference on Compiler Construction (CC 2004)*, volume 2985 of *LNCS*, pages 57–72. Springer, April 2004.

[CLHY02] Tong Chen, Jin Lin, Wei-Chung Hsu, and Pen-Chung Yew. An empirical study on the granularity of pointer analysis in c programs. In *Proceedings of 15th Workshop on Languages and Compilers for Parallel Computing (LCPC'02)*, 2002.

[CM04] John Cavazos and J. Eliot B. Moss. Inducing heuristics to decide whether to schedule. In *ACM SIGPLAN Conference on Program-*

ming *Language Design and Implementation (PLDI 2004)*, pages 183–194. ACM Press, 2004.

[CO05] John Cavazos and Michael F.P. O'Boyle. Automatic tuning of inlining heuristics. In *Proceedings of the 2005 ACM/IEEE conference on Supercomputing (SC '05)*, page 14, Washington, DC, USA, 2005. IEEE Computer Society.

[CSS99] Keith D. Cooper, Philip J. Schielke, and Devika Subramanian. Optimizing for reduced code space using genetic algorithms. In *ACM SIGPLAN workshop on Languages, Compilers, and Tools for Embedded Systems (LCTES'99)*, pages 1–9. ACM Press, 1999.

[CT04] Keith D. Cooper and Linda Torczon. *Engineering a Compiler*. Morgan Kaufmann, 2004.

[Das00] Manuvir Das. Unification-based pointer analysis with directional assignments. In *ACM SIGPLAN Conference on Programming Language Design and Implementation (PLDI 2000)*, pages 35–46, New York, NY, USA, 2000. ACM Press.

[DCF+07] Christophe Dubach, John Cavazos, Björn Franke, Grigori Fursin, Michael F.P. O'Boyle, and Olivier Temam. Fast compiler optimisation evaluation using code-feature based performance prediction. In *Proceedings of the 4th conference on Computing Frontiers (CF '07)*, pages 131–142, New York, NY, USA, 2007. ACM.

[DH96] Brian L. Deitrich and Wen-Mei W. Hwu. Speculative hedge: Regulating compile-time speculation against profile variations. In *29th Annual ACM/IEEE International Symposium on Microarchitecture (MICRO-28 1996)*, pages 70–79, 1996.

[DZHY05] Xiaoru Dai, Antonia Zhai, Wei-Chung Hsu, and Pen-Chung Yew. A general compiler framework for speculative optimizations using data speculative code motion. In *3nd IEEE/ACM International Symposium on Code Generation and Optimization (CGO 2005)*, pages 280–290, Washington, DC, USA, 2005. IEEE Computer Society.

[EGK+94] Kemal Ebcioglu, Randy D. Groves, Ki-Chang Kim, Gabriel M. Silberman, and Isaac Ziv. VLIW compilation techniques in a superscalar environment. In *ACM SIGPLAN Conference on Programming Language Design and Implementation (PLDI 1994)*, pages

36–48, New York, NY, USA, 1994. ACM Press.

[ESL89]   Helmut Emmelmann, Friedrich-Wilhelm Schröer, and Rudolf Landwehr. BEG: a generation for efficient back ends. In *ACM SIGPLAN Conference on Programming Language Design and Implementation (PLDI 1989)*, pages 227–237. ACM Press, 1989.

[FE02]   Manel Fernández and Roger Espasa. Speculative alias analysis for executable code. In *Proceedings of the 2002 International Conference on Parallel Architectures and Compilation Techniques (PACT '02)*, pages 222–231, Washington, DC, USA, 2002. IEEE Computer Society.

[Fel90]   Stuart I. Feldman. A Fortran to C converter. *ACM SIGPLAN Fortran Forum*, 9(2):21–22, 1990.

[Ges08]   Lars Gesellensetter. Scalable analysis via machine learning: Predicting memory dependencies precisely. In Florian Martin, Hanne Riis Nielson, Claudio Riva, and Markus Schordan, editors, *Scalable Program Analysis*, number 08161 in Dagstuhl Seminar Proceedings, Dagstuhl, Germany, 2008. Schloss Dagstuhl - Leibniz-Zentrum fuer Informatik, Germany.

[GG08]   Lars Gesellensetter and Sabine Glesner. Interprocedural speculative optimization of memory accesses to global variables. In *Proceedings from the 14th International Euro-Par Conference on Parallel Processing (Euro-Par '08)*. Springer, 2008.

[GLS01]   Rakesh Ghiya, Daniel Lavery, and David Sehr. On the importance of points-to analysis and other memory disambiguation methods for c programs. In *ACM SIGPLAN Conference on Programming Language Design and Implementation (PLDI 2001)*, pages 47–58, New York, NY, USA, 2001. ACM Press.

[Har85]   David Harel. A linear algorithm for finding dominators in flow graphs and related problems. In *Proceedings of the seventeenth annual ACM symposium on Theory of computing (STOC '85)*, pages 185–194, New York, NY, USA, 1985. ACM.

[Hin01]   Michael Hind. Pointer analysis: haven't we solved this problem yet? In *Proceedings of the 2001 ACM SIGPLAN-SIGSOFT workshop on Program analysis for software tools and engineering (PASTE '01)*, pages 54–61, New York, NY, USA, 2001. ACM

Press.

[HMR+00] Jerry Huck, Dale Morris, Jonathan Ross, Allan Knies, Hans Mulder, and Rumi Zahir. Introducing the IA-64 architecture. *IEEE Micro*, 20(5):12–23, 2000.

[Hor97] Susan Horwitz. Precise flow-insensitive may-alias analysis is NP-hard. *ACM Transactions on Programming Languages and Systems (TOPLAS)*, 19(1):1–6, 1997.

[HP00] Michael Hind and Anthony Pioli. Which pointer analysis should I use? In *Proceedings of the 2000 ACM SIGSOFT international symposium on Software testing and analysis (ISSTA '00)*, pages 113–123, New York, NY, USA, 2000. ACM Press.

[HP04] Hewlett-Packard. *pfmon – a hardware-based performance monitoring tool, v3.2*, 2004. http://perfmon2.sourceforge.net.

[Int01] Intel Corporation. Intel Itanium software conventions and runtime architecture guide. Document number: 245358-003, Intel Corporation, May 2001.

[Int04] Intel Corporation. Intel Itanium2 processor reference manual for software development and optimization. Order number: 251110-003, Intel Corporation, May 2004.

[Int06a] Intel Corporation. *icc 9.1 20061105*, 2006. http://developer.intel.com/software/products/compilers.

[Int06b] Intel Corporation. Intel IA-64 architecture software developer's manual: Volume 1: IA-64 application architecture. Revision 2.2, Intel Corporation, Jan 2006.

[Int06c] Intel Corporation. Intel IA-64 architecture software developer's manual: Volume 2: IA-64 system architecture. Revision 2.2, Intel Corporation, Jan 2006.

[Int06d] Intel Corporation. Intel IA-64 architecture software developer's manual: Volume 3: Instruction set reference. Revision 2.2, Intel Corporation, Jan 2006.

[Int07] Intel Corporation. *Pin – a tool for the dynamic instrumentation of programs, v2.2, version 14289*, 2007. http://www.pintool.org.

[JNMW00] Roy Dz-Ching Ju, Kevin Nomura, Uma Mahadevan, and Le-Chun

Wu. A unified compiler framework for control and data speculation. In *2000 International Conference on Parallel Architectures and Compilation Techniques (PACT'00)*, Philadelphia, Pennsylvania, October 15 - 19 2000.

[KA02] Ken Kennedy and John R. Allen. *Optimizing compilers for modern architectures: a dependence-based approach*. Morgan Kaufmann Publishers Inc., San Francisco, CA, USA, 2002.

[KR90] Leonard Kaufman and Peter J. Rousseeuw. *Finding groups in data: an introduction to cluster analysis*. John Wiley and Sons, New York, 1990.

[Lan92] William Landi. Undecidability of static analysis. *ACM Lett. Program. Lang. Syst.*, 1(4):323–337, 1992.

[LCH+04] Jin Lin, Tong Chen, Wei-Chung Hsu, Pen-Chung Yew, Roy Dz-Ching Ju, Tin-Fook Ngai, and Sun Chan. A compiler framework for speculative optimizations. *ACM Transactions on Architecture and Code Optimization (TACO)*, 1(3):247–271, 2004.

[LCHY03] Jin Lin, Tong Chen, Wei-Chung Hsu, and Pen-Chung Yew. Speculative register promotion using advanced load address table (ALAT). In *1st IEEE/ACM International Symposium on Code Generation and Optimization (CGO 2003)*, pages 125–134, Washington, DC, USA, 2003. IEEE Computer Society.

[LCM+05] Chi-Keung Luk, Robert Cohn, Robert Muth, Harish Patil, Artur Klauser, Geoff Lowney, Steven Wallace, Vijay Janapa Reddi, and Kim Hazelwood. Pin: building customized program analysis tools with dynamic instrumentation. In *ACM SIGPLAN Conference on Programming Language Design and Implementation (PLDI 2005)*, pages 190–200, New York, NY, USA, 2005. ACM Press.

[LCW08] Pingjing Lu, Yonggang Che, and Zhenghua Wang. An effective iterative compilation search algorithm for high performance computing applications. In *Proceedings of the 2008 10th IEEE International Conference on High Performance Computing and Communications (HPCC '08)*, pages 368–373, Washington, DC, USA, 2008. IEEE Computer Society.

[LHY+06] Jin Lin, Wei-Chung Hsu, Pen-Chung Yew, Roy Dz-Ching Ju, and Tin-Fook Ngai. Recovery code generation for general speculative optimizations. *ACM Transactions on Architecture and Code Optimization (TACO)*, 3(1):67–89, 2006.

[MCH+92] Scott A. Mahlke, William Y. Chen, Wen-Mei W. Hwu, Bantwal Ramakrishna Rau, and Michael S. Schlansker. Sentinel scheduling for vliw and superscalar processors. In *Proceedings of the fifth international conference on Architectural support for programming languages and operating systems (ASPLOS-V)*, pages 238–247, New York, NY, USA, 1992. ACM Press.

[MDCE01] Markus Mock, Manuvir Das, Craig Chambers, and Susan J. Eggers. Dynamic points-to sets: a comparison with static analyses and potential applications in program understanding and optimization. In *Proceedings of the 2001 ACM SIGPLAN-SIGSOFT workshop on Program analysis for software tools and engineering (PASTE '01)*, pages 66–72, New York, NY, USA, 2001. ACM Press.

[Muc97] Steven S. Muchnik. *Advanced Compiler Design & Implementation*. Morgan Kaufmann, 1997.

[MUC+98] J. Eliot B. Moss, Paul Utgoff, John Cavazos, Doina Precup, Darko Stefanović, Carla Brodley, and David Scheeff. Learning to schedule straight-line code. In Michael I. Jordan, Michael J. Kearns, and Sara A. Solla, editors, *Advances in Neural Information Processing Systems*, volume 10. The MIT Press, 1998.

[Mur85] Fionn Murtagh. *Multidimensional Clustering Algorithms*. Physica-Verlag, Vienna, 1985.

[Nic89] Alexandru Nicolau. Run-time disambiguation: coping with statically unpredictable dependencies. *IEEE Transactions on Computers*, 38(5):633–678, 1989.

[NNH99] Flemming Nielson, Hanne R. Nielson, and Chris Hankin. *Principles of Program Analysis*. Springer-Verlag New York, Inc., Secaucus, NJ, USA, 1999.

[NW88] George L. Nemhauser and Laurence A. Wolsey. *Integer and combinatorial optimization*. Wiley-Interscience, New York, NY, USA, 1988.

[PHES05] Thomas R. Puzak, Allan Hartstein, Philip G. Emma, and Viji Srinivasan. When prefetching improves/degrades performance. In

Proceedings of the 2nd conference on Computing Frontiers (CF '05), pages 342–352, New York, NY, USA, 2005. ACM Press.

[PIBS95] Pointer-Intensive Benchmark Suite. Assembled by Todd Austin, 1995. http://www.cs.wisc.edu/~austin/ptr-dist.html.

[PSW04] Vlad-Mihai Panait, Amit Sasturkar, and Weng-Fai Wong. Static identification of delinquent loads. In *2nd IEEE/ACM International Symposium on Code Generation and Optimization (CGO 2004)*, page 303, Washington, DC, USA, 2004. IEEE Computer Society.

[RCT08] R Development Core Team. *R: A Language and Environment for Statistical Computing*. R Foundation for Statistical Computing, Vienna, Austria, 2008. ISBN 3-900051-07-0, http://www.R-project.org.

[RL92] Anne Rogers and Kai Li. Software support for speculative loads. In *Proceedings of the fifth international conference on Architectural support for programming languages and operating systems (ASPLOS-V)*, pages 38–50, New York, NY, USA, 1992. ACM Press.

[RSEW04] Rodric M. Rabbah, Hariharan Sandanagobalane, Mongkol Ekpanyapong, and Weng-Fai Wong. Compiler orchestrated prefetching via speculation and predication. *ACM SIGPLAN Notices*, 39(11):189–198, 2004.

[SA05] Mark Stephenson and Saman Amarasinghe. Predicting unroll factors using supervised classification. In *3nd IEEE/ACM International Symposium on Code Generation and Optimization (CGO 2005)*. IEEE Computer Society, 2005.

[SAG+01] Artour Stoutchinin, José N. Amaral, Guang R. Gao, James C. Dehnert, Suneel Jain, and Alban Douillet. Speculative prefetching of induction pointers. In *10th International Conference on Compiler Construction (CC 2001)*, pages 289–303, London, UK, 2001. Springer-Verlag.

[SAMO03] Mark Stephenson, Saman Amarasinghe, Martin Martin, and Una-May O'Reilly. Meta optimization: improving compiler heuristics with machine learning. In Jr. James B. Fenwick and Cindy Norris, editors, *ACM SIGPLAN Conference on Programming Language*

[SH97]   *Design and Implementation (PLDI 2003)*, pages 77–90, New York, June 9–11 2003. ACM Press.

[SH97]   Marc Shapiro and Susan Horwitz. Fast and accurate flow-insensitive points-to analysis. In *24th ACM SIGPLAN-SIGACT Symposium on Principles of Programming Languages (POPL 1997)*, pages 1–14, New York, NY, USA, 1997. ACM Press.

[SHK04]   Bernhard Scholz, Nigel Horspool, and Jens Knoop. Optimizing for space and time usage with speculative partial redundancy elimination. *ACM SIGPLAN Notices*, 39(7):221–230, 2004.

[SPEC]   Standard Performance Evaluation Company. http://www.spec.org.

[SS06]   Jeff Da Silva and J. Gregory Steffan. A probabilistic pointer analysis for speculative optimizations. *ACM SIGOPS Operating Systems Review*, 40(5):416–425, 2006.

[Ste96a]   Bjarne Steensgaard. Points-to analysis by type inference of programs with structures and unions. In *6th International Conference on Compiler Construction (CC'96)*, pages 136–150, London, UK, 1996. Springer-Verlag.

[Ste96b]   Bjarne Steensgaard. Points-to analysis in almost linear time. In *23rd ACM SIGPLAN-SIGACT Symposium on Principles of Programming Languages (POPL 1996)*, pages 32–41. ACM Press, 1996.

[VL00]   Steven P. Vanderwiel and David J. Lilja. Data prefetch mechanisms. *ACM Comput. Surv.*, 32(2):174–199, 2000.

[Win04]   Sebastian Winkel. Exploring the performance potential of Itanium processors with ILP-based scheduling. In *2nd IEEE/ACM International Symposium on Code Generation and Optimization (CGO 2004)*. IEEE Computer Society, 2004.

[Win07]   Sebastian Winkel. Optimal versus heuristic global code scheduling. In *40th Annual IEEE/ACM International Symposium on Microarchitecture (MICRO-40 2007)*, pages 43–55, Washington, DC, USA, 2007. IEEE Computer Society.

[WL94]   Youfeng Wu and James R. Larus. Static branch frequency and program profile analysis. In *27th Annual International Symposium* on *Microarchitecture (MICRO-27 1994)*, pages 1–11, New York, NY, USA, 1994. ACM Press.

[WM95] William A. Wulf and Sally A. McKee. Hitting the memory wall: implications of the obvious. *ACM SIGARCH Computer Architecture News*, 23(1):20–24, 1995.

[Wu02] Youfeng Wu. Efficient discovery of regular stride patterns in irregular programs and its use in compiler prefetching. In *ACM SIGPLAN Conference on Programming Language Design and Implementation (PLDI 2002)*, pages 210–221, New York, NY, USA, 2002. ACM Press.

Supervised Diploma Theses

[Hee07] Jonas Heese. Lernen von Speicherabhängigkeiten. Technische Universität Berlin, Fachgebiet PES, November 2007.

[Opp07] Jan Oppor. Spekulative Alias-Analyse. Technische Universität Berlin, Fachgebiet PES, November 2007.

[Rol09] Tobias Roloff. Identifikation von Programmklassen mit ähnlichem Speicherzugriffsverhalten. Technische Universität Berlin, Fachgebiet PES, April 2009.

[Sch07] Stefan Schulz. Spekulative Optimierung von Speicherzugriffen in Compilern. Technische Universität Berlin, Fachgebiet PES, November 2007.

[Tet07] Dirk Tetzlaff. Erweitertes Hyperblock-Scheduling für VLIW-Prozessoren. Technische Universität Berlin, Fachgebiet PES, October 2007.

Die VDM Verlagsservicegesellschaft sucht für wissenschaftliche Verlage abgeschlossene und herausragende

Dissertationen, Habilitationen, Diplomarbeiten, Master Theses, Magisterarbeiten usw.

für die kostenlose Publikation als Fachbuch.

Sie verfügen über eine Arbeit, die hohen inhaltlichen und formalen Ansprüchen genügt, und haben Interesse an einer honorarvergüteten Publikation?

Dann senden Sie bitte erste Informationen über sich und Ihre Arbeit per Email an *info@vdm-vsg.de*.

Sie erhalten kurzfristig unser Feedback!

VDM Verlagsservicegesellschaft mbH
Dudweiler Landstr. 99　　　　　　　Telefon　+49 681 3720 174
D - 66123 Saarbrücken　　　　　　　Fax　　　+49 681 3720 1749
www.vdm-vsg.de

Die VDM Verlagsservicegesellschaft mbH vertritt

Printed by Books on Demand GmbH, Norderstedt / Germany